Poe and the Idea of Music

Perspectives on Edgar Allan Poe

General Editor: Barbara Cantalupo,
Pennsylvania State University, Lehigh Valley

The Perspectives on Poe series includes books on new approaches to Edgar A. Poe, his work and influence; all perspectives—theoretical, historical, biographical, gender studies, source studies, cultural studies, global studies, etc.—are invited.

Titles in the Series

Poe and the Idea of Music: Failure, Transcendence, and Dark Romanticism, by Charity McAdams (2017)
The Lovecraftian Poe: Essays on Influence, Reception, Interpretation, and Transformation, edited by Sean Moreland (2017)
Translated Poe, edited by Emron Esplin and Margarida Vale de Gato (2014)
Deciphering Poe: Subtexts, Contexts, Subversive Meanings edited by Alexandra Urakova (2013)
Poe's Pervasive Influence, edited by Barbara Cantalupo (2012)

http://inpress.sites.lehigh.edu/

Poe and the Idea of Music

*Failure, Transcendence, and
Dark Romanticism*

Charity McAdams

LEHIGH UNIVERSITY PRESS
Bethlehem

Published by Lehigh University Press
Copublished by The Rowman & Littlefield Publishing Group, Inc.
4501 Forbes Boulevard, Suite 200, Lanham, Maryland 20706
www.rowman.com

Unit A, Whitacre Mews, 26-34 Stannary Street, London SE11 4AB

Copyright © 2017 by Charity McAdams

All rights reserved. No part of this book may be reproduced in any form or by any electronic or mechanical means, including information storage and retrieval systems, without written permission from the publisher, except by a reviewer who may quote passages in a review.

British Library Cataloguing in Publication Information Available

Library of Congress Cataloging-in-Publication Data

Names: McAdams, Charity author.
Title: Poe and the idea of music : failure, transcendence, and dark romanticism / Charity McAdams.
Description: Lanham : Lexington Books, 2017. | Series: Perspectives on Edgar Allan Poe | Includes bibliographical references and index. | Description based on print version record and CIP data provided by publisher; resource not viewed.
Identifiers: LCCN 2017041134 (print) | LCCN 2017037210 (ebook)
Subjects: LCSH: Poe, Edgar Allan, 1809-1849--Criticism and interpretation. | Music in literature.
LCC PS2642.M87 (print) | LCC PS2642.M87 .M33 2017 (ebook) | DDC 818/.309--dc23
    LC record available at https://lccn.loc.gov/2017041134

ISBN 978-1-61146-204-3 (cloth : alk. paper)
ISBN 978-1-61146-206-7 (pbk. : alk. paper)
ISBN 978-1-61146-205-0 (Electronic)

Table of Contents

Acknowledgments — vii
Introduction — ix

1. Is This Divine? No, This Is the Voice of a Woman — 1
2. Another Kind of Musician Altogether — 19
3. An Almost Magical Melody — 49
4. The Wantonest Singing Birds — 61
5. The Starry Choir (And Other Listening Things) — 79
6. But Gradually My Songs They Ceased — 103

Conclusion — 125
Appendix — 131
Bibliography — 141
Index — 149
About the Author — 155

Acknowledgments

Peter Dayan believed in this project from its inception and showed me how to navigate my portion of theory in music and literature with kind brilliance. Both Peter and Sarah Dunnigan were generous with their time, patient with arguments that eluded articulation, and inspirationally insightful. Because of them, this book was always buoyed by a sense of hope and accomplishment that moved far beyond the words on the page. Alongside Peter and Sarah, I am most grateful to have been guided by Andrew Taylor and Delia da Sousa Correa, who gave me feedback invaluable to the evolution and maturation of this book.

I would also like to extend my thanks to the International Association for Word and Music Studies (WMA) as well as to the members of the Forum of the International Association for Word and Music Studies (WMAF) for their advice and encouragement.

I could not have made it through the final stages of writing this book without the humanity of Alexandra Lawrie, Catherine-Rose Stocks-Rankin, and Kieran Curran. Most especially, I am deeply grateful for the tremendous support of Ryan Somerville.

Much of the research that went into this book was made available through the efforts of the University of Edinburgh's Interlibrary Loan Service and the British Library and the charity of Margaret Hrabe, the reference coordinator for the University of Virginia Library.

Finally, a million thanks to the reviewers and editors for the *Edgar Allan Poe Review*, Lehigh University Press, and Rowman & Littlefield.

Introduction

> Once as yet, and once only, has there sounded out of it all one pure note of original song—worth singing, and echoed from the singing of no other man; a note of song neither wide nor deep, but utterly true, rich, clear, and native to the singer; the short exquisite music, subtle and simple and somber and sweet, of Edgar Poe.
> —Charles Swinburne, "Under the Microscope"

When Poe wrote about music, he wrote about it in the abstract—he wrote about music that we never hear. A book about Poe and heard music would be a relatively short one: he rarely authored literature on music as we experience it, or what I define throughout this book as "real-world music." In the same way, the little we know concerning what music Poe listened to and how he listened to it has arisen circuitously. The same can be said of his creative works: rather than writing about music in ways we relate to it in the ordinary world, only three times does Poe invent literary musical performances reminiscent of music in the real world. All three performances, Usher's in "The Fall of the House of Usher," a young girl's in "The System of Doctor Tarr and Professor Fether," and Lalande's in "The Spectacles," then retreat into the realm of the unheard upon careful reading, as I will show in the first two chapters of this book. Poe nearly universally employs otherworldly, impossible music in his poems and short stories.

Poe's oblique references to music initially seem to mirror Romantic ideals of sublimity, spirituality, and transcendence. For Poe, as for other writers of the period, unheard Song is the highest form of art, heard Music may be the second highest, then comes Poetry, and finally prose falls at the base of the hierarchy. Words are too material and too earthly and too bound to definition for Poe to idealize. Our collective artistic hope lies in Song, which if unheard, occupies a spiritual realm.

The tragedy in this hierarchy for Poe is that it banishes Poe himself to practicing the least ideal of the arts. Poor Poe! He dooms himself to failure, and his perceived failure is the key to understanding Poe's sharp departure from Romantic musical ideals. If placed in the Romantic artistic hierarchy, Poe stays a writer who must accept the inherent failure of his endeavors while still searching to idealize them—to purify prose to the condition of Song—only to fail once more. In a reaction to this hierarchy, I believe that, rather than offering up the Poet as a vehicle for earthly transcendence, Poe systematically rejects the very possibility of that transcendence. Artists instead must find beauty in their struggle.

To make this argument, I must situate Poe in a theoretical context of Romanticism, spirituality, otherworldliness, and madness in connection to music. Poe scholars have written about music and literature, certainly, but they have done so without any centralized approach to it, and almost always they have written about the topic in article-length pieces.[1] Some academics have written about music Poe might have listened to or music Poe later influenced. Some have written of his music in a kind of nineteenth-century poetic fashion—the music of his language. I never have found an in-depth book-length study on Poe's use of music purely in a literary space.

Because of the lack of consolidated scholarship surrounding various studies of Poe and music, I do not extensively engage with other scholars' work on the topic. I outline my reasoning for this omission in detail in the appendix to this book. I offer instead a different theoretical framework for the study of Poe and music that substantiates, first and foremost, Poe's postlapsarian narrative. Reading Poe's works through the lens of word and music scholarship helps one to negotiate Poe's place in the Romantic musical aesthetic (primarily via Daniel Chua, Lawrence Kramer, Peter Dayan, and John Hollander). When writing about literary music, especially that birthed from an aesthetic that rejects text, the language we use to discuss music faces the danger of rapidly losing meaning. Poe's purposefully oblique descriptions of music reinforce, and even ensure, breakdown of analytic terms that directly relate to his use of it: "music," "song," "verse," "hymn," "chant," "madness," "ideality," etc. By placing Poe's sense of a Romantic musical aesthetic in dialogue with Poe scholars (such as Daniel Hoffman, Mutlu Konuk Blasing, Joseph Riddel, and Martin Roth) who identify Poe as an author "properly [located] [. . .] in a textual universe,"[2] I hope to fend off the danger of total collapse of meaning in terms surrounding Poe's literary music, at least for the length of this book.

The primary texts that underpin the book then are Michel Foucault's *Madness and Civilization* (1988), in the first part, and Daniel Chua's *Absolute Music and the Construction of Meaning* (1999), in the second. I do not consult Foucault and Chua as authoritative historians of the treatment of madness and music from ancient to modern times, but rather as practitioners of the kind of discourse in which Poe immerses himself: an ancient state of undifferentiated experience that informs the differentiated modern one in which we live. Like Foucault, who famously describes "that zero point in the course of madness at which madness is an undifferentiated experience, a not yet divided experience of division itself," Chua couches his account of the (re)-emergence of the concept of absolute music in terms of a comparison between the modern world and an ancient Pythagorean universe in which "music tunes the cosmos [. . .] and scales the human soul to the same proportions. This enabled the inaudible sounds of the heavens to vibrate within the earthly soul, and, conversely, for the audible tones of human music to reflect the celestial spheres."[3] Just as Foucault interrogates the modern understanding of insanity as that point "which relegates Reason and Madness to one side or the other [. . .] as things henceforth external, deaf to all exchange, and as though dead to one another,"[4] Chua negotiates a parallel fissure to Reason and Madness, that between the earthly and the heavenly.

Chua envisions this rupture, that in his theory led to modern disenchantment, as a severing of "the umbilical link" between earth and the cosmos, and was a protracted historical moment that dominated post-Galilei, who explicitly "collapsed music into 'reality' as an audible *fact* divorced from celestial *values*."[5] Rather than the "inaudible sounds" of the heavens that vibrated in the "earthly soul," music in its modern condition is vulgarly "heard," "real," and "earthly," and the notion of music as "inaudible" represents a no longer existent connection to the "invisible" and the "otherworldly." While I do not subscribe to Chua's rendering of a musical history that explains a fallen modernity, I believe that Poe's work does. Chua's universe best illustrates Poe's expression of a real, audible, or to use Chua's terms, "demythologised music with an empirical rationality,"[6] which is constantly at war with a celestial inaudible music that he continually tries to reclaim. When using Chua's universe in conjunction with Foucault's *Madness and Civilization*, a crucial dichotomy of reason and madness, audibility and inaudibility, the earthly and the heavenly, and the real and the supernatural emerges. In this tension, the ancient "inaudible sounds" to which the human soul vibrated (a kind of heavenly silence) have made way for another kind of silence, that which reinforces the modern severance from that prelapsarian cosmic tuning. Toward the end of this book, I differentiate between the ancient "inaudible sounds," the heavenly silence, and that silence that represents a severance from that ideal, as a distinction between Silence (the ideal) and silence (the real); these both align with Music (the ideal) and music (the real).

I ground my interpretation of Poe via Chua in Mutlu Konuk Blasing's parallel response to Poe's possible failure, which she also articulates in Platonic terms while maintaining that Poe's "failure—and his success—directly stem from his American displacement."[7] She goes on to argue:

> To borrow Derrida's terms for this Platonic distinction, the raven's language is the "rememoration" of writing, which is non-knowledge, forgetfulness, or oblivion, as opposed to true memory, which is knowledge or a repetition of truth. The only force capable, in postmythological times, of distinguishing between the true poet's "angelic," Orphic music and the failed or fake poet's hellish chatter is the standard, established by history, or craft. [. . .] Without cultural and historical authorization, he works in an echo chamber of forms empty of significance

and is condemned to self-parody—to exposing himself his manipulation of the physical and temporal properties of the language he would sound celestial notes with.[8]

Blasing incorporates into her discussion of Poe's music the recognition of Poe's entrenchment in "postmythological times," just as I have. However, while Blasing sequesters the "true poet's 'angelic,' Orphic music" from the "failed or fake poet's hellish chatter," thereby designating Poe as the singular transatlantic artist working in "an echo chamber of empty forms," I maintain that Poe extends his own sense of failure to a commentary on the modern condition of art, and that music becomes the one art form which best expresses this failure. I argue that his meta-commentary on his "manipulation of the physical and temporal properties of language" not only confines him to "self-parody," but rather the inescapability of the poet's failure paradoxically points back toward the "celestial notes" that he cannot sound.

Incorporating this argument into an analysis of both Poe's poetry and prose fiction, I will progress Blasing's notion that,

> while the poet can hear the music of the spheres—a harmony that precludes sounds [. . .]—he cannot "name" this "silence" without the means of the music of verse [. . .]. The poet has authority over "the circumscribed Eden" of dreams; the circumscribing or defining words subscribe to another authority and are subject to time and history, thus rendering the dreamed-of paradise unspeakable and unrecoverable. This paradise is both a radiant center before time and a nature before history.[9]

Although I agree that Poe's "poet," or representative voice in his tales and prose fiction, finds his "dreamed-of paradise unspeakable and unrecoverable," that "radiant center before time and history," I believe that he cannot "name" that "harmony that precludes sounds" of the music of the spheres precisely because he cannot "hear" it. Rather, Poe's work assumes a prelapsarian world from which we are completely excluded, and music most clearly conveys and incorporates notions of dispossession, an attempt to escape from history and time and return to an undifferentiated and nontemporal past. I divide this book into two parts: chapters 1 through 3 touch upon Poe's short stories, and chapters 4 through 6 focus on his poetry. This organization allows me to contextualize my argument around the little Poe wrote about music that might be heard, or "real-world music." For me, the very few performance scenes in Poe's short stories are vital to understanding Poe's musical obliqueness. These scenes form the foundation for understanding the importance of the ways that he then rejects heard music, beginning by introducing Poe's simultaneous reference to and dismissal of performed, real-world music. In each chapter, I progress the discussion away from these more "real-world" examples and toward examples of the unheard, and the otherworldly.

Using this progression, I argue for a postlapsarian division that underscores Poe's works: failure is a perversity that points heavenward.

NOTES

1. Evans, *Music and Edgar Allan Poe*.
2. Blasing, *American Poetry*, 18.
3. Foucault, *Madness and Civilization*, ix; Chua, *Absolute Music*, 15.
4. Foucault, *Madness and Civilization*, ix.
5. Chua, *Absolute Music*, 16, 18.
6. Ibid., 19.
7. Blasing, *American Poetry*, 17.
8. Ibid., 32.
9. Ibid., 23.

ONE

Is This Divine? No, This Is the Voice of a Woman

> No thinking person, hearing Malibran sing, could have doubted that she would die in the spring of her days. She crowded ages into hours. She left the world at twenty-five, having existed here thousands of years.
>
> —Edgar Allan Poe, "Marginalia"

Poe's tales "The Spectacles" and "The System of Doctor Tarr and Professor Fether" use music differently than any of his other short stories. They feature literary music that comes closest to describing earthly musical performances in anything Poe wrote in his fiction. Earthly musical performances, hereafter denoted as "real-world music," refer to music as Poe would have heard it, and which I define through Richard Leppert's classification of the eighteenth-century culture of domestic musical performances and culture of its public consumption. My argument requires a distinct definition of "real-world music" to clearly indicate the subtle ways Poe shifts away from it.

The phrase "real-world music" is not laden with musical or literary theory, nor is it burdened with a critical past. Rather, the phrase is my own, substantiated by Leppert's *The Sight of Sound: Music, Representation, and the History of the Body*. Leppert writes about home musical performances as having five "interlocking and mutually mediating but inevitably dialectical and different" components.[1] I use the first three of these to convey "real-world music":

> First, and most obvious, music comprises certain phenomena experienced as sound via the sense of hearing. Second, in Western high culture music refers to notated "instructions" for producing such sounds. Third, and here the story becomes more complex, music is a sight, a richly semantic visual phenomenon. It is a sight in performance, thus

an embodied and interactive, hence social, practice (except when performed for the self, out of the hearing of others). [. . .] Music as a sight and sound together, united in performance prior to the advent of recording technology, cannot be fully understood except in this conjunction.[2]

To fulfill the first definition, real-world music (as I define it) must be experienced by a character, in either a story or poem, as "sound via the sense of hearing": it must be recognized and described by a character as a heard sound. Clearly, the reader does not experience the textual description as a heard sound, but real-world music must describe a sound that has been experienced by the reader or could reasonably be experienced by the reader. To fulfill the second definition, a character must perform music that has the potential of being notated in the early nineteenth-century Western tonal tradition, although he or she might not explicitly follow "notated 'instructions' for producing such sounds." Any sound described in a way that would escape notation cannot be considered real-world music by this definition, even if a character in the text describes it with musical terminology, because it would no longer convey music as one could consume it in the nineteenth-century Western world. To fulfill the third definition, real-world music must have a visible source of its performance. This last component is conspicuously absent in many of Poe's pieces—with two possible exceptions. These possible exceptions are the aforementioned "The Spectacles" and "The System of Doctor Tarr and Professor Fether."

MADAME MALIBRAN: THE VERY GENIUS OF MUSIC

The stories superficially differ immensely, but they were first published around the same time, in 1844 and 1845, respectively. Also, both stories draw upon a single source for their material: *Memoirs and Letters of Madame Malibran*. Poe reviewed the *Memoirs and Letters of Madame Malibran* in 1840; in 1844 he published the first edition of "The Spectacles" and wrote his first manuscript of "The System of Doctor Tarr and Professor Fether."[3] Although his review of the memoirs comes four years before the two short stories, the three are closely related and together reveal the creative foundation for Poe's literary gesturing toward real-world music.

Born in 1808, Maria García Malibran was Poe's contemporary, and like Poe, she spent time in both England and America.[4] When she was as young as seventeen to nineteen years old (1825–1827), she performed in New York: on the "1st [of] October, 1825, Garcia and all his family [. . .] embarked in Liverpool for New York, which they reached thirty-seven days later," and on the "28th [of] November, 1827, twenty-eight days after leaving New York, Maria Malibran arrived in France."[5] Poe was in America at the same time as Malibran, but he would not have seen her perform, as he was at home in Richmond and a student at the University of Virginia at that time.[6]

In fact, his experience of opera or concerts altogether is difficult to reconstruct. He does not write in his creative pieces about any musical performers or performances that he could not have read about. In that sense, his tales give us no firm evidence concerning what music Poe actually heard. For instance, he would not have seen Malibran perform, yet Poe uses multiple details of her performances and life from the memoirs in these two tales so that, if one did not know of his reviews of the book on Malibran, one might suspect he had seen her himself. Peculiarly, Poe uses no artist apart from Malibran in this fashion. Besides Malibran (and Henriette Lalande, indirectly), Poe cites only two other famous singers in his creative pieces, Angelica Catalani and Henriette Sontag, and those references to Catalani and Sontag are insubstantial (see the appendix to this book for more).

Knowing that Merlin's *Memoirs and Letters of Maria Malibran* is the only definite source for Poe's knowledge of Malibran herself is central to understanding his literary use of music. The second volume of the memoirs concerns Malibran's personal stories, such as her troubled relationship with her husband, M. Eugene Malibran, and the first volume relates a more public biography, including Malibran's dislike of competing singer Henriette Lalande.[7] The volumes are authored by a friend, who characterizes Malibran as a "fair syren"[8] who not only became famous for her performances in the opera, but who was also popular in private circles:

> I assembled at my house a sort of musical jury—a party of unbelievers. They were, as I expected, struck with astonishment on seeing and hearing her. Maria Malibran was sublime as a dramatic singer, but her most triumphant efforts were those little extempore *fioituri*, with which she was wont to electrify her hearers in small private circles. On these occasions, when she gave free scope to her own inspirations, she seemed like the very genius of music. What a fund of original ideas, what exquisite taste, did Madame Malibran evince, when she imparted new life to a composition, by adorning it, as it were, with the brilliant and vivid hues of the rainbow. Before Madame Malibran had sung her first aria at my party, she had completely converted the little group of unbelievers into devout worshippers.[9]

This "very genius of music" did not merely excel in her private and public performances for high society, however. According to Merlin, Malibran showed a dedicated affection for the less fortunate, and even the outcast. One particularly affecting anecdote conveys how Malibran's even voice touched the inmates of an asylum.[10] While there, Malibran sang for a patient, and then she also received a performance from other patients, in turn. Each of these details of Malibran's personal life that Poe read about for his review in 1840 plays out in the two stories in which Edgar Allan Poe comes closest to using real-world music. F. Eugene Malibran is one possible nominal influence for Eugénie Lalande of "The Spectacles," and Henriette Lalande shares her surname with Eugénie and Stéphanie Lalande in the same story. The asylum that Malibran visits differs from the one portrayed in "The System of Doctor Tarr and Professor Fether," but the singing inmates, the director of the asylum, and the idea of a young woman singing in a private chamber all appear in the story in ways that illuminate Poe's literary music when read in the context of the memoirs that Poe reviewed.

"THE SPECTACLES": IN IMITATION OF MALIBRAN

"It was [on] an opera night" that Napoleon Buonaparte Froissart Simpson sets the scene for "The Spectacles."[11] Refusing to wear glasses for fear that they "[disfigure] the countenance," he heads off with his friend Talbot to attend the "P— Theatre," most likely in New York.[12] The theatre promises "a very rare attraction," which Poe never names, but certainly someone like Maria Malibran would constitute that rarity in New York.[13] Despite the "rare attraction," whatever or whomever it may be, and the "front seats" in which Simpson and Talbot sit, Simpson "amused [himself] by observing the audience," and calls his friend a "a musical *fanatico*" for giving "his undivided attention to the stage."[14] Simpson has not even turned his "eyes to the *prima donna*" when he sees a woman in a viewing box, "grace personified, incarnate."[15] Simpson takes no notice of the opera, but becomes entranced with this woman, who we later discover is an elderly woman named Madame Lalande, whom he describes here as his *"first* love."[16]

Simpson curiously misses the entire performance because he is so entranced by the vision of the "magic of a lovely form in woman—the necromancy of female gracefulness," but also by the sight of a "diamond ring [. . .] of extraordinary value."[17] Overcome by her beauty, which he does not really see correctly due to the absence of his spectacles, and overcome by her wealth, about which he makes no mistake, Simpson never responds at all to the opera, much to the dismay of his companion, who after being subjected to Simpson's questions about Lalande during the performance, scolds Simpson: "*do* hold your tongue, *if* you can."[18] Thus, the tale introduces Simpson to the story as willfully ignorant of music, unmoved by the "rare attraction" of the opera, and drawn instead to the sight of this woman and her wealth.

Still, the opera's "very rare attraction" is not the only musical performer in the story. Simpson later attends Lalande's home for "a little musical *levée*," which promised to showcase "some good singing."[19] As Simpson narrates the story, he takes this opportunity to reaffirm himself as a true appreciator of music, as he now realizes how much music matters to the woman with whom he's become infatuated. He sets the scene in the following manner:

> The evening thus spent was unquestionably the most delicious of my life. Madame Lalande had not overrated the musical abilities of her friends; and the singing I here heard I had never heard excelled in any private circle out of Vienna. The instrumental performers were many and of superior talents. The vocalists were chiefly ladies, and no individual sang less than well. At length, upon a peremptory call for "Madame Lalande," she arose at once, without affectation or demur, from the *chaise longue* upon which she had sat by my side, and, accompanied by one or two gentlemen and her female friend of the opera, repaired to the piano in the main drawing-room. [. . .] I was [. . .] deprived of the pleasure of seeing, although not of hearing her, sing.[20]

Even though Lalande is "accompanied by one or two gentlemen and her female friend" at the piano in the drawing room, Simpson does not follow them; he does not actually see her sing. In terms of "real-world music," the third definition is held in limbo; although the narrator sees the piano, sees Lalande and company retire to it, he does not experience the actual musical production as a "richly semantic visual phenomenon."[21] Herein lies the crux of the story's twist. Because Simpson's pride causes him to refuse to wear his spectacles, Simpson sees and speaks to Eugénie Lalande, the woman he "saw" in the opera and with whom he believes himself to be in love, but he hears Stéphanie Lalande sing. He eventually discovers that Eugénie is his great-great-grandmother, and Stéphanie his age-appropriate faceless, speechless musical performer.

To return for a moment to Malibran's memoirs, if we position the real Eugene Malibran, Maria Malibran's husband, as one of the inspirations for the fictional Eugénie, the quality they have in common is an attachment to material wealth. While Eugénie actually has wealth in the tale, Eugene Malibran "became a bankrupt, the inhabitant of a jail" and continually pursued for financial reasons Maria Malibran, who gave "up even her marriage settlement to the creditors of her husband."[22] "The Spectacles" inverts Malibran's biographical story. Simpson's attachment to material wealth enhances his blindness to any other qualities, so much so that he can clearly see Eugénie's wealth, but mistakes everything else. Readers should question Simpson's fervor for Stéphanie Lalande's performance then, in this inversion of Malibran's memoirs, especially as Simpson acknowledges directly that he was denied the "pleasure of seeing, although not of hearing her, sing."[23] Simpson continues:

> The impression she produced upon the company seemed electrical—but the effect upon myself was something even more. I know not how adequately to describe it. It arose, in part, no doubt, from the sentiment of love with which I was imbued; but chiefly from my conviction of the extreme sensibility of the singer. It is beyond the reach of art to endow either air or recitative with more impassioned *expression* than was hers.

> Her utterance of the romance in Otello—the tone with which she gave the words "*Sul mio sasso*," in the Capuletti—is ringing in my memory yet. Her lower tones were absolutely miraculous. Her voice embraced three complete octaves, extending from the contralto D to the D upper soprano, and, though sufficiently powerful to have filled the San Carlos, executed, with the minutest precision, every difficulty of vocal composition—ascending and descending scales, cadences, or *fioriture*. In the finale of the Sonnambula, she brought about a most remarkable effect at the words—
>
> Ah! non giunge uman pensiero
> Al contento ond "io son piena."
>
> Here, in imitation of Malibran, she modified the original phrase of Bellini, so as to let her voice descend to the tenor G, when by a rapid transition, she struck the G above the treble stave, springing over an interval of two octaves.[24]

This citation makes this tale one of only two tales in which Poe cites operatic pieces (the other being "The System of Doctor Tarr and Professor Fether"). In doing so, Simpson (and thus Poe) appears to exhibit some knowledge of scored music, describing Lalande's vocal range with control and precision, a fact that led Charmenz Lenhart to conclude that this "single passage from the prose tales should prove that Poe [himself] understood much about vocal music."[25] However, as Mabbott soon pointed out, the "proof" of Poe's musical knowledge was nothing more than plagiarism.[26] Burton Pollin elaborated:

> coalesced two descriptions of [Malibran's] voice for part of his review without the benefit of quotation marks. Now in need of material for the vocal enchantments of Madame Lalande, following the suggestion about "a difficult bravura" in the original, he quoted his own borrowing from the *Memoirs of Madame Malibran*, which Poe reviewed for *Burton's Gentleman's Magazine*.[27]

Pollin does not discuss, however, that Poe borrowed something else from the *Memoirs and Letters of Madame Malibran*: the name "Lalande" itself. Far from an arbitrary choice, the name appears in chapter sixteen of the first volume in reference to Henriette Méric-Lalande.

The memoirs describe Lalande's relationship to Malibran as follows: "On her arrival [to London, Malibran] found that Madame Lalande was the prima donna whom she herself was to succeed. This lady had become a considerable favourite in England, which annoyed Madame Malibran not a little."[28] Malibran decided upon seeing Lalande perform, and the memoirs quote letters Malibran wrote to a friend in which she describes Lalande's performance. Malibran describes Lalande's "middle notes [as] wiry, and [as having] a harsh and shrill effect" and her voice as having "trembled so, that none could find out whether it was sweet or harsh"; she "utterly spoiled the pretty cavatina" and "finished her part in the same bad style in which she began it."[29] Malibran gathers her information while viewing Lalande's performance of Bellini's *Il Pirata*, an opera Malibran calls "decidedly feeble."[30] In terms of Lalande's physical appearance, Malibran writes:

> I will give you an account of the *debút* [sic] of Madame Lalande. [. . .] Venga la bella Italiana, said I to my little self. I was all impatience, and as she appeared I stretched over the box to catch a glimpse of her. Alas! what a disappointment! Picture to yourself a woman of about forty, with light hair and a vulgar broad face, with an unfavourable expression, a bad figure, as clumsy a foot as my own, and most unbecomingly dressed.[31]

Malibran's spiteful descriptions of Lalande convey an antagonistic relationship that comes into play in Poe's work when Poe goes on to use Lalande's name in his tale as the attribution for the plagiarized positive and detailed descriptions of Malibran's singing. Rather than camouflaging this sleight-of-hand in exchanging the real Malibran's performances for the fictional Lalande's, Poe draws attention to his plagiarism of the memoirs via his review by illustrating Lalande's performance as an "imitation of Malibran"; the fictional Lalande's singing is a textual "imitation of Malibran," itself copied from Poe's review, copied from the memoirs. In contrast, the voiceless, faceless *"prima donna"* from the story's beginning never returns.

Whatever the "very rare attraction," Simpson does not hear or see it. He sees Eugénie Lalande, his great-great-grandmother, who derives her name from Malibran's hated husband (Eugene) and rival (Henriette Lalande). Moreover, he does not hear or see Eugénie herself sing. Simpson instead goes to a smaller performance and hears another substitution, Stéphanie Lalande, and in his description of her performance, Poe draws attention to it being in "imitation of Malibran," and thus to the stark contrast between the specific, the material, and the completely comprised words of Lalande of the story and the voiceless, faceless "rare attraction" whom she opposes. Simpson can only repeat plagiarized words that relate to the performance of the real "genius of music," Malibran.

In choosing the descriptions for Stéphanie Lalande's "imitation of Malibran," Poe derives the excerpts from two different volumes of the memoirs; the first part of the excerpt (that apart from Lalande's "electrical" effect) comes from the second volume:

> Madame Malibran's voice embraced three complete octaves, extending from the contralto D to the upper soprano D. There is no sound in nature which can convey any idea of her lower notes. Those who never heard her sing the romance in Otello,—those who had never heard her soul-moving tones in that sublime phrase in the Capuletti, *Sul mio sasso*, have not felt the vibration of the tenderest chord of the heart. Her voice, though sufficiently powerful to fill the spacious theatres of San Carlos and La Scala, was capable of executing with precision all the difficulties

of vocal composition: ascending and descending scales, fiorituri, cadences, all were equally easy to her.[32]

Poe rewrites this section with changes demonstrative of the ways I argue are typical of his use of his musical vocabulary in his short stories. Firstly, he changes the idea that there "is no sound in nature which can convey any idea of her [Malibran's] lower notes" to the idea that Lalande's "lower tones were absolutely miraculous." Secondly, rather than "sing the romance in Otello" as Malibran does, Poe changes Lalande's performance to an "utterance of the romance in Otello." Malibran's "soul-moving tones in that sublime phrase [. . .] *Sul mio sasso*" become Lalande's "tone with which she gave the words '*Sul mio sasso*.'" Poe's tale completely omits idea of "the vibration of the tenderest chord of the heart." I will elaborate upon the meaning of these changes shortly.

The second part remains largely unchanged from the original: "But who can describe the electrifying effect she produced in the finale? 'Ah! non giunge uman pensiero / Al contento ond 'io son piena.' By an ingenious transposition of the original phrase of Bellini, her voice descended to the tenor G; then by a rapid transition she struck the G above the treble stave, an interval of two octaves."[33] The major difference is that Poe reiterates that Lalande brings "about a most remarkable effect at the words" themselves. Poe omits the "soul," "nature," the "sublime," and the "heart." As opposed to the Malibran of the memoirs, Poe's literary Lalande is all "utterance" and "words."

Poe's own reaction, published in 1840 separately from this tale, to reading the *Memoirs of Madame Malibran* takes a more passionate tone: "No thinking person, hearing Malibran sing, could have doubted that she would die in the spring of her days. She crowded ages into hours. She left the world at twenty-five, having existed her thousands of years."[34] Rather than repeat this, more mystical, interpretation of the memoirs that omits any specific mention of Malibran's words or the individual notes she sings, Poe opts for plagiarizing those elements he personally avoids from the memoirs themselves, highlighting the description of Lalande's singing as transmitted through words alone. The continual descriptive insistence on comparing Lalande's singing performance with "utterance" and "words" opposes the theoretical idea of song as "broaching the ineffable"—that Romantic notion that Lawrence Kramer describes as "the mythical union of a lower reality embodied in language and a higher one embodied in music."[35] Far from uniting "language" and "music," or even uniting language and descriptions of music, Simpson's description of Lalande's vocal range remains separate from the words she utters, and Poe's plagiarism of the review and of himself highlights this separation by further emphasizing the words themselves.

Moreover, this is the only story in which Poe specifically describes the performance of music in a way that refers explicitly to the notes in a score. That is not to say that elements of real-world music do not occur elsewhere in the stories ("The System of Doctor Tarr and Professor Fether" also refers to a musical note and "The Fall of the House of Usher" (1839) references a musical piece); but this is the only story in which he refers to the specific notes on the material score, the "notated 'instructions' for producing" music.[36] As one of Poe's least supernatural tales, it also exemplifies another rare instance in Poe's oeuvre; it is devoid of an underlying theme of madness. Details of the story might be exaggerated, but overall the tale depicts what could be ordinary life, and it is the only story in which a character gives a private concert performance in the nineteenth-century parlor tradition. Poe plays on custom, and on repetition and imitation, to reinforce the superficiality of the scene. The character Lalande acts as a namesake of the real Lalande and sings "in imitation of Malibran," the description of which in turn repeats multiple textual layers; all these elements of repetition and imitation reinforce the levels of distance and materiality between the reader and musical performance. That technique changes slightly in "The System of Doctor Tarr and Professor Fether."

"The System of Doctor Tarr and Professor Fether": *The Lunatics Wished in Their Turn to Sing*

The connections between the *Memoirs and Letters of Madame Malibran* and "The System of Doctor Tarr and Professor Fether" are not as direct as those between the memoirs and "The Spectacles." In the anecdote of Malibran singing for a patient,

> Madame Malibran approached a piano which stood in the chamber, and ran her fingers over the keys. In an instant the poor maniac was all attention. She sang the romance in Otello. "Is this divine?" exclaimed the young man, and he appeared violently excited. "No," he added, "this is the voice of a woman": then bursting into tears, he threw himself into a chair and sobbed aloud.[37]

In this account and in "The System of Doctor Tarr and Professor Fether," a young woman sings an aria in a madhouse, even if the details are not directly repeated. The crucial element from this anecdote that resonates in this story and many of Poe's others, is the "poor maniac['s]" struggle in hearing Malibran: he initially questions whether the experience is "divine," then realizing it is "the voice of a woman," he weeps. One possible interpretation of this anecdote illustrates an idea that I believe inhabits Poe's use of music in his creative works; initially experienced as "divine," Malibran's singing is immediately recognized as nothing more than the earthly "voice of a woman," and both the acknowledgment and suffering of this duality stem from the "poor maniac."

The anecdote links and embodies in the "poor maniac" questions of the relationship between madness, divinity, failure, and singing, all of which are key in understanding Poe's music. The following anecdote from the memoirs thus takes on a deeper significance, that in which Malibran receives her performance in turn: "Several of the lunatics wished in their turn to sing to Madame Malibran, who very patiently listened to them, although the discordance of their tones was indescribably disagreeable."[38] Malibran's private performance as it is interpreted by one kind of madness relates to divinity, albeit through mortal failure to be divine; the group performance of another kind of madness made public lends itself to a described "discordance," which does not relate to divinity at all.

These themes find their parallel in "The System of Doctor Tarr and Professor Fether," a story that opens with the narrator finding himself in an occupied parlor of the "private Mad House": "At a piano, singing an aria from Bellini, sat a young and very beautiful woman, who, at my entrance, paused in her song, and received me with graceful courtesy. Her voice was low, and her whole manner subdued. I thought, too, that I perceived the traces of sorrow in her countenance."[39] As in "The Spectacles," the aria is by Bellini, although here it remains unnamed.[40] While the narrator of "The Spectacles" is completely cut off from seeing Lalande sing, the young lady of this story implicitly performs long enough for the visitor to recognize her performance, but the young lady also "pause[s] in her song" "at [his] entrance." In this way, both narrators do not describe seeing the performance. As in "The Spectacles," the third definition of real-world music, that "music is a sight," is held in limbo.[41] In both of these tales, the narrators know the source of the singing, but cannot be said to explicitly watch the musical production as it unfolds. Both narrators are removed from the sight of performance, forcing them to describe the visual aspect of the performance as they imagine it, not as they see it.

The narrator never describes the details of the piece because the young lady stops singing once her private playing is exposed, and although the narrator does mention that her "voice was low" when she pauses and receives him into the parlor, she does not sing at this point. Even as he describes her speaking in a "low" voice, the narrator carefully omits her words. A point that will return in stories such as "Ligeia," this "low" quality does not clearly refer to being "low" in pitch or in volume. Due to its ambiguity, Poe generically uses the term to signify some undercurrent of solemnity and mystery.

The two stories have other elements in common. They contain the only two instances in which the characters sing a high art song by a recognized composer presumably accompanied with lyrics.[42] Both evoke concordant and readily imaginable musical performances, although in "The System of Doctor Tarr and Professor Fether" one might not know which Bellini aria she sings. Unlike "The Spectacles," in "The System of

Doctor Tarr and Professor Fether," the music is less specific, less clearly described so that it does not draw so explicitly upon the reader's musical memory. These two stories do share the topic of individual females performing in private spaces: Lalande for company and the young girl of the latter story for herself. Whereas Simpson, however, gives the reader every reason to doubt his description of Lalande, as his abundant attention to the material world renders him blind to interpreting it, the narrator of "The System of Doctor Tarr and Professor Fether" wrestles with a more complex relationship in his story between the expression of madness in terms of public and private musical expression.

The narrator of "The System of Doctor and Professor Fether" later attends the dining room of the asylum and encounters multiple discordant musical performances. Seated at the far end of the room are "seven or eight people with fiddles, fifes, trombones, and a drum. These fellows annoyed [him] very much, at intervals, during the repast, by an infinite variety of noises, which were intended for music, and which appeared to afford much entertainment to all present, with the exception of [himself]."[43] As opposed to the previous examples, this is real-world music in the sense of being "experienced as sound" and as "a sight," with a visible source. However, this instance problematizes the idea of the second definition of real-world music, which refers to "notated 'instructions' for producing such sounds."[44] These "seven or eight people" perform their "intended [. . .] music" in a space made public and not purely for a concert setting; the people provide background "noise" to an already cacophonous dining environment. Their cacophony increases as the dinner progresses, as diners "jested—they laughed—they perpetrated a thousand absurdities" while "the fiddles shrieked—the drum row-de-dowed—the trombones bellowed like so many brazen bulls of Phalaris—and the whole scene, growing gradually worse and worse, as the wines gained the ascendancy, became at length a sort of Pandemonium *in petto*."[45] The noise of the scene builds upon itself, as the people "jested," then "laughed," and then the "fiddles shrieked." The fiddles are depicted with a distinctly vocal description, "shrieking," such that they cannot even be described in terms of their limitations as musical instruments. Poe's attribution of this cacophony to a "Pandemonium *in petto*" describes the scene as Pandemonium in miniature, linking it to a term of musical direction in a way that associates the chest voice with chaotic and cacophonous sound. The musical term becomes intimately tied to the protracted and harsh noises and the concept of a kind of nightmarish earthly struggle.

THE ALCHEMY OF UNREASON:
WELL AND STRENUOUSLY SUNG!

As opposed to the controlled description of Lalande's performance in musical terms, and as opposed to the young lady's "low" voice that opens the story, the "musical performance" of this mad group is neither associated with words nor with concert music, but with noise. At one point, the same orchestra breaks out "with one accord, into 'Yankee Doodle,' which they performed, if not exactly in tune, at least with an energy superhuman, during the whole of the uproar."[46] Mabbott points out the most glaringly out-of-place element of the performance, that in "Poe's day 'Yankee Doodle' was our most popular national air, but its selection by a French orchestra, even if mad, was certainly extraordinary."[47] They perform their bizarre choice of music with "energy" and "during" an "uproar" and "not exactly in tune," all implying dissonance. Moreover, they do so to mask another source of discord. A sudden "series of loud screams, or yells" arise from the inmates (the previous sane managers of the asylum).[48] After the narrator inquires after the nature of the sound, the director of the asylum chalks it up to being "mere *bagatelle*" in which the "lunatics [. . .] get up a howl in concert [. . .] as is sometimes the case with a bevy of dogs at night. It occasionally happens, however, that the *concerto* yells are succeeded by a simultaneous effort at breaking loose; when, of course, some little danger is to be apprehended."[49] The narrator of the story not only depicts the cacophonous "howl" of the so-called "lunatics" in the terminology of music, but this expression of madness also takes a form that resonates with Foucault's description of the development of the perception of madness associated with the caged or the asylum: "Madness borrowed its face from the mask of the beast [. . .] as if madness, at its extreme point [. . .] managed to rejoin, by a paroxysm of strength, the immediate violence of animality. This model of animality prevailed in the asylums and gave them their cagelike aspect, their look of the menagerie."[50] In fact, many of the characters of "The System of Doctor Tarr and Professor Fether" who produce cacophonous sounds described in musical vocabulary, are compared to animals. In this instance, the "mere *bagatelle*" parallels a "bevy of dogs."

One man in particular describes himself in the third person, as a frog, claiming: "Sir, if that man was *not* a frog, I can only observe that it is a pity he was not. His croak thus—o-o-o-o-gh-o-o-o-o-gh! was the finest note in the world—B flat."[51] The narrator goes on to elaborate that then, "again, the frog-man croaked away as if the salvation of his soul depended upon every note that he uttered."[52] Another character believes herself to be a rooster, and would "sing out incessantly, at the top of her voice, 'Cock-a-doodle-de-dooooooh!'"[53] Noticeably, the further the descriptions of the noises descend into the mad and the bestial, the further they move away from real-world music. Even though these examples fit some elements of the rules for real-world music, being experienced as "sound via the sense of hearing" and as "sight," their descriptions associate them with discord rather than musical performance.[54]

Returning to Foucault, he writes: "Here is madness elevated to spectacle above the silence of the asylums, and becoming a public scandal [. . .]. Unreason was hidden in the silence of the houses of confinement, but madness continued to be present on the stage of the world—with more commotion than ever."[55] Although I do not appropriate for this book Foucault's differentiation between perception of "unreason" and "madness," I argue that the distinction between the "silence" of "confinement" and the "commotion" of madness on the "stage of the world" permeates Poe's tales. Understanding this in terms of Foucault's separate discourse in *Madness and Civilization* draws attention to a key element in the relationship between the public musically described madness and cacophony. Unlike madness elsewhere in Poe's works, none of this loud, animalistic public depiction of madness via music points toward spirituality, mystery, or the beyond. To once again turn to Foucault:

> animal metamorphosis is no longer the visible sign of infernal powers, nor the result of a diabolic alchemy of unreason. The animal in man no longer has any value as the sign of a Beyond; it has become his madness, without relation to anything but itself: his madness in the state of nature. The animality that rages in madness dispossesses man of what is specifically human in him; not in order to deliver him over to other powers, but simply to establish him at the zero degree of his own nature. For classicism, madness in its ultimate form is man in immediate relation to his animality, without other reference, without recourse.[56]

This description pointedly sums up a specific kind of relationship between animalism and madness that speaks to one kind of earthly madness and diabolism in Poe. In what this book describes as an earthly madness, a materially based madness, the "animal in man" has no "value as the sign of a beyond; it has become his madness, without relation to anything but itself." This kind of mania diametrically opposes that anecdote of the "poor maniac" who weeps after Malibran sings to him. The madness of the public animalistic display is a madness tied fully to the bestial and not to a sense of the beyond; this madness, and/or this explicit tie to the earthly, when expressed in musical terms in Poe, is continually made more present, whether through emphasis on words, on discord, or on the materiality of the performer or performance instrument. Each of these qualities points back to a notable absence of any "sign of a Beyond."

A few of Poe's tales make a similar connection between meaningless madness and noise. "Four Beasts in One," as Mabbott summarizes it, is a "combination of stories about the freaks of a mad ancient monarch and the caricatures of a nineteenth-century king of France [. . .] the result is one of the best of the tales of the grotesque."⁵⁷ The narrator has the reader "suppose" that "it is now the year of the world three thousand eight hundred and thirty, and [. . .] [we are] at that most grotesque habitation of man," Antioch.⁵⁸ The narrator then leads the reader through the city, through "an infinity of mud huts" and to "the new Temple of the sun" before describing an "extraordinary tumult [. . .] a loud noise even for Antioch" stemming from "the principal street, which is called the street of Timarchus."⁵⁹ The narrator guides the reader from the "huts," or private homes, through to the "Temple" and then to a "principal street," where the public gathers.

Discordant sound emerges from "the principal street": "The uproar increases. Shouts of laughter ascend the skies. The air becomes dissonant with wind instruments, and horrible with the clamor of a million throats."⁶⁰ The dissonance builds as the story's "mad" "king" approaches, a grotesque "king" who is a "cameleopard" that has "the visage of a man."⁶¹ As opposed to the normalized interior of "The Spectacles" and the initially normalized interior of "The System of Doctor Tarr and Professor Fether," the public space of "Four Beasts in One" is grotesquely present, creating a vivid, loud, and bizarre Antioch of the past. In this public space, the "wind instruments" create dissonance parallel, nearly synonymous, with the air becoming "horrible" with the "clamor of a million throats."

Just after this, "a troop of a similar description" to "a thousand chained Israelitish prisoners [. . .] [who] have made a Latin hymn upon the valor of the king, and are singing it as they go" pass by with a "Latin hymn."⁶² Poe gives us their lyrics:

> A thousand, a thousand, a thousand,
> A thousand, a thousand, a thousand,
> We, with one warrior, have slain!
> A thousand, a thousand, a thousand, a thousand,
> Sing a thousand over again!
> Soho!—let us sing
> Long life to our king,
> Who knocked over a thousand so fine!
> Soho!—let us roar,
> He has given us more
> Red gallons of gore
> Than all Syria can furnish of wine!⁶³

Poe prints the hymn in the text and the narrator redescribes it a few times. The story first prints the "hymn" in Latin, then prints it again in this English translation. In the English version, he further draws attention to the words of the "hymn" by using a forced masculine rhyme. He then notes within the tale that "Flavius Vopiscus says, that the hymn here introduced, was sung by the rabble upon the occasion of Aurelian, in the Sarmatic war, having slain with his own hand, nine hundred and fifty of the enemy."⁶⁴ Instead of the lyrics of a more spiritual "hymn," these lyrics call for a "roar" for the "king" who has "given us more / Red gallons of gore." Not only does Antioch have a mad king with a bizarre embodiment, but the tale centers on a gory attachment to the material aspects of death. This perverse hymn, moreover, does not follow any real piece of music, nor does it mention a score. Rather, instead of being tied to music, it is tied to noise. As if this were not pinned enough to the materially diabolical, the narrator describes it being "sung by the rabble" and then moves further away from real-world music by having this "hymn" for and by the "rabble" then reflected in a "song of triumph" that Epiphanes, a kind of supernatural creature, sings for himself:

> Who is king but Epiphanes?
> Say—do you know?
> Who is king but Epiphanes?
> Bravo!—bravo!
> There is none but Epiphanes,
> No—there is none:
> So tear down the temples,
> And put out the sun!

> Well and strenuously sung! The populace are hailing him "Prince of Poets," as well as "Glory of the East," "Delight of the Universe," and "most remarkable of Cameleopards." They have *encored* his effusion, and—do you hear?—he is singing it over again.⁶⁵

The "song of triumph," specifically printed in the text, is "strenuously sung" and then repeated in an encore. Again, the lyrics to this "song" are marked by specific, material, and horrifying images, with the call to "tear down the temples, / And put out the sun," but again the words are specified, and not the music of the "song." Not only is the singing "strenuously sung" by the "rabble" and couched in other forms of discordance in the preceding paragraph, but that discordance is not reflected in musical terms, but in words themselves. The animalism of Epiphanes, the "cameleopard" that has "the visage of a man," does not point to any sort of a beyond. The madness, expressed in musical terminology, does nothing but establish man, in Foucault's terms, "at the zero degree of his own nature."⁶⁶

Like Epiphanes, the creature that is both man and giraffe, there are supernatural characters in Poe's tales closely allied with bestial, diabolical, earthly madness, and the vocabulary of music associated with them follows the same principles. Another story that portrays an instrument of the public sphere in a descriptively material manner is "The Devil in the Belfry." In this story, the devil carries "a fiddle nearly five times as big as himself."⁶⁷ The first time the devil uses the fiddle, he uses it to beat the belfry-man: "lifting up the big fiddle, beat him with it so long and so soundly, that what with the belfry-man being so fat, and the fiddle being so hollow, you would have sworn that there was a regiment of double-bass drummers all beating the devil's tattoo up in the belfry of the steeple of Vondervotteimittiss."[68] The fiddle used as a weapon turns into an untuned instrument, like "a regiment of double-bass drummers." When the devil actually plays the fiddle, he does so in the town belfry such that the public can hear it: "In his teeth the villain held the bell-rope, which he kept jerking about with his head, raising such a clatter that my ears ring again even to think about it. On his lap lay the big fiddle at which he was scraping out of all time and tune, with both hands, making a great show, the nincompoop! of playing 'Judy O'Flannagan' and 'Paddy O'Raferty.'"[69] As in "The Spectacles" and "The System of Doctor Tarr and Professor Fether," the tunes "Judy O'Flannagan" and "Paddy O'Raferty" are quite possibly solely derived from other authors Poe would have read, in this case William Maginn and Washington Irving.[70] These tunes, like "Yankee Doodle," are not high art music, nor are they played in accordance with their notation, for the devil plays by "scraping out of all time and tune."

Moving even further along the trajectory of the diabolical and into hell itself, in "The Duc de L'Omelette" music becomes even less like real-world music while maintaining qualities associated with this earthly madness and diabolism. The Duc arrives in the halls of the devil and hears something described in terms of melody, a description that changes slightly between the first and final versions. In the first version of the story, the Duc looks through an "uncurtained window" and sees the "most ghastly of all fires," to which Poe comments: "Could he have imagined that the glorious, the voluptuous, the never-dying symphonies of that melodious hall, as they passed filtered and transmuted through the alchemy of that enchanted glass, were the wailings and the howlings of the hopeless and the damned?"[71] In the final version of the story, this description changes: "*He could not help imagining* that the glorious, the voluptuous, the never-dying *melodies* which *pervaded that hall*, as they pass filtered and transmuted through the alchemy of the enchanted window-panes, were the wailings and the howlings of the hopeless and the damned!"[72] (In both cases, the shift from "Could he have imagined" to "He could not help imagining" brings more force to the link between the "wailings and howlings" and the music he hears as he looks out into the fire, such that the tale maintains the first definition of real-world music: he experiences the melodies as "sound via the sense of hearing."[73] In terms of the third definition of real-world music, that "music is a sight," the Duc has access to its transmission through the "window-panes," but they are "enchanted," their "alchemy" affects his vision of the musical production such that he could "not help imagining" its source. Even if one assumes the truth of the Duc's interpretation, Poe's changes between editions reveal the importance of obscurity. The first version's "symphonies" become "melodies," and the description of the hall itself is no longer "melodious." Through these changes, Poe renders that which is "melodious" less specific; rather than being a specific series of notes, or even performed pieces in their entireties, as "symphonies" would be, the "melodious" does not signify a complete musical piece. In both versions, however, this description of the "melodious" is associated with torture, hellfire, and the most material versions of death and damnation. More importantly, both versions leave the "wailings and howlings" unarticulated; no words are pinned to the music, but rather the music conveys an unarticulated agony. Thus, as the settings of Poe's stories and as Poe's plots move from the earthly, the sane, and the lack of the supernatural through the earthly and the mad, the deathly and the gory, descriptions of music move from consonant descriptions based on real-world sources to discordant and loud articulations of agony or screams. As the plot and setting move toward the diabolical supernatural, as in "The Duc de L'Omelette," descriptions of music, although maintaining an unarticulated sense of agony, fit less and less into the definition of real-world music, becoming more complex and indefinite.

NOTES

1. Leppert, *Sight of Sound*, 64.
2. Ibid.
3. Poe, "Rev. of *Memoirs*," 248–49; Mabbott, ed., *Edgar Allan Poe: Tales*, 2: 886, 1002.
4. Fitzlyon, *Maria Malibran*, 23.
5. Ibid., 34, 54.
6. Quinn, *Edgar Allan Poe*, 92–113.
7. Merlin and Malibran, *Memoirs and Letters*, 2: 6–8; Ibid., 1: 108.
8. Ibid., 191.
9. Ibid., 38–39.
10. Ibid., 212–14.
11. Poe, "Spectacles," 889.
12. Ibid., 888; Mabbott, ed., *Edgar Allan Poe: Tales*, 2: 917. He never gives a location for the theatre, but Mabbott comments that the "Park Theatre was the leading playhouse of New York."
13. Poe, "The Spectacles," 889.
14. Ibid.
15. Ibid.
16. Ibid., 895.
17. Ibid., 889–90.
18. Ibid., 892.
19. Ibid., 904.
20. Ibid., 904–05.
21. Leppert, *Sight of Sound*, 64.
22. Merlin and Malibran, *Memoirs and Letters*, 2: 8.
23. Poe, "The Spectacles," 905.
24. Ibid.
25. Lenhart, *Musical Influence*, 130.
26. Mabbott, *Edgar Allan Poe: Tales*, 2: 917.
27. Pollin, "The 'Spectacles' of Poe," 188.
28. Merlin and Malibran, *Memoirs and Letters*, 1: 108.

29. Ibid., 110–12.
30. Ibid., 112.
31. Ibid., 110.
32. Merlin and Malibran, *Memoirs and Letters*, 2: 122–23.
33. Ibid., 1: 192.
34. Poe, "Marginalia," 1345.
35. Kramer, *Music and Poetry*, 2.
36. Leppert, *Sight of Sound*, 64.
37. Merlin and Malibran, *Memoirs and Letters*, 1: 214.
38. Ibid.
39. Poe, "System of Doctor Tarr," 1004.
40. See Preston, *Opera on the Road*, 64. There were performances of *La Sonnambula* in Philadelphia in 1839. Poe also lived there in 1839 (see Quinn, *Edgar Allan Poe*, 268). There is no historical evidence available to suggest Poe attended them, however.
41. Leppert, *Sight of Sound*, 64.
42. See Poe, "Fall of the House," 405. In it, Poe cites the "last waltz of Von Weber," and although Roderick Usher may or may not sing lyrics to the piece, the real-world piece itself does not have any lyrics. This will be discussed in the following chapter.
43. Poe, "System of Doctor Tarr," 1009.
44. Leppert, *Sight of Sound*, 64.
45. Poe, "System of Doctor Tarr," 1017.
46. Ibid., 1020.
47. Ibid., 1024.
48. Ibid., 1014.
49. Ibid., 1015.
50. Foucault, *Madness and Civilization*, 72.
51. Poe, "System of Doctor Tarr," 1012.
52. Ibid., 1020.
53. Ibid., 1021.
54. Leppert, *Sight of Sound*, 64.
55. Foucault, *Madness and Civilization*, 69.
56. Ibid., 73–74.
57. Mabbott, *Edgar Allan Poe: Tales*, 1: 117.
58. Poe, "Four Beasts in One," 120.
59. Ibid., 122–24.
60. Ibid., 124–25.
61. Ibid., 123–24, 126.
62. Ibid., 124.
63. Ibid., 124–25.
64. Ibid., 125.
65. Ibid., 126–27.
66. Foucault, *Madness and Civilization*, 74.
67. Edgar Allan Poe, "Devil in the Belfry," 371.
68. Ibid., 372.
69. Ibid., 374.
70. Levine and Levine, eds., *Short Fiction*, 431.
71. Poe, "Duc de L'Omelette [A]," 36.
72. Poe, "Duc de L'Omelette [F]," 36 (my italics).
73. Leppert, *Sight of Sound*, 64.

TWO
Another Kind of Musician Altogether

> I've been working on *La Chute de la Maison Usher* recently and have almost finished a long monologue for Roderick. It's sad enough to make the stones weep for what neurasthenics have to go through. It smells charmingly of mildew obtained by mixing the sounds of the low oboe with violin harmonics.
>
> —Claude Debussy

Debussy never finished *La Chute de la Maison Usher*. Debussy struggled with writing the piece in part because he felt the influence of the "atmosphere" of Poe's stories to the extent that he conflated his own sensitivities with those of Roderick Usher. Jack Sullivan explains that Debussy "was not so much influenced as 'obsessed,' identifying himself repeatedly with Poe's most morbidly isolated hero, with whom he felt a terrible empathy and spiritual kinship," and Debussy exposes this kinship by tying the story's "atmosphere" to the "atmosphere" of his own piece, as though the "low oboe" and the "violin harmonics" arise organically out of Poe's descriptions.[1] The story also lends itself to Debussy's focus. The narrator of "The Fall of the House of Usher" takes a relatively large amount of space to describe the surroundings of the house itself; he takes five extended paragraphs before he even enters the house to portray the landscape and the "atmosphere peculiar" to the setting.[2] Poe's description of the atmosphere in this story, as well as those of stories like "William Wilson," prompts critic Gerhard Joseph to argue that "physical objects are suffused with a mingled aura of ineffable beauty and suffocating gloom; houses and palaces and cities are built to a shadowy music and take upon themselves deathlike associations."[3] Even though for Joseph music mingles with death in the story's "suffocating gloom," no musical descriptions actually arise in the narrator's description of the house. Rather, the crucial element to the setting of "The Fall of the House of

Usher" is the house's situation upon a "silent tarn."[4] Combined with the story's beginning on "a dull, dark, and soundless day in the autumn of the year," silence pervades the environment of the house, seemingly arising from the water itself.[5] The narrator completes his description of the house's setting with a "barely perceptible fissure, which, extending from the roof of the building in front, made its way down the wall in a zigzag direction, until it became lost in the sullen waters of the tarn" so that he emphasizes water's crucial role in the story's opening.[6] That crucial role relates to the narrative climax, as the brewing electrical storm that surrounds the mansion arises from the tarn itself. As the storm gathers from the waters, the narrator attempts to calm Usher by reading from a romance called the "Mad Trist" that Poe invents for the purposes of the tale:

> "These appearances, which bewilder you, are merely electrical phenomena not uncommon—or it may be that they have their ghastly origin in the rank miasma of the tarn. [. . .] Here is one of your favorite romances. I will read, and you shall listen;—and so we will pass away this terrible night together." The antique volume which I had taken up was the "Mad Trist" of Sir Launcelot Canning; but I had called it a favorite of Usher's more in sad jest than in earnest; for, in truth, there is little in its uncouth and unimaginative prolixity which could have had interest for the lofty and spiritual ideality of my friend.[7]

The sources of Poe's "Mad Trist" are uncertain, and there has been little scholarly consensus on the matter, apart from the fact that it represents a medieval romance and symbolizes the events of the frame narrative in one way or another. Rather than being a contentious topic, critics implicitly concur that many sources might have influenced Poe's tale, and I tend to agree. I would like to offer one possible source that scholars may not have discussed explicitly or at length, however: that of the medieval legend of Tristan and Iseult. The invented author "Sir Launcelot Canning" derives his first name from the Arthurian romance intimately connected to the story of Tristan and Iseult. Of course, the specific versions of the Tristan and Iseult myth that Poe might have read or heard of are difficult to discover, and it is beyond the scope of this book and fruitless to trace all the possible variations of the tale to which he may have been exposed.[8] Poe may have known any number of versions.

As David Shirt writes, in "1785 Myller published his edition of Gottfried von Strassburg's *Tristan und Isolde*, although [. . .] in 1776, the appearance of the Comte de Tressan's *Histoire de Tristan de Léonis et de la Reine Iseult* [. . .] based on a 1589 prose compilation, seems to have launched the vogue for the Tristan stories."[9] He goes on to say that the "cause was quickly taken up [. . .] by Sir Walter Scott who published his edition of *Sir Tristrem* in 1804," but that it was not until the end of the nineteenth century that the first critical editions and translations were published of the various versions of the story.[10] Of all the versions of the tale, apart from Malory's, Poe would have most likely been aware of Walter Scott's *Sir Tristrem; A Metrical Romance of the Thirteenth Century* as "written" by Thomas of Ercildoune, or Thomas the Rhymer. Poe read and admired Scott, and Scott most likely influenced a few of Poe's works, most notably "Ligeia."[11] I find that, for these and other poetic reasons, I prefer to use Scott's versions of the tale of "Tristrem" and "Ysolt" for the purposes of comparison with the "Mad Trist," and Scott does write multiple versions of the tale: his version of Thomas the Rhymer's edition and an abstract description of "French metrical romance" versions of the story.[12] When referring specifically to Scott's tale, I will use the names "Tristrem" and "Ysolt" or "Ysond," but when speaking of the tale in general, will return to using "Tristan" and "Iseult."

One need not know the details of Poe's "Mad Trist" to recognize the similarities between the story and the legend of Tristrem; Poe's version involves a hero knight, a hermit's home, a dragon, and a shield, all of which come into play in various permutations of the legend of Tristan and Lancelot. In Poe's version, the hero knight, called "Ethelred," slays a dragon, as Tristrem does in Scott's rendition of Thomas the Rhymer's version of the tale.[13] However, in Scott's version, Tristrem cuts off the dragon's tongue after killing it and is "deprived of his senses" due to its poison.[14] After being reunited with Ysond, his sanity is restored, and he pledges the tongue and his ship as symbols of honor that he truly did kill the dragon.[15] This pledge is crucial, as it represents two of three key elements associated with Tristrem in nearly all of the legends surrounding him: firstly, his madness (represented in this tale by the tongue) and secondly, his continual association with the sea (represented in this tale by the ship). The third key element associated with Tristrem, his musicality, comes into play elsewhere. Scott describes him as "a perfect master of the harp," and in the Rhymer version of the tale, Tristrem "asks from King Mark a ship. Mark reluctantly grants his request, and he embarks with [. . .] his harp as his only solace," such that Tristrem's voyage on the sea and his harp playing coalesce into one mutable symbol.[16] In Scott's other version of the tale (the French fragments), the harp is tied to the sea as well: "I landed with nothing but my harp, which had long been my only consolation. Soon you heard of my skill on that instrument, and I was sent for to court. [. . .] I taught you the sweetest lays on the harp."[17] He does all of this by opting to "feign madness" as a disguise from the king who already knows him, using the mask of the madman to allow him to speak freely in Mark's court, bringing full circle the three elements of his madness, his musicality, and his association with the sea.[18]

If this is read as a possible source of Poe's "Mad Trist," the title refers explicitly to the madness of Tristrem (the "Mad" 'Trist'rem), and Poe's "Mad Trist" itself ties into the frame narrative of "The Fall of the House of Usher."[19] (In Scott's version of the "French Metrical Romances," as in various other versions, the mad or fool Tristrem inverts his name to Tramtrist or Tramtris: "Queen Ysolt, I *am* Tramtris"[20]). In this way, the ties between Tristrem's madness, his musicality, and his connections to the sea evoke an interpretation of "The Fall of the House of Usher" that exposes numerous threads integral to this book. Beginning with the connection between Tristrem, the sea, and madness, let us return to Foucault, who uses the story of Tristan to illustrate the links between water and madness, a madness that precedes and differs from that described in the previous chapter:

> Already, disguised as a madman, Tristan had ordered boatmen to land him on the coast of Cornwall. And when he arrived at the castle of King Mark, no one recognized him, no one knew whence he had come. But he made too many strange remarks, both familiar and distant; he knew too well the secrets of the commonplace not to have been from another, yet nearby, world. He did not come from the solid land, with its solid cities; but indeed from the ceaseless unrest of the sea, from those unknown highways which conceal so much strange knowledge, from that fantastic plain, the underside of the world.[21]

Foucault's interpretation of Tristan uncovers madness both "familiar and distant," a madness that, whether or not it was purposefully adopted, speaks of "strange knowledge" from a "fantastic plain." The myth of Tristan ties into Foucault's overarching description of madness as read through the symbolism inherent in the historical roots of the "Ship of Fools," which he argues becomes part of the "imaginary landscape of the Renaissance."[22] Of this connection between madmen and the sea, Foucault writes:

> to hand a madman over to sailors [. . .] made him a prisoner of his own departure. But water adds to this dark mass of its own values; it carries off, but it does more: it purifies. [. . .] It is for the other world that the madman sets sail in his fools' boat; it is from the other world that he comes when he disembarks. The madman's voyage is at once a rigorous division and an absolute Passage. In one sense, it simply develops, across a half-real, half-imaginary geography, the madman's *liminal* position on the horizon of medieval concern—[. . .] he is kept at the point of passage. [. . .] One thing at least is certain: water and madness have long been linked in the dreams of European man.[23]

The madman that Foucault describes in this passage, the madman that finds root in the middle ages, precedes the division between "the silence of the asylums" and "madness [that] continued to be present on the stage of the world—with more commotion than ever" that tied into the madness described in the previous chapter.[24] The sea places the madman in a "liminal position" that speaks of "the other world," one continually promising embarkation and arrival to and from this "other world," and one which purifies him by making him a "prisoner of the passage," as

Tristan is.²⁵ Yet rather than setting sail for other worlds, Poe's Tristan, Roderick Usher, sits in his mansion instead of a ship, on a tarn instead of the sea. As opposed to the sea, the lake is stagnant, representative not of voyage, but of immobility and circumscription. The water that promised voyage *across* to other worlds for Tristan is the water through which Roderick Usher can only travel *downward*, and thus the sea that purifies becomes a tarn that damns.

Whereas Tristan and Iseult are "cursed" with a love potion, Roderick and Madeline Usher are trapped in an incestuous "sexual curse," as critics such as John Allison have explained.²⁶ Whereas Tristan uses a mask of "madness" to unite himself with Iseult, in Poe's tale, Roderick's madness keeps Madeline at a distance, eventually so far as to put her "living in the tomb."²⁷ Whereas Tristan is a "prisoner of the passage" of the sea, a liminal figure that speaks of other worlds, the "fantastic plain," in Foucault's terms, Roderick is a liminal figure of the tarn, into which the only passage to other worlds is downward. In fact, the story climaxes just after the narrator finishes reading the "Mad Trist," as a supernatural storm gathers by finding root in the "miasma" that arises from the tarn itself. Upon Madeline's rise from the tomb and reunion with Roderick, the narrator flees from the house. Roderick's madness speaks of "other worlds," but those that exchange the heavenly for the hellish, that move from electrical storms and sound to darkness and silence, perversions of the madness associated with Tristan. Roderick Usher is an inversion of Tristan: Roderick Usher's musicality, his "ballad" and his "speaking guitar" especially illustrate the importance of this reversal of the legend of the musical harpist Tristan.²⁸

"THE FALL OF THE HOUSE OF USHER": THE GUITAR AND THE BALLAD

The ties between Roderick, Tristan, and stringed instruments are present from the story's outset. Poe adapts from the poem "Le Refus" the epigraph for the tale: "Son coeur est un luth suspendu; / Sitôt qu'on le touche il résonne," which Mabbott translates as "His heart is a hanging lute; as soon as it is touched, it responds."²⁹ Poe never uses lutes in his prose tales, although they figure in his poetry, most notably in "Israfel," whom he portrays as an angel whose "heart-strings are a lute," a lute that ultimately parallels the poet's "lyre within the sky."³⁰ This again speaks of an inversion of Scott's Tristrem and Ysolt, as Tristrem is a "perfect master of the harp" to the enchantment of all, but Roderick Usher is another kind of musician altogether.³¹

Roderick Usher's inclination toward stringed instruments is subtly indicated before he ever picks up his guitar, as his mental sensitivities take form in a "morbid acuteness of the senses" so that "there were but peculiar sounds, and these from stringed instruments, which did not inspire him with horror."[32] J. O. Bailey posits that Roderick's "horror of all sounds except those of stringed instruments seems natural for anyone who senses the presence of a demon. Poe often associates stringed instruments with angelic forces."[33] While maintaining that Poe often connects stringed instruments with angels, Roderick Usher's circumscription to tolerating only the sounds from stringed instruments, rather than pointing to his desire to be near the angelic, instead points to his sensing a demonic presence. This inversion ties back to the series of inversions of the Tristan legend that Poe's tale invokes; Roderick's madness speaks of "other worlds" of damnation, rather than purification. Poe's use of Roderick"s "music" continues to illustrate this reversal.

In Roderick's separation from Madeline, he passes his time in artistic endeavors with the narrator of the story.[34] The narrator first mentions Roderick's guitar as he describes the days following Madeline's sequestering: "I listened, as if in a dream, to the wild improvisations of his speaking guitar. And thus, as a closer and still closer intimacy admitted me more unreservedly into the recesses of his spirit, the more bitterly did I perceive [. . .] a mind from which darkness [. . .] poured forth."[35] Returning to the definition of real-world music from the previous chapter as a framework for interpreting this introduction of Roderick's "speaking guitar" reveals the ways in which Roderick's "performances" differ from those of the fictional Lalande and the young girl from "The System of Doctor Tarr and Professor Fether." First, real-world music must be experienced as "sound via the sense of hearing" by a character, specifically recognized as a heard sound; the narrator fulfills this definition, saying he "listened" explicitly to Roderick, but his qualification that he "listened, as if in a dream," complicates his experience of Roderick's "improvisations" as a heard sound.[36] If the reader must be able to imagine that sound as it could be reasonably experienced in the real-world, this instance is also a bit more complex than the examples in the previous chapter in that, although one could reasonably imagine hearing a guitar, the phrase "wild improvisations of his speaking guitar" does not relate to a commonly defined or understood real-world experience. Second, real-world music must be experienced by a character as a "sight," a definition that this story also complexly fulfills; the narrator is present with Roderick during his "improvisations," but he describes listening "as if in a dream," rather than seeing him.

Third, to fulfill the definition of real-world music, the character must perform music that either refers to real-world "notated 'instructions'" or has the potential to be notated in nineteenth-century Western tonal tradition. This third definition is complicated in Poe's tale as the narrator continues:

I shall ever bear about me a memory of the many solemn hours I spent alone with the master of the House of Usher. Yet I should fail in any attempt to convey an idea of the exact character of the studies, or of the occupations, in which he involved me, or led me the way. An excited and highly distempered ideality threw a sulphureous lustre over all. His long improvised dirges will ring forever in my ears. Among other things, I hold painfully in mind a certain singular perversion and amplification of the wild air of the last waltz of Von Weber.[37]

The "last waltz of Von Weber" was believed in Poe's time to be Von Weber's last composition, composed just a "few hours before his death" in 1826, even though it was written by Karl Reissiger.[38] Roderick's "perversion and amplification" of the piece resonate with their inescapability, or their entrapping both the narrator and Roderick Usher between the realms of the natural and supernatural. In this way, this scene holds all three definitions of real-world music in limbo: the narrator listens to Roderick "as if in a dream" and he implicitly sees Roderick, but the hell-like "sulphureous lustre" pervades his sight. While he names an actual piece, which itself refers to "notated 'instructions'" for producing the music, Roderick's performance perverts and amplifies it. This portrays Roderick as a liminal character who continually inverts the characteristics of the madman of the sea as described by Foucault and expressed through Tristan. While Scott's Tristrem uses his facility on the harp to obtain Ysolt's love, Roderick can play only in Madeline's distance, and his playing is a "dirge." While Tristrem's playing holds a nearly Orphic power, Roderick's playing is held "painfully in mind" as an inverse power that lends itself to the "dream," to the "otherworldly," in a way that conveys pain and darkness, creating the hellish "sulphureous lustre" that occupies his space. These themes expand in another example of a tale in the story, the inset "ballad" of "The Haunted Palace."

The narrator of "The Fall of the House of Usher" continues to describe Roderick's "speaking guitar" as he introduces an inset poem "The Haunted Palace." (I will refer to "The Haunted Palace" as a poem for simplicity's sake, and because it is published separately as a poem, but it should be noted that the tale carefully avoids calling it a poem just as much as it does calling it a song.) Poe included poems in a few of his tales: "The Conqueror Worm" appears in "Ligeia" from 1845 onward, "To One in Paradise" appears in "The Assignation" from its inception in 1834, and "A Catholic Hymn" appears in the first manuscript of "Morella" in 1835.[39] However, apart from the "Latin Hymn" published in "Four Beasts in One" as discussed in the first chapter of this book, "The Haunted Palace" is the only inset poem that ties into the frame narrative as "verses" that accompany what might be heard as music in the narrative. Yet, unlike the "Latin Hymn" from "Four Beasts in One," "The Haunted Palace" is never called a "song." Poe goes to great lengths to never name it as such, even if critical consensus interprets it as a song:

Roderick "composes and sings 'The Haunted Palace,'" or as Michael Hoffman argues in his 1965 article, the "clue to the narrator's strange reactions to the House of Usher lies in the song."[40] Christopher Rollason posits that "Roderick in 'The Fall of the House of Usher,' presented as a poet and musician, [. . .] may be seen as a prototype of the singer-songwriter whose practice within the text uncannily anticipates early Dylan."[41] Rollason implies that "The Haunted Palace," the printed poem that the narrator of the story writes that Roderick performs, is a song, at least in the context of the story itself, yet the narrator describes it otherwise:

> It was, perhaps, the narrow limits to which he thus confined himself upon the guitar, which gave birth, in great measure, to the fantastic character of his performances. But the fervid *facility* of his *impromptus* could not be so accounted for. They must have been, and were, in the notes, as well as in the words of his wild fantasias (for he not unfrequently accompanied himself with rhymed verbal improvisations), the result of that intense mental collectedness and concentration [. . .]. The words of one of these rhapsodies I have easily remembered. [. . .] [I]n the mystic or under current of its meaning, I fancied that I perceived, and for the first time, a full consciousness on the part of Usher, of the tottering of his lofty reason upon her throne. The verses, which were entitled "The Haunted Palace," ran very nearly, if not accurately, thus: [. . .] I well remember that suggestions arising from this ballad led us into a train of thought.[42]

Roderick Usher's "speaking guitar" was previously described as producing "wild improvisations," which now become "performances" with "fantastic character," "impromptus" with "fervid facility," "rhapsodies" accompanied with "words," and "wild fantasias," which may refer to the "rhymed verbal improvisations" or the guitar itself. When referring only to the words, they become "verses" and, together with Roderick's performance, a "ballad." This is far removed, as were the performances of the previous chapter, from that Romantic notion of song as "the mythical union of a lower reality embodied in language and a higher one embodied in music."[43] The narrator continually describes the "notes" as separate from the "words" of the performances, and when the two become indistinguishable, it is when he describes "The Haunted Palace" as a "ballad." Crucial to Poe's use of this term is that Roderick's "ballad" is just printed in the text without accompanying music.

This depiction of "The Haunted Palace" as a "ballad" invokes crucial references in the story. Tristan the harpist takes the role of a minstrel character in the legend, which becomes self-referential in that the legend itself might have been sung. The fact that legends, from the Greek myths to the medieval romances, were meant to be sung, would not have escaped Poe's attention. Scott himself notes in his edition of *Sir Tristrem*:

several of the romances bear internal evidence that they were occasionally chaunted to the harp. [. . .] It is evident, indeed, that the minstrels, who were certainly authors of the French romances, and probably of the English also, could derive no advantage from these compositions, unless by reciting or singing them. Some traces of this custom remained in Scotland till of late years. [. . .] Within the memory of man, an old person used to perambulate the streets of Edinburgh, singing, in a monotonous cadence, the tale of Rosewal and Lilian, which is, in all the forms, a metrical romance of chivalry.[44]

Scott also famously published his own version of a collection of "Historical and Romantic Ballads" in his *Minstrelsy of the Scottish Border*. The obvious connection between Scott's collection of ballads and the metrical romances he describes in the above note is the fact that the accompanying music is either lost or unprinted. When Tristan plays his lays on the harp, he represents the minstrel who performs his own romance, but Poe writes his tale when only the words of the ballads and romances remain, without the music. As Daniel Chua writes of music in the broader historical context of the movement toward absolute music, "modernity, by disenchanting the world, divides it. Modern music is therefore divided. One of the first signs of this division is the expulsion of music from language," and thus "music's future becomes a matter of recovery; its drive towards the new is haunted by an idealised past."[45] Setting aside for the moment the possibility of music's "drive towards the new" in Poe, the two key emergent themes here involve music's division from language. First, music separates from language because it inhabits a disenchanted world estranged from an "idealised past," and second, traces of that "idealised past" itself haunt the text. Poe's perverse Tristan, Roderick Usher, cannot marry his "rhymed verbal improvisations" and his "speaking guitar" in anything but a "wild fantasia" that directly relates to neither. The "ballad," a poem transmitted through the memory of the narrator rather than through Roderick himself, points back to Roderick's madness, the "tottering of his lofty reason upon her throne."[46]

The Case of the Ballad

Poe only uses the title of "ballad" for three other poems: "Bridal Ballad," "Ulalume—A Ballad," and "Annabel Lee—A Ballad," and the use of the term "ballad" in relationship to poetry published without musical score is not uncommon in the nineteenth century. Wordsworth's and Coleridge's *Lyrical Ballads* at the turn of the century and Scott's collection of ballads are only two famous examples of the word's proliferation. Poe's "ballads" still differ from Scott's, for instance, because they do not engage explicitly with a historical framework of minstrelsy or singing. Poe's "ballads" also refuse to participate in poetic depictions of real-world music. The use of the title "ballad" both engages with and differs from what Terence Hoagwood describes as the use of musical terminology in poetry of the Romantic period, arguing:

> Two sorts of pseudo-songs proliferate in the Romantic period: those that, like many of the lyrics by Burns and Clare, are sold as if they were songs when they are entirely scriptorial or typographical objects; and those that refer to music and use rhetorical resources to conjure imaginary musical effects, without pretending to be, really, music.[47]

Both of Hoagwood's notions of the Romantic "pseudo-song" work on some level with Poe. In the following chapters, this book will absorb an ongoing dialogue with the second kind of "pseudo-song" Hoagwood mentions, those that refer to music "without pretending to be, really, music." For the purposes of this chapter, Hoagwood's description of "lyrics" that are "sold as if they were songs" corresponds with some critical interpretations of Poe's "ballads."

Burton Pollin reasons that many of Poe's later poems, including his ballads, were intended for publication with music. He argues that there were "reasons other than the philosophical or aesthetic for Poe's veering toward the lyrics of song and thinking of himself as a 'song writer' in his 'latter years.' First, there was a powerful economic motive: the high emolument paid to song writers, far greater than to magazine poets."[48] The idea that poems written as "ballads" must be set to music or somehow use musical techniques intended to evoke real-world music is a common one, although not representative of all critical viewpoints on the matter. As Hoagwood argues regarding Letitia Landon's poetry,

> Landon's pseudo-songs exemplify common features of the genre in the Romantic period. Coming late as they do in that period, they also help to illustrate the progression that the genre undergoes historically. In the poetry trade, music often disappears under its typographical simulation. The imaginariness of the music is part of its charm, its sales appeal. While bringing about this evanescence of actual song—the turn from song-sheets to entirely letterpress commodities—the pseudo-songs of Moore and Byron make a theme of their own emptiness and absence, treating lyrically the emptiness and absence in their narrative situations; so too do Landon's pseudo-songs, both with and without musical scores.[49]

As Hoagwood observes, the "genre" of the song or the ballad goes through a real historical transformation in which the music associated with the lyrics disappears, and that "imaginariness of the music" becomes part of its economic appeal. This chapter will explore the notion that the "imaginariness of music," whether or not part of the economic appeal for Poe, has another appeal altogether. The "imaginariness of music" in the case of the ballad points back to a kind of "idealised past," as Chua describes, in which music and lyrics were united.[50]

The ballad may have had two important and opposing historical attributes for Poe, the first typifying associations with real-world music described in the first chapter and the second illustrating associations with music described in this chapter. First is the association with the "balladmonger," the lower form of balladeer, and the second is the association with a mythical lost art that brings together history, superstition, and mythology. The first type of ballad exists as commodity that united public performance of lyrics and music. As Michael Bristol observes,

> ballad-mongers were small-time entrepreneurs or sub-contractors who earned their livelihood selling mechanically reproduced entertainment to a mainly lower-class buying public. Ballads were wares or commodities, and the ballad-monger was a kind of pitchman who found his market at the edges and interstices of organized economic activity.[51]

This definition of the ballad hearkens back to the public performance of music in the previous chapter and is a definition that continues nearly to Poe's time. Rather than representing the mythical unification of lyrics and music, it represents public performance that places economic value on song as a hawked ware. Exemplifying this definition, the narrator of Poe's "The Man of the Crowd" describes the crowd of the title in one extraordinarily long sentence extending to an entire page. The description ends with: "organ-grinders, monkey-exhibiters and ballad mongers, those who vended with those who sang; ragged artizans and exhausted laborers of every description, and all full of a noisy and inordinate vivacity which jarred discordantly upon the ear."[52] This concept of the "ballad monger," tied to the clashing juxtaposition of "those who vended with those who sang" implies that there is nothing more than a motley, "discordant" outcome to placing economic value on a "ballad," or "those who sang," by positioning them in a public sphere, rendering them grotesquely materially present.

This first kind of ballad from "The Man of the Crowd" does not occur in Poe's poetry. Rather, Poe's poetic "ballads" position themselves in relation to a second type of ballad. In his *Minstrelsy of the Scottish Border*, Scott paints a picture of the Scottish ballad setting of the middle ages, that the "tales of tradition, the song, with the pipe or harp of the minstrel, were probably the sole resources against *ennui*."[53] He goes on to say that the more "wild the state of society, the more general and violent is the impulse received from poetry and music. [. . .] Verse is naturally connected with music; and, among a rude people, the union is seldom broken. By this natural alliance, the lays, 'steeped in the stream of harmony,' [. . .] produce upon his audience a more impressive effect."[54] This "union" between "poetry and music" that is "seldom broken" in the romanticized "wild" Scotland of the middle ages has already come undone by Poe's time, even though the essential relationship between ballad and public performance continues for the next few centuries. Hoagwood argues of Sir Walter Scott's *Minstrelsy of the Scottish Border*, "As influential and widely admired as Scott's *Minstrelsy* has been, the work joins a long history of printed simulations of folk songs, works that are forgeries in two senses: editors feign authentic folk origins for their own writing or for other modern works, and they pretend that literary texts are 'songs.'"[55] Unlike Scott, Poe does not preface his poetry with folk origins, but like Scott's "ballads," Poe's are also not songs.

As Maureen McLane writes of the English and Scottish Romantics, they had to consider "the fate of poetry as a cultural project set adrift from its imagined origins in speech and gesture [. . .]. Scott derived his own poetic genealogy from minstrels who, he maintained, served the Scottish 'National Muse' even as Homer served that of the Greeks."[56] This idealized ballad again opposes what Steve Newman describes as the ballad one could see and hear: "from 1728 [the ballad is] [. . .] a 'song commonly sung up and down the streets.' For those attracted to the ballad, 'commonly' signifies in two ways. [. . .] the ballad lacks the prestige of high genres. [. . .] But this very lowness makes the ballad attractive to elite authors."[57] Newman continues that, as the eighteenth century progresses, the "music of the ballad broadens its reach and intensifies its grasp on an audience [. . .] [and] even those who do not write songs for musical performance [. . .] draw on the communal orientation intimated by the ballad's ontology as song."[58] Whatever the given critical reason for using the term "ballad," often acknowledged as either economically motivated or motivated by audience, the key factor is that real-world music is not necessary for its production and is detrimental to its significance as hearkening back to an idealized past.

"ULALUME": FAËRY BALLET

In addition to not being printed with music, Poe's ballads also do not necessarily use musical terminology. "Ulalume—A Ballad" does not use musical imagery or music as a subject at all. Neither condition stops critics from interpreting the poem in terms of its relationship to music, as it is evoked by the title. Daniel Hoffman writes,

> Not until I took seriously the full title of the piece—"Ulalume—A Ballad"—did I recognize what he was up to. A ballad has incremental repetition, tells its story *in song*. Poe's tale can't move any faster than the music, the music is more important than any of the words. Poe even scores his words for a particular composer—for who is Auber but Daniel-François-Esprit Auber, whose piece "Le Lac des Fées" was in the popular repertoire at the time. [. . .] So I have to conclude that Poe, setting his scene with the help of a faëry ballet and a wispy painting, [. . .] is already in an ideal landscape imaginable only to artists and bereaved lovers.[59]

While I absolutely agree with Hoffman that Poe surely references Auber, I would like to offer two alterations to Hoffman's reading of the reference. First, Poe's "ballad" does not tell "its story *in song*" more than any of his other poems. Whatever his rhythmic and sound effects, the poem's music, in a real-world sense, does not exist. Moreover, his argument that Poe "scores his words" from his short poem for Auber's extended ballet-opera seems rather unlikely. Going so far as to call the speaker of the poem "Edgarpoe's melancholy ballad-singer," Hoffman makes a common assumption.[60] Hoagwood explains the common assumption as follows:

> Often in the nineteenth and twentieth centuries, readers and writers apparently confuse textual and typographical products with actual music. My point is not that commentators have been mistaken about the poem, but rather that [. . .] his [Shelley's] poem "Music, when soft voices die" is an especially clear example of a printed text which, internally, is about the absence of music, but which, externally, becomes an apparently convincing illusion of the music whose absence it declares in plain English.[61]

Poe's "Ulalume—A Ballad" does not explicitly make music its subject in the way that Shelley's poem does; however, Poe's invocation of the title "ballad," rather than invoking "song" in a real-world sense, highlights music's absence, whether or not it "becomes an apparently convincing illusion of the music whose absence it declares in plain English."

Second, Hoffman supposes that if the Auber of the poem is related to the composer of the same name, Poe explicitly calls upon the reader's musical memory. As I pointed out in the case of *La Sonnambula*, it is difficult to say to what performances Poe was ever actually exposed. Mabbott notes that Auber's opera-ballet was "presented at the Olympic Theater, New York, on December 1, 1845," at the same time that Poe lived in New York. There is, however, no historical evidence available to suggest he attended. He may have known it through reviews.[62] For instance, "Auber and His New Opera" was printed in *The Evergreen* in New York in 1840.[63] Even if Poe did call upon his musical memory of the opera in the poem, the idea that the reference was used to somehow summon the ghost of real-world music undermines the subject of the poem itself. The poem begins:

> The skies they were ashen and sober;
> The leaves they were crispéd and sere—
> The leaves they were withering and sere:
> It was night, in the lonesome October
> Of my most immemorial year:
> It was hard by the dim lake of Auber,
> In the misty mid region of Weir:—
> It was down by the dank tarn of Auber,
> In the ghoul-haunted woodland of Weir.[64]

No musical terms describe the "dim lake" or the "dank tarn" of Auber. If the "dim lake of Auber" does indeed relate to the composer Auber's "Fairy Lake," the connection is one of imagery reversal, as in the inversion of the Tristan legend in "The Fall of the House of Usher." Like the "Mad Trist" pointing to the Ushers' perversion of the myth of Tristan and Iseult, the "dim lake of Auber" or the "dank tarn of Auber" is anything but a "Fairy Lake"; it is a lake haunted by ghouls. Described in nearly identical terms to the body of water upon which the Usher house is situated, the situation of the poem on Auber prefigures that perverse madness evident in Poe's tale—the madness that points not to worlds beyond, but to worlds underneath.

There is one interpretation of the poem's setting, including the lake Auber, which ties together the subject of the poem and the title. As Eric Carlson summarizes, building his argument upon James Miller's article "'Ulalume' Resurrected," the

> unreality of the opening scene, for instance, is intentional: the panel of images (*ashen* skies, leaves *crisped* and *sere*, Auber, Weir, etc.) reflects the speaker's torment of frustration. The first stanza functions as a part of a non-logical, impressionistic sequence [. . .]. As such, in Miller's words, it "underscores the abnormal or dream-like state of the mind of the speaker."[65]

The interpretation of the poem as reflecting or "underscoring" the "abnormal" or the "dream-like mind of the speaker" is crucial; Miller's relation and opposition of the terms "abnormal" and "dream-like" highlights a relationship between madness and a liminal positioning that works parallel to that described in "The Fall of the House of Usher." Carlson quotes Miller as arguing that the poem's "hypnotic effect, emphasizes the non-rational state of the speaker's mind where the real and the unreal intermingle and become indistinguishable. It is a point midway between waking and sleeping, sanity and insanity."[66] In describing this liminal positioning, Carlson makes a passing observation that the poem's "very vagueness or 'indefinitiveness' makes for a desirable artistic delay."[67] In describing the poem's subject and texture as that of a liminal madness, Carlson appropriates a term invented by Poe, "indefinitiveness," but does not proceed to explain the context of his use of the word.

Indefinitiveness: The True Musical Expression

Poe's only famous use of the term "indefinitiveness," a word he invents, is in relation to music.[68] In his published "Marginalia," Poe leads into his use of the term "indefinitiveness" by way of Tennyson:

> I am not sure that Tennyson is not the greatest of poets. [. . .] Other bards produce effects which are, now and then, otherwise produced than by what we call poems; but Tennyson an effect which only a poem

does. [. . .] There are passages in his works which rivet a conviction I
had long entertained, that the *indefinite* is an element in the true
ποιησις.⁶⁹

Before Poe uses the term in question, he sets it up by using Tennyson as
an example of a truly great poet. He then argues that poems have the
capacity to "produce effects" that other works of art do not. He appears
to qualify this particular kind of poetry as the "true ποιησις" and that a
crucial element of it is "the *indefinite*." Heidegger describes the Greek
term ποιησις as "'making' that which *is not yet*; what is 'made' is not the
poetized—for the inceptuality, only truth procures a *making one's way* to
and for."⁷⁰ In Nikolopoulou's explanation of the term, it is translated as
"poeisis," where

> poeisis and praxis [are] two mutually exclusive modes of production—
> creating or making versus doing or operating. Agamben writes, "In the
> *Symposium* Plato tells us about the full original resonance of the word
> ποιησις: "any cause that brings into existence something that was not
> before is ποιησις." Every time that something is pro-duced, that is,
> brought from concealment and nonbeing into the light of presence,
> there is ποιησις, pro-duction, poetry."⁷¹

Poe's use of the term ποιησις, rather than "poetry," is critical. Poe does
not refer so much to the finished product of a poem, but relates poetry to
a larger concept of bringing something "from concealment and nonbeing
into the light of presence." The "*indefinite*" is then an element of a poetic
production in a God-like manner of creation, the "true ποιησις." Poe
continues:

> Why do some persons fatigue themselves in attempts to unravel such
> fantasy-pieces as the "Lady of Shalott?" As well unweave the *"ventum
> textilem."* If the author did not deliberately propose to himself a sugges-
> tive indefinitiveness of meaning, with the view of bringing about a
> definitiveness of vague and therefore of spiritual *effect*—this, at least,
> arose from the silent analytical promptings of that poetic genius which,
> in its supreme development, embodies all orders of intellectual capac-
> ity. I *know* that indefinitiveness is an element of the true music—I mean
> of the true musical expression. Give to it any undue decision—imbue it
> with any very determinate tone—and you deprive it, at once, of its
> ethereal, its ideal, its intrinsic and essential character. You dispel its
> luxury of dream. You dissolve the atmosphere of the mystic upon
> which it floats. You exhaust it of its breath of fäery [sic]. It now be-
> comes a tangible and easily appreciable idea—a thing of the earth,
> earthy. It has not, indeed, lost its power to please, but all which I
> consider the distinctiveness of that power.⁷²

Poe smoothly moves from the premise based on Tennyson, that "the
indefinite is an element in the true ποιησις," or of what might be described as poetic production, to the notion that "indefinitiveness is an

element of the true music," which he again qualifies as the "true musical expression."

Much of Poe's explanation of indefinitiveness coalesces in the idea of the "ventum textilem," a term that a few of Poe's editors have traced to Isaac D'Israeli. Mabbott notes that "Poe might have found [. . .] [the term] in D'Israeli's *Curiosities of Literature*."[73] When D'Israeli writes about the "ventum textilem," he cites Apuleius, a citation that according to Mabbott is a misattribution, and so Poe very likely read the term in D'Israeli or D'Israeli's source, *Ménagiana* (the meaning of the term is the same in both). In his *Curiosities of Literature*, D'Israeli writes: "Apuleius calls those neck-kerchiefs so glassy fine, (may I so express myself?) which, in veiling, discover the beautiful bosom of a woman, *ventum textilem*; which may be translated *woven air*. It is an expression beautifully fanciful."[74] No matter which source it was in which Poe first saw the phrase, he would have known it to be from Apuleius, famous for *The Golden Ass*, but he would not have found the source in a particular story from the volume. Poe makes his own connections and gives us a hint about them in "The Spectacles," when he draws upon the story of Cupid and Psyche. When the narrator mistakenly takes in the sight of Eugénie Lalande and falls in love with her, he says, "The head, of which only the back was visible, rivalled in outline that of the Greek Psyche, and was rather displayed than concealed by an elegant cap of *gaze äerienne* [sic], which put me in mind of the *ventum textilem* of Apuleius."[75] In both D'Israeli and Poe, the ventum textilem or the gaze äerienne represents that which, in attempted concealment, paradoxically reveals. This association will return in "Ulalume."

Unraveling a poem unweaves the "ventum textilem," and depriving the poem of indefinitiveness deprives it of its "ethereal" character, the "atmosphere" upon which it "floats," its "breath of fäery." Dispelling a poem's indefinitiveness dispels it of its "true musical expression," which is described only in terms of the ethereal, or the air woven. To return once more to the division between the music of the ancients and modern music, such that "modernity, by disenchanting the world, divides it" and thus modern "music is therefore divided." "In the enchanted world of the ancients, music was an airy substance, it did not occupy space, it was its very essence."[76] As one looks toward that idealized past, represented as linked to the otherworldly, music becomes intrinsically tied with notions of ether, atmosphere, and breath. The opposite of the "true musical expression" is a "tangible and easily appreciable idea" that Poe crucially describes as "a thing of the earth, earthy." Any attempt to divine what Poe means by the "true musical expression" will be deferred for a while. For now, the division between the "thing of the earth, earthy," and the "indefinitiveness" associated with the ethereal that characterizes the "true musical expression" is crucial in returning to Carlson's interpretation of "Ulalume—A Ballad."

When Carlson describes the poem's "very vagueness" as "indefinitiveness," he invokes the context described, implicitly using a term that summons Poe's description of the key element of the "true musical expression," whatever it may be, and a term that Poe elsewhere associates with the myth of Psyche and Cupid.[77] Bringing this all together and returning to the Auber connection, Miller argues that "it is important that there *not* be any geographical locations of Auber and Weir except in the imagined world of the narrator," as both the poem's setting and the narrator's consciousness separate themselves as much as possible from the "earth, earthy," to use Poe's phrase.[78] If the composer Auber's "Fairy Lake" is invoked, it is in title only, as his real-world music is not mentioned, nor is music in a real-world sense ever suggested. Rather, music remains a few steps removed from the poem. As Hoagwood argues of other Romantic poems, "the speaker's references to music foreground its unreality or illusions, its comforts and pleasures not really being there. In all of these texts, there is no music, but only reference to it. It is the absence that counts."[79] Poe's lake Auber does invoke the composer in a sense, to highlight the absence of the music anywhere but in the title's suggestion, as much as it illustrates the perversity of the ghoul-haunted tarn opposing the composer's "Fairy Lake." Carlson's recognition of its "indefinitiveness" highlights the vital link between the poem and Poe's description of the "true musical expression": that of the relationship between the earthy and the ethereal in the liminal setting.

After introducing the setting of the poem, the speaker describes roaming the landscape with the mythological Psyche, who he also refers to as his "Soul":

> Here once, through an alley Titanic,
> Of cypress, I roamed with my Soul—
> Of cypress, with Psyche, my Soul.
> These were days when my heart was volcanic
> As the scoriac rivers that roll—
> As the lavas that restlessly roll
> Their sulphurous currents down Yaanek,
> In the ultimate climes of the Pole—
> That groan as they roll down Mount Yaanek,
> In the realms of the Boreal Pole.[80]

Akin to the "sulphureous lustre" that pervades the scene in "The Fall of the House of Usher" when Roderick performs his "long improvised dirges," the "sulphurous" is associated with the speaker's heart in this poem.[81] The speaker describes his heart as "volcanic," as volcanic as "lavas" that "groan." Rather than music, one of the only sound descriptors in the poem is the sound of a groan as the heart's expression. The speaker's heart, compared to the groaning rivers of lava, opposes his description of Astarte in a following stanza, as the speaker and Psyche watch the rising of Astarte in the sky:

> And I said—"She is warmer than Dian;
> She rolls through an ether of sighs—
> She revels in a region of sighs.
> She has seen that the tears are not dry on
> These cheeks where the worm never dies"[82]

As Astarte, the goddess of fertility and the sea, becomes synonymous with the star Venus, she also exists in an "ether of sighs," unearthly opposite to the "groan" that represents the sound of the speaker's heart. Psyche acts as Astarte's antithesis in the poem, bringing full circle the Apuleius connection from the "ventum textilem" reference. If indefinitiveness imbues "true musical expression" with its ethereal character, it is notable that ethereality in this poem is associated with the slightest of sounds, the "ether of sighs," or the "region of sighs." This duality sets up the narrator's forthcoming failure to discover for himself the "region of sighs" in telling ways.

The speaker believes Astarte to be a good sign. Journeying with Psyche, he interprets Astarte as an ethereal sign that will "point us the path to the skies— / To the Lethean peace of the skies."[83] The falsehood of his hope is inherent in its very description. The "path to the skies" leads to a "Lethean peace," one not only of forgetfulness, but also one associated with the river of the Underworld, the opposite of the mirage of the heavenly ideal toward which the poet looks. Like the tarn of "The Fall of the House of Usher" that pulls Roderick Usher and his house downward as though to the underside of the world, this poem is situated on a dank tarn that is mirrored in the sky not by a heavenly escape, but by another watery gate to the underworld. This is doubled in the figure of Psyche, who appears in this poem without Cupid, so she exists outside of her mythological context and is trapped in the point in her story between her fall and her transcendence. Another sign that the narrator's desire to follow Astarte's perverse "path to the skies" is inherently flawed is Psyche's reaction:

> But Psyche, uplifting her finger,
> Said—"Sadly this star I mistrust—
> Her pallor I strangely mistrust—
> Ah, hasten!—ah, let us not linger!
> Ah, fly!—let us fly!—for we must."
> In terror she spoke; letting sink her
> Wings till they trailed in the dust—
> In agony sobbed; letting sink her
> Plumes till they trailed in the dust—
> Till they sorrowfully trailed in the dust.[84]

Psyche's call for escape, "let us fly!," only highlights their circumscription to the ghoul-haunted woodland and the tarn, their inability to escape by sky or sea reiterated as she speaks in "terror" as her wings trail literally in the dust of the world. Despite the supernatural elements surrounding the narrator, his separation from (his own) Psyche, who warns him with her wings trailing in his world's dust, only reveals the narrator's inability to escape the darkness and sorrow of his earthly plight, represented by his heart's "groan" and his "cheeks where the worm never dies."

As some critics interpret it, this struggle also embodies the "relation between sensual love and spiritual love," which may be the case, but it is more complicated than that.[85] The opposition of Eros and Psyche reframes itself in terms of the myth in its various forms, both Apuleius's and others, a connection which introduces themes vital to this poem and Poe's other ballads. As Joel Relihan explains, Apuleius's tale begins "with the introduction of the beautiful youngest daughter of an unnamed king and queen; [. . .] we are told her name, and we are supposed to be startled: *So this fairy tale is about Soul?*"[86] He goes on to explain that Cupid, at first, also is not named, describing him as "Psyche's demon lover," who once revealed, disappears as Venus takes up "the role of the tormenter."[87] Relihan notes that there are multiple transformations of other renditions of the Cupid and Psyche myth in Apuleius: Psyche is "butterfly-winged," implying a connection between her wings and the "human soul," Psyche is both tortured and torturing, and most importantly, in the Platonic tradition, there are two "Aphrodites," represented as Psyche and Venus, the "Heavenly and Vulgar. There is much talk of multiple Venuses." [88] Poe's poem takes this doubling a step further. Rather than Psyche being the earthly replica of the Heavenly Venus, Venus as Astarte is also both the tormented and the tormenter, the dark iteration of a heavenly ideal that does not exist in the poem. Psyche's wings neither allow her to fly nor are taken away, but in their connection to the soul, only drag in the dust, pointing back to their functional failure.

The doubling of Psyche's and Astarte's torment, like the dank tarn mirroring the Lethean skies, reflect this concept of a madness trapped in a liminal position; like Roderick Usher, the speaker of "Ulalume" has a madness that points to other worlds, which perversely and paradoxically point back to a demonic loop, to the absolute underworld that reminds him of his fallen nature. When the speaker of "Ulalume" attempts to follow Astarte, Psyche seems to be aware of her mythological heritage as she remembers Astarte's jealousy. Only partially taking in Psyche's warnings, the speaker urges them on, guided by Astarte's light, but their path leads them to "the end of the vista" where they "were stopped by the door of a tomb— / By the door of a legended tomb:—" where Ulalume lies.[89] In his attempt to follow Astarte's light to the "path in the skies," the speaker arrives at its complete opposite, a tomb that, like the tarn, moves toward an absolute and dark death.

As the narrator reaches Ulalume's vault, his voice unites with Psyche's and ends the poem:

> "Ah, what demon hath tempted me here?"
> [...]
> Said we, then—the two, then—"Ah, can it
> Have been that the woodlandish ghouls—
> The pitiful, the merciful ghouls,
> To bar up our way and to ban it
> From the secret that lies in these wolds—
> Have drawn up the spectre of a planet
> From the limbo of lunary souls—
> This sinfully scintillant planet
> From the Hell of the planetary souls?"[90]

Like Roderick Usher, the narrator is set in an inescapable liminal space that inevitably leads to the tomb. The madness of this narrator and of Roderick attempts the otherworldly, but remains in a demonic infinite loop of seeing only "spectres" of ideals, "ghouls" instead of fairies, the "Hell of the planetary souls" rather than the ventum textilem. More than this, the mad narrator places this infinite loop in the mythological framework that positions vulgar and ideal love in mutual opposition and jealousy of one another, a theme that recurs in "Annabel Lee—A Ballad."

"ANNABEL LEE": THE SOUNDING SEA

Daniel Hoffman posits that there are two types of ballads in Poe's writing. One set, including "Annabel Lee," deals "with the putatively successful escape of the speaker from the 'horrible throbbing / At heart,' from 'the fever called living.'"[91] The other set of ballads, including "Ulalume," describes a speaker "desperately trying to burst out of the prison of his passions, but he cannot do so; he is trapped."[92] He argues that, like Poe's "For Annie," in which "the speaker has been delivered into the quietude of his death-sleep, freed at last from the torments of passion," the "quest" of the narrator of "Annabel Lee" "is likewise successful although the speaker is still alive."[93] While I love the beauty of Hoffman's argument, I think rather that the latter escape is impossible and that "Annabel Lee" has the same themes, the same story, as "Ulalume."

"Annabel Lee" is often compared to "Ulalume." Both are "ballads," and both lend themselves to biographical readings of the relationship between Edgar and Virginia. The problem that this creates is that most interpretations of "Annabel Lee" take it at face value; the speaker falls in love with Annabel Lee when they are both children, but to be "the would-be lover, of Annabel Lee, or Annabel Leigh [of Nabokov], is a fate not easily avoided. On the one hand you end up yearning to lie down by her side in a sepulchre: necrophilia! On the other, you can't get her, can't get *at* her."⁹⁴ Even Hoffman, who in this quote ties together the Annabel Leigh of *Lolita* and Poe's Annabel Lee, and in doing so implicitly acknowledges that complex themes become intimately connected with the character, does not directly discuss the implications of Poe's speaker's liminality:

> It was many and many a year ago,
> In a kingdom by the sea,
> That a maiden there lived whom you may know
> By the name of Annabel Lee;—
> And this maiden she lived with no other thought
> Than to love and be loved by me.⁹⁵

He speaks after "many and many a year," which figures into the madness associated with his liminal position once the reader discovers that every night for "many and many a year" he dreams of her as he sleeps by her tomb on the sea. His solipsism imposes his own will onto hers, that she "lived with no other thought / Than to love and be loved by me." He continues:

> *I* was a child and *she* was a child,
> In this kingdom by the sea;
> But we loved with a love that was more than love—
> I and my Annabel Lee—
> With a love that the wingéd seraphs of Heaven
> Coveted her and me.⁹⁶

The setting of the poem in the "kingdom by the sea" starts to become foregrounded here so that the prominent returning image of the poem is that of the sea. Like "Ulalume" and "The Fall of the House of Usher," the story's setting is on a body of water, this time in a "kingdom by the sea," like Tintagel of Arthurian legend. As Foucault writes, the madman "is kept at the point of passage. [. . .] One thing at least is certain: water and madness have long been linked in the dreams of European man."⁹⁷ For the speaker of this poem, however, he is kept on the water's edge, associated continually with the sea, with that space that looks across to other worlds; he is kept eternally as a figure of the shore. Like the narrator of "Ulalume," he is arrested in a seemingly infinite loop of madness that attempts to look into the world beyond, but stays chained to a dark and mad earthly plight. The seemingly infinite loop is then mirrored again in the theme of heavenly jealousy.

Like Astarte of "Ulalume," who was both tormented by and the tormenter of Psyche, the "wingéd seraphs" apparently "went envying" the love of the speaker and Annabel Lee, which figures critically into the poem:

> And this was the reason that, long ago,
> In this kingdom by the sea,

> A wind blew out of a cloud, chilling
> My beautiful Annabel Lee;
> So that her high-born kinsmen came
> And bore her away from me,
> To shut her up in a sepulchre,
> In this kingdom by the sea.
> The angels, not half so happy in Heaven,
> Went envying her and me—
> Yes!—that was the reason (as all men know,
> In this kingdom by the sea)
> That the wind came out of the cloud by night,
> Chilling and killing my Annabel Lee.[98]

As Quinn writes, the theme of heavenly envy of earthly love in this poem speaks of "spiritual passion that transcended human limits."[99] The transcendence in this case again brings the narrator back to a cycle of madness. The narrator maintains that earthly air, a "wind," kills Annabel Lee so that instead of there being a ventum textilem that uplifts the speaker and Annabel Lee, a gale ends her. Like the speaker of "Ulalume" who follows Astarte's light only to arrive at Ulalume's vault, the tomb of her physical remains, the speaker of "Annabel Lee" sleeps by Annabel Lee's mortal crypt. He "dreams" of her when the "moon [. . .] beams," and he "feel[s]" the "eyes" of Annabel Lee as the "stars [. . .] rise," but all that he sees in the heavens, all that the heavens leave him with, is her "tomb by the sounding sea."[100] When he claims that "neither the angels in Heaven above, / Nor the demons down under the sea, / Can ever dissever my soul from the soul" of Annabel Lee, the speaker reinforces his own liminality.[101]

Neither "Ulalume" nor "Annabel Lee" have any musical terminology, but both have nearly identical themes. Poe's "ballads" are linked by a mad liminality that ties together the impossibility of voyage to the otherworldly and of an explicitly perverse desire for ideal love that only returns the one filled with desire to an infinite earthly cycle of absolute suffering. Bearing these themes in mind, by returning to "The Haunted Palace," one can see how this liminal quality tied into this kind of madness affects the expression of musical terminology when it does arise.

"THE HAUNTED PALACE": SPIRITS MOVING MUSICALLY

As mentioned earlier, "The Haunted Palace" in "The Fall of the House of Usher" is a "ballad" that refers to Roderick Usher's madness, the "tottering of his lofty reason upon her throne."[102] The "ballad" itself is a poem transmitted through the memory of the narrator rather than through Roderick Usher himself, but still the generally accepted interpretation of this poem is that it represents, in Poe's own words, "a mind haunted by phantoms—a disordered brain."[103] As Mabbott explains, the poem "is an allegory, very exact in detail" in which a palace is described as a face: "The protagonist has golden hair and—at first—intelligent eyes, fine teeth, and lips whence flows intellectual conversation. But madness seizes him, his eyes are bloodshot, and there come from his lips only raving and insane laughter."[104] Of the poem's six stanzas, three explicitly use musical terminology. The third stanza describes the "intelligent eyes" of the subject:

> Wanderers in that happy valley
> Through two luminous windows saw
> Spirits moving musically
> To a lute's well-tunéd law,
> Round about a throne, where sitting
> (Porphyrogene!)
> In state his glory well befitting,
> The ruler of the realm was seen.[105]

This stanza harks back to the image of the hanging lute from the epigraph of the story. As in that epigraph, the lute is not presented as a played musical instrument. Rather, the lute holds an ideological place as the instrument to whose law "spirits" are "moving musically." This idea of the "spirits" moving, as opposed to the ghouls of "Ulalume" or even the covetous seraphs of "Annabel Lee," provides an image reminiscent of the ventum textilem, or the "breath of faery" that Poe describes in relationship to "indefinitiveness" as an element of the "true musical expression."[106] Rather than a "thing of the earth," the "spirit" is tied to the "musical" in this passage.[107] The lute does not play "musically," but the "spirits" move musically to a "law" of the "lute" that cannot be said to be actually played or to produce a sound, unlike Roderick's "speaking guitar," which produces "dirges" that the narrator holds "painfully in mind."[108]

As Daniel Chua argues, "Romantics did call instrumental music 'pure music', [. . .] for its purity was deemed to be the essence of music itself [. . .]. So for the Romantics music became equated with Spirit, something too ethereal to have a history and too transcendent to be soiled by the muck of contextualisation."[109] Poe adopts and transmutes this notion of instrumental music as "pure" by substituting instruments that one could hear performed in a concert hall for instruments that take on symbolic, rather than real-world, significance. Lutes, lyres, and harps are what "became equated with Spirit" in Poe, giving them the quality of that which is ethereal and transcendent. Poe goes even further, however, to highlight the inescapability of this "muck of contextualization." That "pure music" associated with the "Spirit" almost instantly disintegrates, devolving into representation in musical imagery of that which is "haunted by an idealised past."[110] For Darrel Abel, the "lute's well-tunéd law":

symbolizes ideal order in the "radiant palace," and the whole of that song is an explicit musical metaphor for derangement of intellect. For Poe, music was the highest as well as the most rational expression of the intelligence, and string music was quintessential music (wherefore Usher's jangled intellect can endure only string music). Time out of mind, music has symbolized celestial order. [. . .] The derangement of human reason, then, "sweet bells jangled out of tune and harsh," cannot be better expressed than in a musical figure.[111]

The divine and the demonic implications of music coexist in Abel's analysis of Poe, the divine being reflected in music in tune, and the demonic (expressed as derangement) being reflected in discordance. The lute's law acts as a symbol of an "ideal" that is not articulated, a symbol whose inversion falls into the framework of Ophelia's famed description of Hamlet's madness, "Like sweet bells jangled, out of time and harsh," a comparison that has major implications in Poe's works.[112] The liminal madness described throughout this chapter finds unarticulated expression in "The Haunted Palace" that Abel chooses not to reiterate in Poe's terms, but by appropriating the phrase of "sweet bells" that "jangled" discordantly. Like Bailey, who argues that Roderick Usher's endurance of only string music (associated with the angelic) perversely points to the presence of a demon, Abel appears to argue that the lute symbolizing "celestial order" highlights the mad discordance of "The Haunted Palace" and its echo in the frame narrative.

Richard Wilbur provides a similar reading of the following stanza, which is the last to illustrate the concordant mind. As when the speaker of "Ulalume" reads the sign of Astarte in a way that foreshadows her falsity, the description of the allegorical mouth in this stanza of "The Haunted Palace" contains within it a prefiguring of the mind's collapse:

> And all with pearl and ruby glowing
> Was the fair palace door,
> Through which came flowing, flowing, flowing,
> And sparkling evermore,
> A troop of Echoes whose sweet duty
> Was but to sing,
> In voices of surpassing beauty,
> The wit and wisdom of their king.[113]

The "wit and wisdom" of this haunted mind communicates through a symbolic singing accomplished by multiple Echoes, both incorporeal and inherently representative of duplication. This is one of two instances in Poe's poetry in which he uses Echoes in both the plural and formal sense. The other is in "The Coliseum," and the ways in which he employs the Echoes in that poem shed light on his use of Echoes in "The Haunted Palace." On the subject of the coliseum, Kent Ljungquist argues that, for "Poe in particular, ruins, in their mystery, silence, and desolation, served a prophetic function, offering premonitions, suggestions, and submerged meanings that resisted representation in ordinary language."[114] Fundamental here is the idea of the ruins as representative of earthly decay. The "submerged meanings that resisted representation in ordinary language" embrace the expression of decay and failure:

> These stones—alas! these gray stones—are they all—
> All of the famed, and the colossal left
> By the corrosive Hours to Fate and me?
> "Not all"—the Echoes answer me—"not all!
> "Prophetic sounds and loud, arise forever
> "From us, and from all Ruin, unto the wise,
> "As melody from Memnon to the Sun."[115]

"Melody" arises from "Memnon," which Mabbott explains as an ancient Greek statue that "gave out, when struck by the rays of the morning sun, a sound like the breaking of a harpstring."[116] Mabbott does not cite his source for this myth, but the legend of its sound can be found elsewhere.[117] Robin Dix gives a thorough account of the legend, citing Pausanias as having said that the "sound which issued from the statue was 'very like the twang of a broken lyre-string or lute-string.'"[118] Whether the term "melody" is used to refer to a specific series of notes, or whether it is used to refer to an unspecific series of notes, Poe's use of the term in this instance defies both. "Melody" in this case refers to a "twang," a hum, or a sound of unspecified pitch and unspecified length.

The "morning sun" striking the column to produce the sound ties into the idea that the legend is cited by "Echoes." In this case, as Hollander points out, the "stone image was given voice by the light of its mother, Dawn, falling upon it, and thereby parallels Echo, whose body became stone," providing an image of the simultaneous creation and destruction of sound.[119] This unspecified pitch described as a "melody" is an earthly sound produced by the statue of a man, giving the impression that the statue has a voice, when the statue is not actually articulating any words in the way a person would. The "melody" does not represent the "melody" of a specific series of notes, and although it is based upon the idea of a sound, it is "unheard" and unreal in its present context. Like ancient ballads, Memnon's sound is only legend; while one might imagine that sound, one does not perceive it as articulated melody. Memnon's "melody" is used only as an analogy to the "prophetic sounds" that "arise forever" from the "Echoes." Thus, not only must these "prophetic sounds" be silent to the listener or "the wise," but they are paradoxically by definition repetition of previous sounds. The listener is further and further removed from an ancient ideal, but these "prophetic sounds," akin to "melody," continually point to an unheard repetition of the ideal past source. Music as the language of decay points back toward its otherworldly roots. Rather than its audible manifestations gesturing toward the ideal itself, they point to the lost idea of the ideal.

Similarly, in "The Haunted Palace," there is implied repetition of the Echoes, but what they sing, how they sing, and the words they use (if they use words at all) remain unknown. The "troop of Echoes" may appear to sing in a more audible or articulated sense, but they stem from a mythological character whose voice dissipates, and who is doomed to repeat only the "heard" voices of others. Their "beauty" is undefined, adding an unarticulated and "surpassing" quality to the "singing," which itself is only a duplication of a nonexistent ideal. It should come as no surprise, then, that the "flowing" Echoes quickly change to a "hideous throng" in a nightmarish fashion:

> But evil things, in robes of sorrow,
> Assailed the monarch's high estate.
> [...]
> And travellers, now, within that valley,
> Through the encrimsoned windows see
> Vast forms that move fantastically
> To a discordant melody,
> While, like a ghastly rapid river,
> Through the pale door
> A hideous throng rush out forever
> And laugh—but smile no more.[120]

These lines of the poem reveal the embodiment of "madness," as "the encrimsoned windows" are the subject's "bloodshot" eyes. It is in the "encrimsoned windows," or "bloodshot" eyes of the subject that one sees "Vast forms" that "move fantastically" to the "discordant melody." Whereas the lute's law that represented the concordance of the mind acted in a symbolic fashion without being played, the "melody" arising amid the mind's decay becomes explicitly "discordant." "Melody" relates to an implicit sound more directly than "music."

The "melody" may be something to which beings more than mortal, or "Vast forms," move, but one does not necessarily hear it, or them. Douglas Anderson argues that their "'discordant melody' is not identical to mere discord but to a perpetual flood of ghastly laughter that may signal an embittered wisdom as readily as madness."[121] Indeed, the "discordant" quality of the melody conveys a sense of "madness," but that "discordant melody" cannot be confused with the sound of "ghastly laughter," as Anderson interprets it. Gerhard Joseph makes a similar argument, relating the "discordant melody" to "madness":

> the occupation of Thought's mansion by "evil things, in robes of sorrow" has blasted the lute's harmony with a "discordant melody" that the story itself shows to be madness, whether of Roderick Usher or of

the narrator (if they are not the same kind of "doubles" that Poe brings together in "William Wilson").[122]

Richard Wilbur writes of this transition to the discordant:

> The beautiful Echoes which issue from the pearl and ruby door are the poetic utterances of the man's harmonious imagination, here symbolized as an orderly dance. [. . .] As for the mouth of our allegorized man, it is now "pale" rather than "pearl and ruby," and through it come no sweet Echoes, as before, but the wild laughter of a jangling and discordant mind.[123]

Wilbur analyzes this scene with straightforward musical association. The sane mind is beautiful, harmonious, and the voice itself is lovely. When the mind becomes insane, the "sweet Echoes" disappear and the "wild" and "jangled" metaphor of the "discordant mind" that Abel articulates reemerges, but neither the term "jangled" nor bells appear in the poem itself. Yet it is not without reason that Wilbur and Abel make this comparison. This relationship between the discordant and the "wild" and "jangled" notion associated with the bells parallels the liminal madness associated with bells in Poe's works as a whole, which will be discussed in the second part of this book. Unlike Poe's other ballads, "The Haunted Palace" uses musical terminology, which reflects the themes presented in Poe's other ballads as they work inside the mind as they approach the dark space of what cannot be articulated. The tale of "The Haunted Palace" is one of the mind, and music, the concordant but not necessarily played lute that becomes musical as spirits move to it or the discordant melody to which unknown vast forms move, represents the heavenly and the demonic. But the initial ideal state points ironically back toward the elements of the demonic that were always present from the start.

NOTES

1. Sullivan, "New Worlds," 62.
2. Poe, "Fall of the House," 399.
3. Joseph, "Poe and Tennyson," 420.
4. Poe, "Fall of the House," 400.
5. Ibid., 397.
6. Ibid., 400.
7. Ibid., 413.
8. See Howey and Raimer, eds., *Bibliography of Modern Arthuriana*, for the sheer number of permutations of the story.
9. Shirt, *Old French Tristan Poems*, 13.
10. Ibid.
11. Mabbott, *Edgar Allan Poe: Tales*, 1: 306.
12. See Scott, *Sir Tristrem*, 203.
13. Poe, "Fall of the House," 414; Scott, *Sir Tristrem*, 66.
14. Ibid.
15. Ibid.
16. Ibid., cvi, 63.

17. Ibid., 211.
18. Ibid., 207.
19. Ibid., 211.
20. Ibid.
21. Foucault, *Madness and Civilization*, 12.
22. Ibid., 7.
23. Ibid., 10–12.
24. Ibid., 69.
25. Ibid., 11.
26. See Allison, "Coleridgean Self-Development," 43.
27. Poe, "Fall of the House," 416.
28. Ibid., 404, 408.
29. Poe, "Fall of the House," 397, 417.
30. Poe, "Israfel [G]," 2; ibid., 51.
31. Scott, *Sir Tristrem*, cvi.
32. Poe, "Fall of the House," 403.
33. Bailey, "What Happens," 454.
34. Poe, "Fall of the House," 404.
35. Ibid.
36. Leppert, *Sight of Sound*, 64; Poe, "Fall of the House," 404.
37. Ibid., 405.
38. Mabbott, *Edgar Allan Poe: Tales*, 1: 418.
39. Poe, "Ligeia," 318–19; Poe, "Assignation," 162–63; Poe, "Morella [A]," 227–28.
40. Bailey, "What Happens," 456; Michael Hoffman, "House of Usher," 160.
41. Rollason, "Tell-Tale Signs," 45.
42. Poe, "Fall of the House," 406, 408.
43. Kramer, *Music and Poetry*, 2.
44. Scott, *Sir Tristrem*, 286.
45. Chua, *Absolute Music*, 23; ibid., 31.
46. Poe, "Fall of the House," 406.
47. Hoagwood, *From Song to Print*, 4–5.
48. Pollin, "Poe as a Writer," 61.
49. Hoagwood, *From Song to Print*, 138–39.
50. Chua, *Absolute Music*, 31.
51. Bristol, "In Search of the Bear," 163.
52. Poe, "Man of the Crowd," 510.
53. Scott, *Minstrelsy*, 44.
54. Ibid., 45.
55. Hoagwood, *From Song to Print*, 25.
56. McLane, "Ballads and Bards," 423. McLane has written a brilliantly expanded book on this topic, taking it far beyond the scope of my book, in her *Balladeering, Minstrelsy, and the Making of British Romantic Poetry* (Cambridge: Cambridge UP, 2011).
57. Newman, *Ballad Collection*, 2.
58. Ibid., 3.
59. Daniel Hoffman, *Poe*, 70–71.
60. Ibid., 70.
61. Hoagwood, *From Song to Print*, 5–6.
62. Mabbott, ed., *Edgar Allan Poe: Complete Poems*, 420.
63. "Auber and His New Opera," 86.
64. Poe, "Ulalume," 1–9.
65. Carlson, "Symbol and Sense," 26.
66. Ibid., 26.
67. Ibid., 29.
68. Pollin, *Poe, Creator of Words*, 5–6.
69. Poe, "Marginalia," 1331.
70. Heidegger, *The Event*, 279.

71. Nikolopoulou, *Tragically Speaking*, 74.
72. Poe, "Marginalia," 1331.
73. Mabbott, *Edgar Allan Poe: Tales*, 2: 917.
74. Isaac D'Israeli, ed., "Some Ingenious Thoughts," 1: 132.
75. Poe, "Spectacles," 324.
76. Chua, *Absolute Music*, 23, 52.
77. Carlson, "Symbol and Sense," 29.
78. See Miller in ibid.
79. Hoagwood, *From Song to Print*, 8.
80. Poe, "Ulalume," 10–19.
81. Poe, "Fall of the House," 405.
82. Poe, "Ulalume," 39–43.
83. Ibid., 45–46.
84. Ibid., 51–60.
85. In Carlson, "Symbol and Sense," 34.
86. Relihan, trans., *Tale of Cupid and Psyche*, xvii.
87. Ibid.
88. Ibid., xviii.
89. Poe, "Ulalume," 75–77.
90. Ibid., 90, 95–104.
91. Daniel Hoffman, *Poe*, 66.
92. Ibid.
93. Ibid., 67–68.
94. Ibid., 23.
95. Poe, "Annabel Lee," 1–6.
96. Ibid., 7–12.
97. Foucault, *Madness and Civilization*, 10–12.
98. Poe, "Annabel Lee," 9–26.
99. Quinn, *Edgar Allan Poe*, 123.
100. Poe, "Annabel Lee," 34, 36, 41.
101. Ibid., 30–32.
102. Poe, "Fall of the House," 406.
103. Poe, "Letter 112," 272.
104. Mabbott, *Edgar Allan Poe: Tales*, 1: 312.
105. Poe, "Haunted Palace," 17–24.
106. Poe, "Marginalia," 1331.
107. Ibid.
108. Poe, "Fall of the House," 405.
109. Chua, *Absolute Music*, 4.
110. Ibid., 31.
111. Abel, "Key to the House," 52.
112. Shakespeare, *Hamlet*, 3.1.158.
113. Poe, "Haunted Palace," 25–32.
114. Ljungquist, "'Coliseum': A Dialogue," 32.
115. Poe, "Coliseum," 30–36.
116. Mabbott, *Edgar Allan Poe: Complete Poems*, 231.
117. See Dix, "Harps of Memnon," 289. As Dix points out, more than one theorist has suggested that the statue could have actually produced this sound, as "when the colossus was damaged [in an earthquake] fissures may have been created in the stone and [. . .] any air trapped in them would be set in motion by a sudden temperature change. [. . .] [A]s the trapped air escaped, a noise would be produced." In other words, the heat of the morning sun could effectively produce the sound.
118. Ibid. See Mabbott, ed., *Edgar Allan Poe: Complete Poems*, 78.
119. Hollander, *Figure of Echo*, 13.
120. Poe, "Haunted Palace," 33–34; ibid., 41–48.
121. Douglas Anderson, *Pictures of Ascent*, 137.

122. Joseph, "Poe and Tennyson," 422.
123. Wilbur, "House," 262–63.

THREE
An Almost Magical Melody

> What was meant by the invective against him who had no music in his soul?
>
> —Edgar Allan Poe, "Letter to B —"

As in the case of the ballads discussed in the previous chapter, Poe sometimes calls forth a musical term only to reject it in the subject of a piece. Substituting tumult for melody, Poe develops a function for music—for musical vocabulary—that rejects real-world music. I also believe that Poe offers a parallel to this specific use of musical terms: he uses wailing, howling, and shrieking as descriptors that evoke a sense of the earthly, the diabolical, death, and the type of madness described in the first chapter of this book. This is that madness that "no longer has any value as the sign of a Beyond," madness "without relation to anything but itself: [. . .] madness in the state of nature."[1] The water-lilies of the story "Silence—A Fable" "shrieked within their beds" after being cursed.[2] In "A Descent into the Maelström," the ocean's surf "reared high up against it its white and ghastly crest, howling and shrieking for ever" and "sending forth to the winds an appalling voice, half shriek, half roar, such as not even the mighty cataract of Niagara ever lifts up in its agony to Heaven."[3] The descriptions of shrieking water-lilies and the ocean present personified synesthetic images of horror that also convey an unarticulated "agony." Moreover, the flowers and the water are descriptively chained to the material world, the water-lilies shrieking from "their beds" and the ocean waves, struggling in their emergence from the body of the sea, forming a "white and ghastly crest."

In "The Black Cat," it is a shriek that reveals the murdered corpse:

> No sooner had the reverberation of [his] blows sunk into silence, than [he] was answered by a voice from within the tomb!—by a cry, at first muffled and broken, like the sobbing of a child, and then quickly swell-

ing into one long, loud, and continuous scream, utterly anomalous and inhuman—a howl—a wailing shriek, half of horror and half of triumph, such as might have arisen only out of hell, conjointly from the throats of the damned in their agony and of the demons that exult in the damnation.[4]

The narrator depicts this "wailing shriek," like that of "A Descent into the Maelström," as a "voice." This voice, rendered indefinite in being "half of horror and half of triumph," points toward the horrifying physical remnants of death. As Jonathan Auerbach observes, "the black cat's demonic howl is still an 'informing voice,' communicating what its owner himself wants to betray all along."[5] The cat's revelation is redoubled by the metaphorical expansion of its single "wailing shriek" into the multitudinous "throats of the damned and of the demons that exult in the damnation," which contrasts with the multitudinous sound of the waters in "The Fall of the House of Usher." That story ends: "this fissure rapidly widened [. . .] there was a long tumultuous shouting sound like the voice of a thousand waters—and the deep and dank tarn at my feet closed sullenly and silently over the fragments of the 'House of Usher.'"[6] Roderick is enveloped into other worlds below with a sound that adopts apocalyptic Biblical imagery: "Then I heard what seemed to be the voice of a great multitude, like the sound of many waters and like the sound of mighty thunder-peals, crying out."[7] Lawrence Kramer describes a similar reference in Wordsworth's "Prelude," as with the

> "fixed, abysmal, gloomy breathing-place" from which mounts the "roar of waters, torrents, streams / Innumerable, roaring with one voice" [. . .] nature transcends itself literally, with a roar. The nature that imagines and unfolds in this dark cleft [. . .] has found that region in itself which no merely human imagination can find, envision, or subdue. What breathes in its gloomy breathing-place is nothing human, not even a vatic "pneuma" of inspiration; and what rises from its breathing is a voice that has nothing to say to the human mind. The "roar of waters . . . innumerable" announces a revelation, translating into a "natural" language the divine voice "as the sound of many waters" that reveals itself to John on Patmos [. . .]; yet [. . .] nothing at all is revealed. Not, at any rate, to human ears: [. . .]. Wordsworth, already imaginatively superfluous, is merely privileged to overhear the sounds of nature's creative Word, a sublime Logos neither human nor divine.[8]

The narrator of "The Fall of the House of Usher," like Kramer's interpretation of Wordsworth, stands on the edge of the scene, "imaginatively superfluous" and "merely privileged to overhear" that which is "neither human nor divine." While not all of the elements of Kramer's interpretation are integral to this book's argument, his association of the "roar" with the "sound of many waters" and with a voice from beyond that translates to a different form that I see reiterated in Poe's works. This works only by complicating Kramer's notion that the voice is explicitly "divine," however, and that "nothing at all is revealed" from this "voice that has nothing to say to the human mind." Instead, the multitudinous, revelatory, apocalyptic voice announces that which cannot be named, defined, or articulated by the human mind, translating to an absolute terror, the terrifying unknown of death. Placed in opposition to this "informing voice" of an incorporeal, more absolute, death is the black cat's "wailing shriek [. . .] such as might have arisen only out of hell," tied explicitly to the "throats of the damned in their agony and of the demons that exult in the damnation."[9] Rather, the wailing shriek draws attention to the vulgar, material remnants of an earthly corpse; it "informs" both the characters of the story and the story's readers of a ghastly and utterly earthly death. Still, the "voice" is still "informing" in this way without the influence of articulated words.

In fact, in none of these instances does a shriek accompany articulated words. Apart from in "Ligeia," the only other story in which a character's shrieks accompany speech is "The Fall of the House of Usher," and as in the other examples, no musical vocabulary is used in the description of it. In the climax of this story, Roderick Usher renders his confession through a shriek subsequent to the narrator's reading of the "Mad Trist":

> "I dared not speak! We have put her living in the tomb! [. . .] Do I not distinguish that heavy and horrible beating of her heart? Madman!"—here he sprang furiously to his feet, and shrieked out his syllables, as if in the effort he were giving up his soul—"Madman! I tell you that she now stands without the door!"[10]

Roderick Usher "shrieked out his syllables, as if in the effort he were giving up his soul." His shriek not only prefigures his own death, but it also metaphorically evacuates his soul, his spirit—his breath. His shriek, and not his utterance, is what informs the narrator of something akin to Roderick's "giving up his soul." His words articulate his sister's position, but his shriek "informs" us of the unarticulated internal state. Like Roderick Usher, after she finishes her "half shriek," Ligeia too "returned solemnly to her bed of Death."[11] D. H. Lawrence argues that Ligeia "would rather do anything than die. [. . .] No wonder she shrieks with her last breath."[12] But she does not shriek with her last breath; her "half shriek" accompanies her physical movement toward "Death" and toward her horror (or the narrator's horror) at her physical death. Rather, Ligeia has a second utterance.

As many critics have pointed out, Ligeia is only partially, if at all, mortal.[13] Consequently her return "to her bed of Death" produces a different manner of speech prior to her "last breath": "And as she breathed her last sighs, there came mingled with them a low murmur from her lips. [The narrator] bent to them [his] ear and distinguished, again, the concluding words of the passage" attributed to Joseph Glanvill, including the claim that "Man doth not yield himself [. . .] unto death utterly," which also serves as the epigraph of the tale.[14] In this second utterance, which is quoted in the text, Ligeia's "sighs [. . .] mingled with [the words] a low murmur," which the narrator then interprets as he "bent [his ear] to them." The "half shrieked" ejaculation stands on its own, whereas the "sighs" that combine with "a low murmur" must be distinguished and interpreted by the narrator for the reader.

This use of "sighs" and "a low murmur" also recurs elsewhere in Poe's tales. In fact, the "low" tone, the "murmur" and the "sighs" arise time and time again. One significant instance appears in "Eleonora," narrated by a character who describes himself at the outset of the story:

> Men have called me mad; but the question is not yet settled, whether madness is or is not the loftiest intelligence [. . .]. They who dream by day are cognizant of many things which escape those who dream only by night. In their grey visions they obtain glimpses of eternity, and thrill, in awaking, to find that they have been upon the verge of the great secret. [. . .] They penetrate, however rudderless or compassless, into the vast ocean of the "light ineffable" and again, like the adventures of the Nubian geographer, "*agressi sunt mare tenebrarum, quid in eo esset exploraturi.*" We will say, then, that I am mad.[15]

In emphasizing his madness, the narrator of "Eleonora" invokes that madness described in the previous chapter, that which is tied to the image of the sea. In the italicized quotation, the narrator quotes Jacob Bryant.[16] In his *A New System; or, An Analysis of Ancient Mythology*, Bryant writes:

> The vast unfathomable abyss, spoken of by poets, is the great Atlantic ocean; upon the borders of which Homer places the gloomy mansions, where the Titans resided. The ancients had a notion, that the earth was a widely-extended plain; which terminated abruptly, in a vast cliff of immeasurable descent. At the bottom was a chaotic pool, or ocean; which was so far sunk beneath the confines of the world [. . .] Agressi sunt mare tenebrarum, quid in eo esset, exploraturi. They ventured into the sea of darkness, in order to explore what it might contain.[17]

The narrator explicitly associates himself with the sea to best illustrate his madness. As opposed to the material, natural, bestial madness represented by the shrieks of other tales, in "Eleonora" the narrator's madness is one of the sea. Not an inverted figure of the tarn, like Roderick Usher, this narrator moves back to the image of the sea as a "widely extended plain," which speaks of that "strange knowledge, from that fantastic plain, the underside of the world."[18] There still exists in this description the undercurrent of the theme from "Annabel Lee" of "spiritual passion that transcended human limits," as if when one travels too far across this plain, it terminates "in a vast cliff of immeasurable descent," and the sea that one ventures into becomes "the sea of darkness."[19]

No shrieks, discordance, nor the harsh and protracted soundscape of the diabolical emerge when the narrator of the story "Eleonora" describes the valley that he and his love (Eleonora) inhabit. Instead, the valley rests liminally between earth and the spiritual beyond. In this valley, the narrator "heard the sounds of the swinging of the censers of the angels; and streams of a holy perfume floated ever and ever about the valley; and at lone hours, when [his] heart beat heavily, the winds that bathed [his] brow came unto [him] laden with soft sighs; and indistinct murmurs filled often the night air."[20] All of these sound-based images are, like the shrieks of the previous section, synesthetic and otherworldly. The images of the angels and the streams of holy perfume, coupled with the implied movement of air around a swinging censer and the "indistinct murmurs" and "soft sighs" of the personified wind "bath[ing]" the narrator's brow, imply an implicit meaning understood by the narrator alone, a meaning perhaps delayed for the reader until the rest of the story plays out, much as in "Ligeia" the full import of Ligeia's sighs and murmurs does not appear until her vampire-like return in the body of the narrator's second wife. In this way, the murmur seems to be an "informing voice" as well. In "Eleonora," the narrator has not yet interpreted whatever unarticulated meaning exists, but the reader might deduce that it too has something to do with death, with that awaiting "sea of darkness" after their love has transcended human bounds—Eleonora's death. Now, however, the death is different. Rather than the material, horrifying death, this death deals with questions of the beyond, the ethereal.

There is yet another source for a murmur in "Eleonora," that of a river, another moving body of water, unlike the dank and stagnant waters of the tarn. The river that runs through the valley is described as having a "bosom" "out of which issued [. . .] a murmur that swelled, at length into a lulling melody [. . .] softer than the wind harp of Æolus and more divine than all save the voice of Eleonora."[21] Poe's reference to the ubiquitous Romantic symbol of the Æolian harp is no accident. Not only does the symbol directly correlate the softly sighing wind and the murmuring of the river with music, but the suggestion that the protagonist, through Eleonora's companionship, recognizes the Æolian harp, also connotes his ability to interpret unarticulated meaning in music, nature, and Eleonora's "voice." The wind becomes an unnamed otherworldly sound that remains indefinite, becoming even more vague as it is defined through the breath-inspired notion of the river dying away after Eleonora's death "in murmurs growing lower and lower."[22] That the murmurs dwindle in this way clarifies their previously unarticulated meaning. They, the murmurs, dim rather than disappear, always "informing" the narrator of Eleonora's death; they subside as his life moves forward. Both the murmurs and Eleonora's low voice reflect the disappearance of her breath, but the imparted meaning of her voice remains behind for the narrator so that the association of death with murmurs and the low voice does not create an effect of horror, as shrieks do. The murmurs "inform" the narrator and the reader of some indistinct notion of Death as an absolute ideal, whereas the shrieks "inform" the physical, material remnants of death on earth. Thus, just before Ligeia dies, with her "half shriek" over, her "low murmurs" and "sighs" must be interpreted as speech by the narrator, who hears her words emerging from her "bed of Death," not from her corpse.

"LIGEIA": SIREN WHO NEVER SINGS

Ligeia imparts unarticulated meaning to the narrator by means other than her murmur and her shriek. The narrator writes of the "thrilling and enthralling eloquence of her low musical language," the "dear music of her low sweet voice," the "almost magical melody, modulation, distinctness, and placidity of her very low voice," and her "melody more than mortal."[23] In every case, her "melody" and the "music" of her "low voice" work separately from the words of her utterance. The "almost magical melody" of her "voice" is, in the narrator's interpretation, only amplified by "the fierce energy (rendered doubly effective by contrast with her manner of utterance) of the wild words which she habitually uttered."[24] As her "voice grew [. . .] more low," says the narrator, he "would not wish to dwell upon the wild meaning of the quietly uttered words"; instead, that to which he "hearkened, entranced" was "a melody more than mortal."[25]

The narrator consistently describes this "voice," working separately from utterance, in terms of music. The narrator interprets the "melody more than mortal" for his audience so that this "melody" is equivalent, not to sound, but to "assumptions and aspirations which mortality had never before known," or rather to unarticulated "assumptions and aspirations" that cannot exist in language.[26] As Auerbach notes, Ligeia's "eloquence," like that of other characters in Poe, retains "some absolute power, imperishable and unmediated, beyond personal identity and the contingencies of interpretation. Aspiring to the condition of music, the voice's mystical quality depends on its enchanting effects. Yet this buried utterance [. . .] only moves when it is the object of a second kind of utterance, the social voice of the narrating self."[27] The voice, thus understood, depends on its "enchanting effects" more than on any other quality. Ligeia embodies music without producing any musical sounds, and it is this peculiar "eloquence" that retains "some absolute power" in the narrative. Although one must add to Auerbach's formulation the recognition that the voice's "mystical quality" acts separately from "utterance," it is true that the reader is privy to neither.

This idea of a "melody" and "music" unheard by anyone but the narrator of the story, and of a half-woman, half-immortal who imparts some dangerous "knowledge" to the narrator, has of course been played out in literature time and time again. It is no surprise that several critics have connected Ligeia to siren mythology. In her 1967 article, Joy Rea interpreted Poe's "Ligeia" as "the describing of a siren as if she were a reality."[28] In 1981, Maurice Bennett linked the Ligeia of the tale to the Ligeia of Poe's poem "Al Aaraaf," noting that "the name Ligeia belonged to one of the sirens who sang to Odysseus."[29] In 1983, Daryl Jones justifies reading Ligeia as a siren by arguing, "Poe undoubtedly was acquainted with the lore surrounding the Sirens, as his reference to them in the epigraph to 'The Murders in the Rue Morgue' clearly attests."[30] But although critics repeatedly make this connection and offer textual evidence for it, they do not generally analyze Poe's framework for the unnamed narrator-cum-Odysseus. Instead, they read the connection thematically, using it, for instance, to argue that the "paradox" implicit in the "'wild words' and 'more than mortal melody' [. . .] is like Homer's paradox in his description of the voices of the sirens [. . .] these contradictory qualities may be associated with [. . .] the Greek word for 'siren': a savage person and a divine being."[31] Similarly, Joan Dayan, who analyses the manner of the narrator's speech instead of Ligeia's, and who observes that "we never hear Ligeia," nevertheless focuses on Ligeia's sirenic power: "'Ligeia' is the feminine of the Homeric Greek adjective ligys, meaning canorous, high-sounding or shrill. Ligeia, then, is a siren; no mere singer, she is a sorceress who enthralls men with her spells."[32] There are two facts that all of these critics continually evade. One is that Ligeia, like Roderick Usher, is never said to "sing" at all; the word "song" never appears in the text, and as already discussed in detail, the narrator's interpretation of Ligeia's tone as "musical" may have nothing to do with music in the real-world sense. The other is that she materially evades the narrator. Her communication with him relies upon her distance; it is her contact with him and the concretizing of her words that bring about her demise.

These qualities point to another type of siren. In his interpretation of "a key passage from Nietzsche's The Gay Science," Lawrence Kramer describes sirens who do not sing.[33] In teasing out why they do not, he suggests:

> Their silence is not a stratagem [. . .], but part of a broader pattern of reversal, or reversion, that endows the Odyssean quester with the sirens' own character. The quester in this passage is a centered figure, not a voyager; a figure of the shore, not of the ship; and a figure who does not hear, but sees, the object(s) of his desire. In each of these respects, the quester trades places with the sirens. [. . .] The song is enchanting precisely because it must thus be dreamed. It is not the sailor who must elude the sirens, but the sirens who must elude the beached sailor—but who do so precisely so that, paradoxically, in their

distance he can be moved by them, in their silence he can hear their song, and more, can, in the very texture of his prose, sing their song.[34]

The narrator of Ligeia, like the "Odyssean quester" Kramer describes, is also endowed "with the sirens' own character." As Joan Dayan points out, in "Ligeia" the flow of the narrator's voice "joins the sirenic cadences of the lady. In fact, [. . .] his sing-song disquisitions and monotonous intonings are ironically mirrored in the mystic lady's own sonorities. Through the curious colloquy between subject and object, the narrator seems to imbibe a certain talent for muttering obscure, equivocal and unsteady terms."[35]

In "Ligeia" we are primarily given the "texture" of the narrator's "prose," to adopt Kramer's terminology. Moreover, the narrator of the story awaits Ligeia's return on his own metaphorical isle, "habitually fettered in the shackles" of opium, chained to the earth and hoping to set his mind free to find Ligeia once more in his drugged, otherworldly state.[36] Although he remains "circumscribed," as Richard Wilbur points out, in a circular room that Poe describes in great detail, this room may nonetheless "symbolize a triumphantly imaginative state of mind in which the dreamer is all but free of the so-called 'real' world."[37] But it is Ligeia who bears the power to leave and to return. Even before she dies and (at the end of the tale) returns through the body of her nominal replacement Rowena, "the narrator reports that he is subject to alternating moods of great optimism and deep despair. The times he feels most optimistic appear to be when Ligeia is closest to him and he seems nearly able to grasp the wisdom he imagines she possesses."[38] The narrator is chained to the earth; it is Ligeia who drifts toward and away from him, as if following the waves of the sea. The narrator-cum-quester is, as in Kramer's reading of Nietzsche, "a centered figure [. . .] a figure of the shore," who dreams of Ligeia's "song" and who imagines and recapitulates it in his own prose and in his own descriptions of her "musical voice."

As in "The Fall of the House of Usher," the narrator then represents an inversion of the metaphorical sailor; rather than his madness speaking that "strange knowledge, from that fantastic plain" that moves in voyages from the known to the unknown,[39] he transforms into a liminal figure that speaks of the "sea of darkness." Like the false Astarte, the false angels of "Annabel Lee," and like Roderick Usher's Echoes that turn into throngs of horror, the narrator of "Ligeia" fears Ligeia's physical return at the end of the tale as it becomes a "hideous drama of revivification" that "had chilled [him] into stone," such that the final words of the tale, confirming Ligeia's hideous resurrection, are "shrieked aloud."[40] Murmurs and music, the unarticulated voice, are continually associated with the beyond, death, the otherworldly absolute, but often in a way that foregrounds falsity, or failure to achieve an ideal; in this falsity, however, the failure still points toward the otherworldly, even as it is continually embodied in the demonic.

Much like Ligeia, Morella holds a power over the narrator of her story. When the narrator finds himself "poring over forbidden pages" of Morella's studies, Morella would "rake up from the ashes of a dead philosophy some low, singular words, whose strange meaning burned themselves in upon [his] memory," and he lingers beside her to "dwell upon the music of her voice—until, at length, its melody was tainted with terror,—and there fell a shadow upon [his] soul—and [he] grew pale, and shuddered inwardly at those too unearthly tones. And thus, joy suddenly faded into horror, and the most beautiful became the most hideous."[41] In this excerpt, the "music" of Morella's voice is intrinsically related to its "melody." Not only is this "melody" and "music" described separately from her utterance, as in Ligeia's, but Morella's "music" in her "voice" holds some power to which the reader is not privy, apart from the fact that it throws a "shadow" upon the narrator's "soul" as he interprets its implicit terror. The "music" of her voice informs the narrator of what cannot be articulated, something otherworldly and demonic.

Like Ligeia, it is also the concretizing of Morella's words that brings about her demise. She "says," "I repeat that I am dying. [. . .] thou shalt bear about with thee thy shroud on earth."[42] Once she dies, he writes, "I heard her voice no more."[43] When, like Ligeia who is reborn as Rowena, Morella is reborn in her child, the narrator recognizes her "in the sad musical tones of her speech, and above all—oh, above all—in the phrases and expressions of the dead on the lips of the loved and the living, I found food for consuming thought and horror—for a worm that would not die."[44] Like the distinction between utterance and voice, between words and music, the "musical tones" of the incarnated Morella's "speech" refute the "phrases and expressions" that relate to the narrator the image of a "worm that would not die," gesturing toward horrifying materiality. The only sound associated with utterance in the entire tale comes at the end of the story, when the narrator names their child "Morella":

> What fiend spoke from the recesses of my soul, when, amid those dim aisles, and in the silence of the night, I whispered within the ears of the holy man the syllables—Morella? What more than fiend convulsed the features of my child, and overspread them with hues of death, as, starting at that scarcely audible sound, she turned her glassy eyes from the earth to heaven, and falling prostrate on the black slabs of our ancestral vault, responded — "I am here!" Distinct, coldly, calmly distinct, fell those few simple sounds within my ear, and thence, like molten lead, rolled hissingly into my brain. Years—years may pass away, but the memory of that epoch—never! [. . .] The winds of the firmament breathe but one sound within my ears, and the ripples upon the sea murmured evermore—Morella.[45]

The narrator identifies his own perverse "whisper" of Morella's name with the possibility of a "fiend" within his soul. The reincarnated Morella's utterance "I am here" in response rolls "hissingly into" his brain such that it holds a painful power over his mind, like the "perversions" Roderick Usher plays hold a power over his narrator's mind. The liminal spaces of the seas still "murmur" with their perverse promise of the otherworldly, but when that name is uttered by the narrator, it becomes the utterance of the "fiend" of his "soul."

In "Morella," as in "Ligeia," a liminal kind of music begins to appear. Madness begins to communicate death in a shadowy, demonic, and terrifyingly unknown fashion. Music is heard and seen as though in a dream, perversions of that voice that cannot be articulated, while maintaining the associations of movement away from an original ideal, integrating Echoes and ballads as part of a mythology that once united words and music in a way it no longer does. Murmurs and shrieks parallel unarticulated music and discordance that speak to a split between the otherworldly and the earthly elements of death. Musicality separates completely from real-world music; the characters embody musicality without ever performing music, their musical voices never singing songs. They continually invert expectations and inform the narrator of spiritual transgression. Yearning for any ideal love, understanding of the beyond, unification with the unknown, points back to death and the tomb; music becomes a failure that perversely points heavenward. All of these themes come into play in Poe's poetry, which takes this trajectory further from the diabolical and demonic unknown to the heavenly, beautiful unknown. Real-world music is automatically problematized in Poe's poetry, and the following chapters will construct the connection between liminality and the otherworldly beautiful and demonic with stronger and deeper implications. As with Poe's tales, the best way to position his poems in terms of this emerging trajectory is by beginning with the instances closest related to a real-world musical understanding, instances of song and singing.

NOTES

1. Foucault, *Madness and Civilization*, 74.
2. Poe, "Silence," 197.
3. Poe, "Descent into the Maelström," 579–80.
4. Poe, "Black Cat," 859.
5. Auerbach, *Romance of Failure*, 44.
6. Poe, "Fall of the House," 417.
7. Rev. 19: 6 AV.
8. Kramer, "Ocean and Vision," 216–17.
9. Poe, "Black Cat," 859.
10. Poe, "Fall of the House," 416.
11. Poe, "Ligeia," 319.
12. Lawrence, "Edgar Allan Poe," 118.

13. See Davis and Davis, "Poe's Ethereal Ligeia," 170–86; Gargano, "Poe's 'Ligeia,'" 337–42.
14. Poe, "Ligeia," 319.
15. Poe, "Eleonora," 638.
16. See Ljungquist, "Poe's Nubian Geographer," 73–75. Ljungquist effectively makes the case for this connection in his article.
17. Butler, *Matter of the Page*, 75.
18. Foucault, *Madness and Civilization*, 12.
19. Quinn, *Edgar Allan Poe*, 123.
20. Poe, "Eleonora," 643.
21. Ibid., 641, 643.
22. Ibid., 643.
23. Poe, "Ligeia," 310, 311, 315, 317.
24. Ibid., 315.
25. Ibid., 317.
26. Ibid.
27. Auerbach, *Romance of Failure*, 44.
28. Rea, "Classicism and Romanticism," 25.
29. Bennett, "Madness of Art," 3. This is not strictly true, however, as Homer's sirens are unnamed. Most sources attribute the naming of the sirens to Eustathius and his writing on the Odyssey. As Robert Bell points out, one of these names, however, is indeed "Ligeia." See Bell, *Women of Classical Mythology*, 283.
30. Jones, "Poe's Siren," 34. This epigraph from that 1841 tale is attributed to Sir Thomas Browne: "What song the Syrens sang, or what name Achilles assumed when he hid himself among women, although puzzling questions, are not beyond all conjecture." See Poe, "Murders," 527.
31. Rea, "Classicism and Romanticism," 25–26.
32. Joan Dayan, "Poe, Locke, and Kant," 36.
33. Kramer, "Longindyingcall," 203.
34. Ibid., 204.
35. Joan Dayan, "Poe, Locke, and Kant," 36.
36. Poe, "Ligeia," 323.
37. Wilbur, "House of Poe," 270.
38. Davis and Davis, "Poe's Ethereal Ligeia," 173.
39. Foucault, *Madness and Civilization*, 12.
40. Poe, "Ligeia," 328–30.
41. Poe, "Morella [G]," 226.
42. Ibid., 233.
43. Ibid.
44. Ibid., 234–35.
45. Ibid., 235–36.

FOUR
The Wantonest Singing Birds

> I do not believe that any thought, properly so called, is out of the reach of language [. . .] There is, however, a class of fancies, of exquisite delicacy, which are *not* thoughts, and to which, *as yet*, I have found it absolutely impossible to adapt language. [. . .] These "fancies" have in them a pleasurable ecstasy as far beyond the most pleasurable of the world of wakefulness, or of dreams, as the Heaven of the Northman theology is beyond its Hell. [. . .] Now, so entire is my faith in the *power of words*, that, at times, I have believed it possible to embody even the evanescence of fancies such as I have attempted to describe.
> —Edgar Allan Poe, "Marginalia"

Poe struggled as a poet. His "poetic sentiment" led him to write "The Raven," an immediate and lasting phenomenon of popularity. That same "poetic sentiment" also pigeonholed him as an amateur lyricist at best, with Ralph Waldo Emerson famously deriding him as "the jingle man." Aldous Huxley, one of Poe's harshest critics, famously decries the sonority of Poe's works, arguing of "Ulalume" that "the walloping dactylic metre is all too musical. Poetry ought to be musical, but musical with tact, subtly and variously. Metres whose rhythms, as in this case, are strong, insistent, and practically invariable offer the poet a kind of short cut to musicality. They provide [Poe . . .] with a ready-made, reach-me-down music."[1] This is what Pamela Faber attributes to Poe's success in France, the deletion of Poe's "music": "the music of Poe's prose is not translated," and the "French translation spares us many of Poe's alliterations (e.g., 'thrilling and enthralling' becomes *'pénétrante et subjugante'*)."[2] As Riddel aptly summarizes, "In English Poe is Emerson's jingle man; transcribed into French, he inaugurates the revolution of the word."[3] Poe's own reckoning with popularity and personal aesthetic comes across most drastically in his verse. Poe relies upon his readers' sympathies, and those who love Poe often attempt to find an explanation for some of his heavy-handed prosody. Surely, they believe, some of his most juvenile poetry was written with some express intent—someone so enamored with poetry as a high art simply could not be that bad at writing verse—and one of the first places anyone looks for an explanation of bad poetry is in songwriting.

POEMS AS SONGS IN LANGUAGE, AIM, AND PURPOSE

A few of Poe's poems were published at one point (often retitled later) with titles that tied them to musical pieces, for example, "Song," "A Pæan," "Eulalie—A Song," "The Bells—A Song," and "Serenade." As I alluded to in chapter 2 of this book, these titles have led some critics to believe that Poe intended the poems to function as actual lyrics to musical scores. Poems without titles referring to song, written with demonstrable word music and language of music, could then reveal Poe's intention that they function as lyrics to a score he must have had in mind. Burton Pollin most clearly articulates this argument, contending that Poe's poems were certainly originally intended as songs to be sung and that Poe actually went to great lengths to publish them with sheet music. After all, Poe's "To Ianthe in Heaven," also titled "To One in Paradise," was included in George Pope Morris's anthology *National Melodies in America* (reviewed by Poe in 1839). Moreover, Morris prefaced the volume by noting his understanding that some of the included "lyrics" were "adapted to music." Because of this preface, Pollin maintains that Poe's inclusion in the volume was "obviously not [as] a 'potential' song, but a published piece."[4] Pollin remains undeterred by his self-described "problem" with his own claim, that "problem" being his difficulty in finding the absent musical score itself:

> for in the book there is no hint of the composer or even of the exact date [. . .]. I searched through all the possible titles in every prominent music collection and catalogue, sought the help of all the resources in the music section of the Library of Congress, and looked through all the copyright registration volumes (kept now in Washington) for New York and Philadelphia for the last half of the 1830s. I have examined lists of all the music of major song writers of the period and of major music publishers. All in vain![5]

Throughout the article, Pollin remains convinced that Poe wrote many of his poems, especially this one, as songs with specific music in mind; yet, Pollin's own enormous efforts, seeking "the help of all the resources in the music section of the Library of Congress," were fruitless in finding any musical score attached to the songs.

Apart from Pollin's reasoning, as discussed in this book in the second chapter, that "there was a powerful economic motive" for Poe's publication of his poems as songs, Pollin turns to a textual argument, defining twenty-two of Poe's poems as "lyrics" to songs because he claims that they "show strong tinges of either a song inspiration or a song projection. All bear the word "song" or its equivalent in the title or are unmistakably a song in their language, aim, and purpose."[6] Assuming that the title "song" or the word's incorporation in a poem might mean that the poem is meant to be a song published with sheet music, Pollin does not elaborate upon his reasoning for the poems being "unmistakably" songs in their "language, aim, and purpose," apart from implying that certain prosodic elements necessitate reading them as such. He claims that the understanding of certain of Poe's poems as songs:

> helps to explain his extraordinary stress—almost an obsession—on repetition in prosody: the refrains [. . .] the chiming and echoing of rhymes [. . .] the imagined or assumed music will both blunt the weakness and carry along the effect of the rhyme to the uncritical ear of the listener. This view explains the simplicity of the conveyed thought, the slow accretions of development, as in the traditional ballads, and gaps in the sequence of logic. It also explains the use of invented or warped names, almost meaningless otherwise.[7]

Pollin implicitly defines song by "repetition," "refrains," and "rhymes." He then reintegrates this "imagined or assumed" music into his argument, maintaining that it will "blunt the weakness" of Poe's poetry, bringing together the contentious elements of Poe's versification into one category that "imagined or assumed music" would rectify. He assumes that "Poe's prosodic writings [. . .] all [manifest] a poet who hoped or even longed for collaboration with a composer or some arrangement with a publisher of music," but apart from Pollin's own interpretation of Poe's "hope" for collaboration, he gives no real evidence for this.[8] Besides titles and versification, none of Poe's poems offer a thematic parallel to "The Spectacles." His poems never explicitly reference real-world music; none of them take on the parlor music setting, or the human performance, as a subject, which other authors of the period were interested in conveying. Erland Anderson writes, for instance, about Romantic poetry concerned with the writer's "own experience of music in the concert halls and private salons of the period [. . .] [such as] the poem, 'To the Rev. W.J. Hort while teaching a Young Lady some Song-tunes on his Flute.'"[9]

Rather, like Poe's "ballads," Poe's "songs" cohere in subject rather than anything else.[10] The two poems that maintain the title without change, "Song" and "Eulalie—A Song," are love stories, but with happy endings that are otherwise rare in Poe. In "Song," the narrator describes seeing a woman on her "bridal day," and although there is some implied jealousy on the speaker's part, ultimately "happiness" around the woman "lay, / The world of all love before" her.[11] In "Eulalie—A Song," Eulalie marries the speaker, and "Doubt—now Pain / Come never again."[12] Neither contains musical terminology. "The Bells—A Song" consists of only eighteen lines. Split into two stanzas, the first describes the "merry wedding bells," and the second describes the "heavy iron bells," which contain the germ for the full version of the poem into which Poe expands these lines soon after.[13] Within a year, Poe develops these into their full 112 lines that become a completely new poem from this earlier edition. In doing so, the poem moves far beyond real-world associations of love and happiness and sanity—and then loses the title that references "song." These complexities will be discussed in the section of this book on "The Bells" in chapter 6.

"Serenade," however, takes this same theme, a simple narrative of earthly love, and introduces musical terminology in the body of the poem in ways that impact its shift in subject and meaning. The perspective is explicitly that of a man in love, and like in Poe's other "songs," the woman he loves still lives. Poe gives this poem the title of a piece of played or sung music often "given at night in the open air, [. . .] such as a performance given by a lover under the window of his lady."[14] Presumably the title implies that the poem itself is the serenade, as the words are those of a lover addressing his love "Adeline" as she sleeps.[15] The poem begins:

> So sweet the hour—so calm the time,
> I feel it more than half a crime
> When Nature sleeps and stars are Mute,
> To mar the silence ev'n with lute.[16]

Tying the body of the poem to its title, the speaker sets the scene with the image of the lute, one of the few instruments that recur in Poe's poetry. Apart from bells, it is only lutes, lyres, and harps that arise in his poems. The three function relatively interchangeably in Poe, and the combination of the stringed instruments Poe invokes draws upon a number of poetic traditions, traditions that John Hollander describes when he writes,

> The "lute-harp-lyre" constellation, uniting the contemporary string instrument with those of David and Orpheus, for example, represents no capricious substitution of one term for another. Rather, it depends upon a constant habit of figurative association of the instruments and what they stand for.[17]

Hollander describes a more modern substitution of the lute (played more recently) for the lyre (associated with the ancient) that unite into a similar symbolic image. Even though it is more modern than the lyre, however, the lute was nearly obsolete by Poe's time, its actual employment relegated primarily to the sixteenth and early seventeenth centuries, so Poe uses neither the lute nor the lyre to represent musical instruments that he and his contemporaries would have commonly heard.[18] Rather than "uniting the contemporary string instrument with those of David and Orpheus," Poe unites the absence of any played "contemporary string instrument" with the mythological remembrance of "David and Orpheus." Hollander goes on to explain, "A metonymic use of the lute (for the lyre) to represent poetry as well as music is a familiar one; occasionally a harp will be used in a similar context to refer to a religious muse."[19] Poe draws upon the dual notion of the lute as a symbol for poetry and the lute as symbol for music in these lines, drawing attention to the double nature of his "Serenade" as imagined music and as poem. He complicates this symbol, however, by giving the surrounding "silence" primacy—even his symbolic "lute" would "mar" it.

This silence sets the scene for the poem's ending with the following lines:

> But list, O list!—so soft and low
> Thy lover's voice tonight shall flow
> That, scarce awake, thy soul shall deem
> My words the music of a dream.
> Thus, while no single sound too rude,
> Upon thy slumber shall intrude,
> Our thoughts, our souls—O God above!
> In every deed shall mingle, love.[20]

Initially, this particular instance of "music" appears to be connected with utterance. "Music," in this case, at first seems to be the speaker's "words," drawing upon the poem itself being a "Serenade." Upon first glance, it might appear that the speaker's "words" are "the music of" Adeline's "dream" as she sleeps. Yet the "music" of the speaker's "words" is not heard or listened to in the real-world musical sense, as experienced as "sound via the sense of hearing," but is responded to by a communication with Adeline's "soul."[21] Adeline might receive the sounds as she sleeps, but it is her "soul" that "shall deem" his "words the music of a dream." More than this, the speaker's "voice" is "soft and low," and "no single sound too rude" should "intrude" upon Adeline's "slumber," emphasizing the lowness, the softness, of the voice, adding to the obfuscation of the "Serenade" being heard as music. The musical quality of the speaker's voice relies upon the interpretation of her soul, rather than any inherent quality.

Ventum Textilem: The Veil of the Soul

This ability of Adeline's soul to render the poet's "words" the "music of a dream" reflects a comment Poe made on Art in his "Marginalia": "Were I called on to define, *very* briefly, the term 'Art,' I should call it 'the reproduction of what the Senses perceive in Nature through the veil of the soul.' [. . .] The naked Senses sometimes see too little—but then *always* they see too much."[22] A few fundamental elements to this claim correspond with the trajectory of this chapter. First, Poe describes the capitalized "A" Art, the idea of Art in an ideal, rather than in a practical sense. Second, rather than being purely mimetic, Art necessitates a filtering through what Poe calls the "veil of the soul." Poe does not elaborate upon what the "veil of the soul" may be, but his use of the phrase reintroduces themes already emergent in this book. Returning to the connection introduced in chapter 2 between Psyche and the ventum textilem, as it was summarized in "The Spectacles," the narrator remarks, "The head, of which only the back was visible, rivalled in outline that of the Greek Psyche, and was rather displayed than concealed by an elegant cap of *gaze äerienne*, which put me in mind of the *ventum textilem* of Apuleius."[23] In comparing the elder Lalande's outline to Psyche, the narrator describes her cap, illustrated as the ventum textilem, as displaying, rather than concealing, her Psyche-like profile. This leads to another interpretation of the soul as it is evinced in "Serenade." If the woven air of Apuleius is intimately related to Psyche (the Soul), then the soul in other contexts (i.e., the "veil of the soul") can take on a dual incarnation as breath. Nicky Losseff has argued of other pieces of literature: "The physical means of expelling the voice from the 'soul' is the breath, and the relationship between soul, breath and voice has formed the focus of an enormously wide range of spiritual discussion," including the consideration of the "voice to be articulated and controlled by our inmost soul, the central Spirit located in the heart."[24] Both claims are reminiscent of Chua's notion that for Romantics "music became equated with Spirit."[25] Poe goes further than this though, as the spirit, the soul, the breath and music merge into a single undefined symbol, like that of the "lute-harp-lyre constellation," that must continually escape articulation.

When Adeline's soul takes the speaker's words and interprets them as seeming like "the music of a dream," there is an implied communication between souls, so that which is attempted through song is interpreted through the soul. Although in Losseff's argument this relates directly to the "physical means of expelling the voice," in Poe this expulsion works along a hierarchy: the more symbolic the expulsion, the more distinctly musical. As in "Ligeia," in which utterance is depicted in diabolical terms whereas unarticulated voice is described with musical terminology, there exists in Poe's works a continual separation between heard sounds in a real-world sense, often connected with words, shrieks, or hisses, and that which is musically voiced, which is experienced through the "soul," or through interpretation. This rift between audible sounds and unarticulated music will continually arise throughout the rest of this book in connection with the spirit, the soul, the breath, and the voice.

MERE WORDS: BIRDSONG

None of Poe's other poems invoke the word "song" or its equivalent in the title, but a few of them implicate it in their subject. The most explicit example comes in Poe's "Eldorado," in which a knight is described as "singing a song."[26] This is the only poem in Poe's body of work in which a human sings a song, and it will be taken up later in this book; the only other earthly creatures, the only other nonsupernatural creatures, who sing or who are associated with song in Poe's poetry are birds. The poem "To—" begins:

> The bowers whereat, in dreams, I see
> The wantonest singing birds,
> Are lips—and all thy melody
> Of lip-begotten words—[27]

This poem is set in that liminal space of "dreams," returning to the setting that relates to a tension point between the earthly and the otherworldly. Rather than hearing the "melody" in the scene, the speaker sees a possible visible source of melody in his subject's lips as "bowers" and immediately recognizes that the melody he has interpreted is only of "lip-begotten words." Whereas so often in Poe's tales the visibility of music's source is not made explicit, the sight of the lips is clear in these lines, and they are instantly related to a sense of deflation; the speaker realizes that "all" the "melody" is only of "lip-begotten words." As Mabbott argues, the poem "seems to [. . .] reproach the person addressed," and the "implication is of falsity, *mere* words."[28] The next stanza of the poem continues:

> Thine eyes, in Heaven of heart enshrined
> Then desolately fall,
> O God! on my funereal mind
> Like starlight on a pall—[29]

As in Poe's ballads in which some sign of a false ideal or some spiritual transgression leads the protagonist in an infinite loop leading back to the tomb, the "melody," here associated with words, represents a kind of failure that leads back to the "funereal," to death. As soon as the source of the melody is realized, is made explicit, the melody transmutes into a sight of words.

This reference to "singing birds" is only one of multiple references to birds in Poe's works. Richard Wilbur points out that "dark and voracious birds are continually associated with time in Poe [. . .]. An attentive reader can, in short, compile a small dictionary of symbolic constants which will give some access to Poe's 'under current.'"[30] Wilbur addresses only "dark and voracious birds" in this context, but the birds mentioned in this chapter all have some relationship with song, and this idea that one can "compile a small dictionary of symbolic constants" also points toward the multiple possibilities of symbolism inherent in each subject. As Edmund Stedman and George Woodberry show,

> Poe liberally drew upon the rather small stock of pet words, epithets, names, and phrases, which he invented, or kept at hand, for repeated use throughout the imaginative portion of his writings. The "albatross" and "condor" are his birds, no less than the raven [. . .]. It has been pointed out that his familiars are chiefly angels and demons, with an attendance of dreams, echoes, ghouls, gnomes, and mimes, for characteristic service.[31]

For the most part, each of these "symbolic constants" is in some sense ethereal or mythological. That is, every single one of these named constants, angels, demons, ghouls, gnomes, mimes, and dreams is metaphysical or supernatural, with the exception of the birds. The birds, on the other hand, exist in the real world. Poe's birds all have symbolic significance, however: they are all associated with time, as Wilbur argues, and as this book argues, they are associated with time in the form of death.

"Fanny": Wild Death Song, Sweet and Clear

Often, the theme of death is not necessarily explicit, but emerges through a continually musical association with the idea of paradoxical birth in death, or its reverse: death in life. These themes recur in the poem "Fanny":

> The dying swan by northern lakes
> Sings its wild death song, sweet and clear,
> And as the solemn music breaks
> O'er hill and glen dissolves in air;
> Thus musical thy soft voice came,
> Thus trembled on thy tongue my name.[32]

Even more than "To —," this stanza problematizes the three rules for real-world music. As opposed to the "wantonest singing birds," which are immediately associated with "lip-begotten words," in "To —," the swan song is a metaphor for Fanny's "musical" and "soft voice" and the "name" that "trembled" on her "tongue," complicating on different levels the concept of music experienced as a "sound via the sense of hearing."[33] In the metaphorical image itself, the mythical swan song that does not exist in the real world paradoxically emerges in the swan's death, simultaneously being born as its source dies. This unique and bittersweet "song," or "solemn music," draws upon a larger context that has various implications for music's "solemnity." John Hollander explains the association between music and solemnity:

> Medieval writers would often contrast "lewd fiddling minstrels" with the music of the spheres, the distinction there drawn was primarily

between the common-active as opposed to the learned-contemplative models of music. The distinction under discussion here eventually becomes trivialized into one between the serious and the frivolous, perhaps paralleling the change in meaning of "solemn." An example [. . .] might be seen in the words of "Mr. H. Wanley," [. . .]: "A young man may make a better *Minuet* or *Jigg*; but the elder a more sound Service or *Anthem*. [. . .] [T]hat of the latter excites the Devotion, moves the Affections, and raises the Passions of those truly religious Souls, who take pleasure in singing Praises to the Honour and the Glory of His Name, who lives for ever and ever." Here the doctrine of the affections is reserved for the solemn music.[34]

The concept of "solemn music" and the "anthem" will return in the following chapters in ways that relate to this distinction between the "common" and the "contemplative models of music." Just as birds are often associated with death in Poe's works, as in this poem, music's association with "solemnity" draws upon notions of prayer and the divine. In this instance, the "solemn music" serves as the comparison to Fanny's voice, who is neither described as speaking nor singing, but who acts as the medium for the author's name that "trembled." In fact, the poem "Fanny" is full of paradoxical images that uphold this "musical," yet unheard, sound. The image is indicative in the first sense of a Romantic instance of song in poetry as the reverse of a song text in a real-world musical sense. Lawrence Kramer argues that

> the poet hears a song that assumes epiphanic power precisely because it is unintelligible, and often at the very point where it passes the threshold of intelligibility. The singer in these poems is usually either a bird [. . .], or a girl [. . .]. The poet's imagination is initially aroused by the impulse to insert his own words in the linguistic gap opened by the song. Once in place, these words gradually dissolve like the song's own, leaving the poet mute and transfixed, usually in a posture of intenser listening.[35]

Poe's poem "Fanny" takes this a step further: not only is the song the poet hears "unintelligible"; it is not even necessarily heard. Fanny's "musical voice" does not even make a clear utterance, the poet filling this "linguistic gap" with the words of his poem. The metaphor Poe uses of the swan song further intensifies the image of the song and the musical voice as unheard yet nearly present, leaving the poet in a continual "posture of intenser listening" to what he cannot hear. The swan's "death song" is not necessarily a song in the sense of a dirge or requiem, or any scored funereal song, but rather is a song that acts as an unarticulated voice that conveys a symbolic paradoxical birth and death of love. The descriptors of "wild," "sweet," and "clear" conceal as much as they reveal, compounded by the dissolution of the "solemn music" and the comparison to the equivalently ambiguous name trembling on Fanny's tongue.

"Romance": Unless It Trembled with the Strings

The implication in this instance is that Fanny's voice remains musical so long as it does not utter anything definite. Once it becomes utterance and definitely heard, the musicality dies, as the metaphorical swan song reveals. These themes recur and are elucidated in "Romance":

> Romance, who loves to nod and sing
> With drowsy head and folded wing,
> Among the green leaves as they shake
> Far down within some shadowy lake,
> To me a painted paroquet
> Hath been—a most familiar bird—
> Taught me my alphabet to say—
> To lisp my very earliest word [36]

The poem then ends on an equally musically described image:

> And when an hour with calmer wings
> Its down upon my spirit flings —
> That little time with lyre and rhyme
> To while away—forbidden things!
> My heart would feel to be a crime
> Unless it trembled with the strings. [37]

A common interpretation of the poem is of the speaker's frustration, as Daniel Hoffman argues, "lamenting the loss of that power" he had as a child "and invoking the recurrence of imaginative vision."[38] As Richard Wilbur points out about Poe's works generally, there is

> warfare within the poet's very nature. [...] Prior to his earthly incarnation, and during his dreamy childhood, Poe's poet enjoyed a serene unity of being; his consciousness was purely imaginative [...]. But with his entrance into adult life, the poet became involved with a fallen world in which the physical, the factual, the rational, the prosaic are not escapable. Thus, compromised, he lost his perfect spirituality, and is now cursed with a divided nature.[39]

If the poem "Romance" is read in the context of this interpretation, the division discussed earlier in this book between "a lower reality embodied in language and a higher one embodied in music," between utterance and the musical voice, emerges in the poem.[40] This disunion, in turn, which is signified in "the expulsion of music from language," demonstrates a modern separation from "the enchanted world of the ancients."[41] It is crucial then that Wilbur's division between the "purely imaginative" state of childhood and the "physical, the factual, the rational" state of adulthood is described in a metaphor of music. As Daniel Hoffman argues, the poem begins when "Poe has summoned an image at once autonomous and archetypal, a *reflection* of a *shadowy, painted* bird—thus already at two or three removes from reality. That bird is one which, when tamed, can speak. And from it he learned 'my alphabet to say.'"[42] The poem begins with a bird "at once autonomous and archetypal," an unreal bird called "Romance" that oddly "loves to nod and sing," which might be viewed as physical evidence of the point between waking and sleeping as representative of the liminal (reminiscent of "The Raven," the narrator of which "nodded, nearly napping").[43] Romance does not speak, does not even sing a specific tune, but nods and sings, such that its singing becomes symbolic of a kind of communication that is unheard. The poet does not see the bird itself, but sees its reflection, which appears to him to sing in its liminal space.

As in "Fanny," in which the idea that "the poet hears a song that assumes epiphanic power precisely because it is unintelligible" complicates its own obscurity in that the poet does not hear the song at all, the "autonomous and archetypal" image of the bird of "Romance" is "already two or three removes from reality."[44] The bird mutates to an imitation that the poet can see however, a "painted paroquet," a "familiar bird" that teaches the poet not even to speak, but to "lisp" his "earliest word." As for what bird the "paroquet" represents, Audrey Lavin effectively argues:

> Though the Carolina paroquet has been extinct since 1913, dense flocks of these small, raucous, fast-flying birds inhabited the [. . .] United States in the nineteenth century, from Florida through Virginia, giving Poe ample opportunity to sight them. Their range and frequency indicate that Poe could well mean what he clearly says, the "painted paroquet hath been—a most familiar bird—". With its large, white beak, the Carolina paroquet was a highly "painted" bird whose orange and blue colors bled off into shades of green and yellow.[45]

The Carolina paroquet might have been beautiful, seemingly "painted" in orange and blue, green and yellow, but tied into it is the poet's sinking realization that even this bird that borders on a natural work of art is all too familiar and, more disappointingly, a mere replica of an ideal that cannot be accessed. Thus, the poet becomes associated with falsity, with imitation of an ideal, which transmutes the otherworldly singing bird into the worldly lisping utterance of the poet. Moreover, even this division begins to become less clear by the end of the poem if we consider Kramer's notion that the poet is "aroused by the impulse to insert words in the linguistic gap opened by the song," as once "in place, these words gradually dissolve like the song's own, leaving the poet mute and transfixed, [. . .] in a posture of intenser listening."[46] This dissolution comes into play through Daniel Hoffman's interpretation that the bird Romance of the first stanza transforms to the lyre of the last.

Hoffman claims that there is a "mixed metaphor" of the bird and the lyre in the poem.[47] More specifically, this poem works with a mixed metaphor to confuse the image of the singing bird "Romance" and the poet who "trembled with the strings." The mixed metaphor of the bird and the lyre obscures the instrument as played and the instrument as "singing" independently of player (or poet). In this instance, "lyre and rhyme" are paired together, and the heart of the poet is compelled to "[tremble] with the strings." Rather than posing the speaker as sitting and playing the lyre, singing a rhyme, the speaker's heart responds to the strings directly, conflating them into one musical signifier that escapes a signified musical sound. Reminiscent of the epigraph to "The Fall of the House of Usher," which compares a heart to a suspended lute, the mixed metaphor of the bird, lyre, and poet in "Romance" anticipates the "heartstrings" as musical instrument, which Poe adopts elsewhere in his poetry.

This connection draws from a long-standing poetic notion of the heartstrings as musical: as John Hollander explains,

> A numerological symbol, a particular interpretation of harmonic unity, a sustained conceit here and there, illuminated points of metaphysical and cosmological doctrine. [. . .] Traditional word-lays helped to sustain and proliferate such images: a pun on *chorda* ("string") and *cor, cordis* ("heart"), [. . .] became so deeply imbedded in habitual thinking that the very origins of the word "concord" [. . .] often even today are mistaken for being musical.[48]

This speaks to a broad historical background constructed of "various notions of the soul as an instrument, or the body as the instrument upon which the soul plays, or the soul as the melody or chordal effusion of the body's strings."[49] Moreover, it reintroduces this mixed metaphor of the song, the lyre, the soul, and the breath in a symbolic image that moves away from heard sound. If the "physical means of expelling the voice from the 'soul' is the breath," then one considers the "voice to be articulated and controlled by our inmost soul, the central Spirit located in the heart."[50] As mentioned earlier, however, this metaphor does not come into play in Poe's poetry in terms of the performed song. As in this example, it simply becomes a part of a central mutable, symbolic, and silent image of the bird Romance, who sings unheard song, metamorphosing to the poet's lyre as heart, which trembles as by an unseen wind, at the end of the poem. This association will recur throughout the rest of this book.

In the only poem in which the harp or the lyre is associated with sound in Poe's poetry, we return to that idea of paradox as in "Fanny." In "[Stanzas]" the speaker describes a thought that comes bidden "With a strange sound, as of a harp-string broken / T'awake us—'Tis a symbol and a token / Of what in other worlds shall be."[51] The "strange sound" of a "harp-string broken" is doubly strange in that it conveys a sound, again used as a comparison to an idea, being made and broken simultaneously, a paradoxical sound whose beginning signifies its end, like the swan song of "Fanny." A single "strange sound," that which is couched in musical language without ever becoming music, particularly the single note, returns in Poe's poems (most explicitly in "The Bells"). It voices without articulating "what in other worlds shall be." Returning to "Romance," the bird seems to sing only when it exists in an unreal world, and when the poet attempts to imitate it on earth, he can only "lisp" at first and ultimately "tremble with the strings," held in an eternal posture of making and nonmaking, of listening and nonlistening. The paradoxical making and breaking of a single note becomes that which can imply "what in other worlds shall be," without overly defining it. Returning momentarily to the passage discussed in chapter 2 of this book in which Poe argues that "the *indefinite* is an element in the true ποιησις," Poe appears in his poetry to use music to represent the poet's grandest attempts: "'making' that which *is not yet*."[52] The otherworldly, unknown, beyond, or even ideal can be brought into being only if kept away from utterance and definition, and music represents the paradoxical attempt at its communication through words.

"Nameless Here For Evermore": To Sing Well Is to Avoid Naming

These themes are illustrated even more strongly, ever more strangely, in "The Raven." Turning then from ideal and otherworldly bird figures not obviously allied to death to the common raven and its fatal symbolism, Poe associates the idea of singing with a kind of inversion and explication of the themes so far described.[53] Poe writes:

> "Doubtless," said I, "what it utters is its only stock and store
> Caught from some unhappy master whom unmerciful Disaster
> Followed fast and followed faster till his songs one burden bore—
> Till the dirges of his Hope that melancholy burden bore
> Of 'Never—nevermore.'"[54]

"The Raven," as well as "Fanny" and "Romance," has as its theme the unutterable visions, questions, and dreams, ethereal and immaterial concepts identified with singing, which itself remains not only undefined, but not described as well. Just as in "Romance," in which the shadowy and ideal eponymous creature becomes a painted paroquet, its nodding and singing reifying as the poet's lisping utterance, the raven of this poem sits "croaking 'Nevermore.'"[55] The speaker at first assumes the raven had an "unhappy master" and has repeated that "one burden" caught from the master's "songs." Thus, the reader is given "nevermore" as the implicit "burden" of these "songs," which become synonymous with "dirges of his [master's] Hope." In doing so, the raven paradoxically presents "songs" and "dirges" "nevermore" (in meaning, timing, and substance).

While critics have written on the subject of repetition and deconstruction in Poe's poetry, specifically in "The Raven," Blasing is one of the rare critics who attempts to tie this into music in Poe's "The Raven":

> His emblems are birds that rob the poet's language of transcendent significance or of the possibility of such significance, just as they deprive it of a significant history. [. . .] Yet Poe's raven is no golden bird of artifice, either; his croaking song parodies as much a transcendent artifice as the transcendent meanings we are impelled to attach to certain combinations of certain phonemes.[56]

The raven's croaks themselves cannot really be described as songs at all, their transcendence rejected at every level. The raven is described as "croaking 'Nevermore'" only once, in a stanza removed from that which describes his "songs," and in neither case is it entirely clear whether the raven croaks the word "Nevermore," but it is certain that the raven never sings.[57] The "songs" neither the reader nor the speaker of the poem ever hear, but the speaker of the poem interprets the heard or unheard "Nevermore" as informed by preexisting song; in the song's stead is a "burden" whose relationship to the songs is unclear, and this burden ("Nevermore") is croaked. Like the bird Romance who appears to the speaker of that poem to sing, whose real-world incarnation can teach the poet only an alphabet and to lisp his first words, the speaker of this poem imagines an assumed original song that has condensed into a word that can only be croaked. Again, the subject is immaterial, and the phrase "dirges of his Hope" says less than it evades, namely, questions of mortality paralleled in questions of what the listener actually hears.

Freedman argues that "as a Coleridgean fusion of contraries, as the speaker of a single repeated sound, the raven seems to figure the ultimate ideal of poetic unity: the dissolution of its component oppositions, indeed of all content, into a single ethereal utterance."[58] While the argument is that this "fusion of contraries" results in the "dissolution [. . .] of all content," the remaining "single ethereal utterance" still voices or informs as a token of the otherworldly. That is not to say that there is ever a direct connection between the "songs" and the utterance of the raven itself. The raven's utterance, rather than "ethereal," continually draws attention to its own falsity and repetition, which opposes the fleeting idea of the "song" that neither the reader nor the speaker ever hears.

David Hirsch argues that, instead "of calling on the singer out of Greek mythology [the nightingale], melancholy or happy, Poe turns, rather, to the biblical scavenger bird symbolising the 'carnal heart.' Poe's disjunctive imagination exchanged the Romantic metaphors of flight and Dionysian song for metaphors of stasis and monotony."[59] Hirsch goes on to posit that, in

> place of a lushly singing ethereal bird there is a croaking, fluttering, black raven that is all too physically present. Instead of a speaker who

wants to dissolve himself so that he can fuse with the song of the bird, we have a speaker who is possessed by the bird which will not release him.[60]

Hirsch positions Poe as the inverse of the Romantic poet, as Kramer describes, whose words are inserted into "the linguistic gap opened by the song" and "gradually dissolve like the song's own, leaving the poet mute and transfixed."[61] For Hirsch, the transformed Romantic image of the poet results in a mythological decline in "the orphic power of song" in Poe's works.[62] Instead of "winning his way to the underworld on the wings of song, [the subject of "The Raven"] finds that an apparent messenger from the underworld breaks in on his consciousness."[63] For Hirsch, the paradoxical "song" of the poem is empty, devoid of meaning, representing only a continual decline in the power of "song" from mythology. Hirsch maintains that "Orpheus, charming his way into the underworld, almost overcomes death. Keats's nightingale chants a powerful music that almost charms his speaker into immortality. But Poe exchanges nightingale for raven, real or illusory song for real or illusory croak."[64] Although Hirsch's interpretation of Poe's raven as a kind of inversion works on multiple levels, his series of substitutions implicitly negates the possibility that Poe might be engaging more directly with Orphic myth than Hirsch admits.

I believe that Poe does summon Orpheus in his poem, but I also think that for Poe, the power of the Orphic myth is not just that Orpheus "almost overcomes death," but precisely that he cannot. In this interpretation, there is no affection left for his "almost" doing so. As Peter Dayan explains in terms of Barthes's relationship to the myth,

> Orpheus represents literature because he does not speak, he sings; and he sings of what he cannot see, of a ghost, of one who returns, of a "revenant". Barthes never names Eurydice. He never even genders as feminine the shade that follows Orpheus up from the underworld; that shade is simply defined as what Orpheus loves or desires. And that lack, or rather erasure, of a name and gender seems to me to embody the Barthesian twist to the Orpheus myth. For Barthes, what follows Orpheus is not to be called Eurydice. It is what he loves, and what he sings; and what we love and sing must remain, in Poe's words, "Nameless *here* for evermore." The moment at which Orpheus turns and sees her is the moment (unspoken by Barthes) in which the shade would turn into a woman, and acquire a name; at that same moment, literature would die. To sing well is to avoid that naming.[65]

What Dayan interprets as the "Barthesian twist to the Orpheus myth" has resounding implications in Poe. As mentioned in the first part of this book, Poe himself professes to "*know* that indefinitiveness is an element of the true music—I mean of the true musical expression."[66] The bird Romance, once seen, becomes a "painted paroquet" rendered in all too specific words. In "Fanny," the swan song reveals an unheard musical voice that cannot utter a name. In "The Raven," the croaked "Nevermore" is all that remains of dirges, songs unknown and unsourced, imagined by the speaker; moreover, as Dayan points out, the speaker himself mourns the loss of "the rare and radiant maiden whom the angels name Lenore" who is "Nameless *here* for evermore."[67] In these poems, as in Dayan's interpretation of the Barthesian Orpheus, that "moment" when what the poet or speaker or subject "loves, and what he sings" is seen, the moment it would "acquire a name," is the same moment the musical terminology, the singing or the song, dies. As Dayan goes on to argue,

> Underlying this Barthesian myth is a perfectly clear (and quite traditional) opposition between two types of language. On the one side, the side of both life and death, we have the ordinary use of language, which names, which gives a signified sense, a named sense, a sense of the real, a sense of that which can be seen and possessed. On the other side, on the side of the "revenant" not clearly alive or dead, doubtless moving from death towards life but never simply arriving there, we have literature. Literature, the "parole juste", is identified with music, "le chant"; it allows us to lead that which we love out of obscurity; but only for so long as we continue not to name it, not to look at it.[68]

Setting aside for the moment Dayan's defining "literature" as the opposite of the "ordinary use of language," the key component of this argument lies in the separation between the "ordinary use of language" and that which is "identified with music." The liminal settings, the reiteration of madness, the "angels and demons, with an attendance of dreams, echoes, ghouls" all reflect in subject this idea of the "'revenant' not clearly alive or dead," and in this stage we find suddenly musical terms.[69] As Poe argues, "Give to it any undue decision—imbue it with any very determinate tone—and you deprive it, at once, of its ethereal, its ideal, its intrinsic and essential character. [. . .] It now becomes a tangible and easily appreciable idea—a thing of the earth, earthy."[70] *The threads tying together in Poe music, indefinitiveness, the ethereal, the ventum textilem, the breath, the soul, the murmur, and the unheard continually and unequivocally oppose language, definitiveness, the earthly, the shriek, the diabolical, the loss of the soul, and the explicitly heard, or that which can be named.* These themes and the reiteration of their tension will come continually into play in the remaining poems discussed in this book in ways that will be positioned in terms of the ideal or the divine demonic and heavenly, the falsely ideal or the imagined divine, and the earthly.

For the most part, the creatures most clearly associated with song in ways that move toward real-world music are birds, and Poe's use of bird song reiterates and expands upon themes that have been building throughout this book. Leading these themes is the growing division between music and language, which also mirrors a few other crucial ruptures in Poe's works. That "mythical union between a lower reality embodied in language and a higher one embodied in music" remains mythical in Poe's poetry and highlights the split between the lower reality of language and the higher one of music.[71] In a continual hearkening back to an idealized past that unified the two, Poe's poetic imagery reveals the failed earthly rendering (lisping, uttering, croaking) of an ideal unheard singing or symbolic mutation of lute, lyre, or swan song. Through this divide, Poe plays upon the notion that in "the enchanted world of the ancients, music was an airy substance, it did not occupy space, it was its very essence"; Poe's works associate spirit, soul, and breath with symbolic musical imagery.[72] Opposing these are croaking, groaning, and discordance, which represent a disruption of that ideal. These themes will be reiterated and furthered in the next chapter, which moves from liminal and dream settings to the explicitly otherworldly.

NOTES

1. Huxley, "Vulgarity in Literature," 162.
2. Faber, "Charles Baudelaire," 256.
3. Riddel, "'Crypt' of Edgar Poe," 118.
4. Pollin, "Poe as a Writer," 59.
5. Ibid.
6. Ibid., 61–62.
7. Ibid., 62.
8. Ibid., 63.
9. Erland Anderson, *Harmonious Madness*, 4–5.
10. Poe's "A Pæan" is a singular and more complex example of a poem with a musically themed title and will be discussed in the context of "The Bells" in the chapter 6 of this book.
11. Poe, "Song," 1, 3–4.
12. Poe, "Eulalie—A Song," 15–16.
13. Poe, "Bells—A Song," 2, 9.
14. "Serenade, n." *Oxford English Dictionary*.
15. Poe, "Serenade," 17.
16. Ibid., 1–4.
17. Hollander, *Untuning of the Sky*, 45.
18. Partridge, "Lute," in *Oxford Companion to Music*.
19. Hollander, *Untuning of the Sky*, 46.
20. Poe, "Serenade," 18–25.
21. Leppert, *Sight as Sound*, 64.
22. Poe, "Marginalia," 1458.
23. Poe, "Spectacles," 324.
24. Losseff, "Voice, the Breath," 7–8.
25. Chua, *Absolute Music*, 4.
26. Poe, "Eldorado," 5.
27. Poe, "To —," 1–4.
28. Mabbott, *Edgar Allan Poe: Complete Poems*, 133.
29. Poe, "To —," 5–8.
30. Wilbur, "Poe Mystery Case."
31. Stedman and Woodberry, eds., *Poems of Edgar Allan Poe*, xxi.
32. Poe, "Fanny," 1–6.

33. Leppert, *Sight of Sound*, 64.
34. Hollander, *Untuning of the Sky*, 256.
35. Kramer, *Music and Poetry*, 139.
36. Poe, "Romance," 1–8.
37. Ibid., 16–22.
38. Daniel Hoffman, *Poe*, 50.
39. Wilbur, "House of Poe," 258.
40. Kramer, *Music and Poetry*, 2.
41. Ibid., 23, 52.
42. Daniel Hoffman, *Poe*, 50.
43. Poe, "Raven," 3.
44. Kramer, *Music and Poetry*, 139; Daniel Hoffman, *Poe*, 50.
45. Lavin, "Birder's Re-Reading," 200.
46. Kramer, *Music and Poetry*, 139.
47. Daniel Hoffman, *Poe*, 51.
48. Hollander, *Untuning of the Sky*, 42.
49. Ibid., 268.
50. Losseff, "Voice, the Breath," 7–8.
51. Poe, "[Stanzas]," 23–25.
52. Poe, "Marginalia," 1331; Heidegger, *The Event*, 279.
53. Blasing, *American Poetry*, 17, 32.
54. Poe, "Raven," 62–66.
55. Ibid., 82.
56. Blasing, *American Poetry*, 26–27.
57. Poe, "Raven," 72, 64.
58. Freedman, "Poe's 'Raven,'" 29.
59. Hirsch, "Raven and the Nightingale," 197.
60. Ibid., 199.
61. Kramer, *Music and Poetry*, 139.
62. Hirsch, "Raven and the Nightingale," 202.
63. Ibid., 202.
64. Ibid.
65. Peter Dayan, *Music Writing Literature*, 97.
66. Poe, "Marginalia," 1331.
67. Peter Dayan, *Music Writing Literature*, 11–12.
68. Ibid., 98.
69. Stedman, *Poems of Edgar Allan Poe*, xxi.
70. Poe, "Marginalia," 1331.
71. Kramer, *Music and Poetry*, 2.
72. Chua, *Absolute Music*, 52.

FIVE
The Starry Choir (And Other Listening Things)

> (Such as into himself at last Eternity changes him,
> The Poet arouses with a naked hymn
> His century overawed not to have known
> That death extolled itself in this strange voice!
> But, in a vile writhing of the hydra, (they) once hearing the Angel
> To give too pure a meaning to the words of the tribe
> They (between themselves) thought (by him) the spell drunk
> In the honorless flood of some dark mixture.
> Of the soil and the ether (which are) enemies, O Struggle!
> If with it my idea does not carve a bas-relief
> Of which Poe's dazzling tomb be adorned
> Stern block here fallen from a mysterious disaster
> Let this granite at least show forever their bound
> To the old flights of Blasphemy (still) spread in the future.)
>   —Mallarmé, "Tombeau d'Edgar Poe"

One can trace the origins of some of Poe's complex uses of music all the way to his earliest poems. Poe's first published book of poems begins with "Tamerlane," a long narrative poem spoken in Tamerlane's "dying hour."[1] Tamerlane soliloquizes:

> O, human love! thou spirit given,
> On Earth, of all we hope in Heaven!
> Which fall'st into the soul like rain
> Upon the Siroc-wither'd plain,
> And, failing in thy power to bless,
> But leav'st the heart a wilderness!
> Idea! which bindest life around
> With music of so strange a sound
> And beauty of so wild a birth —

Farewell! for I have won the Earth.[2]

As he dies, Tamerlane does not bid farewell to "human love" itself, which "leav'st the heart a wilderness," but he bids farewell to the "Idea" of the ideal form of "love," presumably to move toward the actual ideal form of that love itself in heaven.

Once "love" is an "Idea," rather than a defined human emotion, all of "life around" comes together with "music of so strange a sound / And beauty of so wild a birth." The connotation of both the "music" and the "beauty" is not that of "the Siroc-wither'd plain"; rather, the "Idea" has unifying, "binding" properties, although these are left undefined. The "life around" is interwoven with "music" and "beauty" as offshoots of an "Idea": they are both associated with the "Idea" of "love," but the "music of so strange a sound" is unarticulated and unspecific. That the "beauty" is "of so wild a birth" does not add any definitive audible meaning for music. This reiterates a distinction in Poe's works between different types of music, a distinction parallel to that which Peter Dayan finds in the works of Mallarmé:[3]

> Mallarmé makes an absolutely clear, rigorous and rigid distinction between two types of music: the audible kind, that exists in physically present sound, created, for example, by the instruments of the orchestra; and the silent kind, which may be produced by poetry. (Note that he is careful to exclude the actual sounds of words from the latter. Mallarmé's Music is not to be confused with the audible qualities of verse. It has no physical existence accessible to any of the five senses.)[4]

Dayan goes on to explore the relationship between the "silent kind" of music and "Greek Music," or what he later describes as "the paradigm of the music that cannot be heard."[5] Dayan also adopts in this quotation the distinction that Mallarmé and other artists make between music and Music: music can allude to audible, real-world music, and Music can allude to inaudible music, silent music, which Dayan describes in an interart context of depending "on two things: the presence of reference to music, of an evocation of music which will resonate with the audience; and the careful removal of our ability to be sure of what might have been the sound of that resonating music."[6] Inaudible music, that which evokes musical imagery without explicitly identifying with music in a real-world sense, complicates itself in poetry. Dayan illustrates how this happens in an interart context by quoting Braque, as his words are remembered by André Verdet: "music [. . .] in accordance with the great tradition of the representation of music by the poets of the interart appeal, going back to Keats and Mallarmé, [is] silent. 'To reach that higher silence where music itself can no longer be heard because it is silence, that mute fervour of space.'"[7] "M"usic, silent or inaudible, takes a hierarchical position over "m"usic, heard in the real-world sense. That "higher silence," or Silence, is represented by "that mute fervour of space," the plane that in some contexts draws from the mythology of the music of the spheres.

MUSIC OF THE SPHERES: MUSIC, IN OUR OWN MORE LIMITED SENSE OF THE WORD

The meaningful assembly of silence, Silence, and the music of the spheres has been established historically for a number of reasons and in different ways. John Hollander explains one of these by describing a few versions of the music of the spheres myth: the Pythagorean, the Socratic, and the Aristotelian. In the Pythagorean, "Certain intervals, such as the octave, fourth and fifth, were shown to result from dividing the string in the most 'perfect' ratios, such as 1/2, 2/3, etc."[8] He goes on to explain that,

> Up through the Renaissance and even later, the harmony of the parts of the cosmos, on the one hand, and of the parts of the human psyche, on the other, were seen as the basic elements of the same universal order. [. . .] In terms of this "harmony," the old myth of the music of the spheres as representing the sounds of heavenly perfection could be reinterpreted as a metaphysical notion, characterizing not only the order of the universe but the relation of human lives to this cosmological order.[9]

The experimentation with ratios, directly related to real-world music, has resonances in two directions: into the human soul and outward through the universe. This then develops into more illustrative myths of the universe, including that which "describes the heavenly spheres bearing 'on the upper surface of each' a siren, [. . .]. The singing siren that produces the tone on each sphere, of course, becomes beautifully adaptable, eventually, to membership in a Christian angelic choir."[10] In this perfect universal tuning from the soul to the outer reaches of the cosmos, the music of the spheres still attracts the inaudible: in "answer to the objection that no mortal had ever heard that music [of the spheres], it was often retorted that the constant droning of the noise deadened the ears of earthly inhabitants by custom alone, and that because it was so constant, it was inaudible."[11] While in Poe, this notion of silence or inaudibility becomes more complex, inaudible not due to "constant droning" but rather due to Silence's inaccessibility; as this chapter will show, the link between Greek music and the inaudible has a few implications in Poe's poetry.

Poe himself directly addressed this "Greek Music" in a couple of his works. In "The Colloquy of Monos and Una," two spirits hold a dialogue with one another in being "born again" after the end of the material world.[12] In this dialogue, Monos speaks "in regard to man's general condition at this epoch" of the world's demise.[13] In his speech regarding this era, Monos laments: "But alas for the pure contemplative spirit and majestic intuition of Plato! Alas for the μουσική which he justly regarded as an all-sufficient education for the soul! Alas for him and for it!—since both were most desperately needed when both were most entirely forgotten or despised."[14] Poe introduces as "education for the soul" the term "μουσικη," which refers in Plato's *The Republic* to "mousikē" in the sense that "Instrumental music [. . .] directly accompanied or otherwise complemented song, chant and declamation rather than being developed for its own sake. The single word *mousikē* can therefore denote accomplishment in both music and poetry."[15] Or as John Hollander explains, like "the folk balladeer's identification of the notions of 'song' and 'story,' the Greek word *mousike* designated neither a linguistic nor a tonal art but the craft of composing *song*, considered as a unified entity."[16] Taking these explanations of "mousikē" into account, we can see that Poe integrates into his tale the idea that the modern world has lost the ancient, primitive, unification of words and music and now is left in a state of failure that can no longer unify the two. Poe draws attention to this with a footnote to the quotation from "The Colloquy of Monos and Una" just cited:

> "It will be hard to discover a better (method of education) than that which the experience of so many ages has already discovered; and this may be summed up as consisting in gymnastics for the body, and *music* for the soul."—Repub. lib. 2. "For this reason is a musical education most essential; since it causes Rhythm and Harmony to penetrate most intimately into the soul, taking the strongest hold upon it, filling it with *beauty* and making the man *beautiful-minded* . . . He will praise and admire *the beautiful*; will receive it with joy into the soul, will feed upon it, and *assimilate his own condition with it.*"—Ibid. lib. 3. Music (μουσικη) had, however, among the Athenians, a far more comprehensive signification than with us. It included not only the harmonies of time and of tune, but the poetic diction, sentiment and creation, each in its widest sense. The study of *music* was with them, in fact, the general cultivation of the taste—of that which recognizes the beautiful—in contra-distinction from reason, which deals only with the true.[17]

This tale was, according to Mabbott, "probably written in May or June 1841" and was published in August 1841, which means that it was written just after the publication of an article in *The American Eclectic* entitled "Education of the Intellect, the Taste and the Imagination, in English Public Schools."[18] Although Poe would have been familiar with the classics in more than one form, his translation bears particular resemblance to this article, which appears to be a possible source, or to draw from the same source, for Poe's translation of Plato:

> "What shall be our method of education?" asks Plato, in the outset of his Republic.—"It will be hard to discover a better than that which the experience of so many ages has already discovered; and this may be summed up as consisting in gymnastic for the body, and *music* for the soul." *Plat. Repub. lib. 2. Music was a word of more extensive signifi-

cation in Athens than with us. It comprehended the ideal creations, the sentiments, the representations and the diction of the poet, as well as the harmonies of time and tune. [. . .]

"For this reason," adds Plato, "is a musical education (rightly conducted) most essential, because it makes Rhythm and Harmony to settle most deeply into the inner soul, and take the strongest hold of it, carrying with them comeliness, and making the man comely-minded. Also because one so nurtured will have the quickest perception of all faults and imperfections in art or nature, and regarding them with a just aversion will praise and admire the beautiful; this he will receive with joy into his soul, will feed on it, and assimilate his own nature to its beauty—will learn to censure and hate deformity even in early youth, while yet incapable of understanding the reason why, and when the reason comes will embrace it gladly, and recognize it as a familiar thing." *Plat. Repub. lib. 3.[19]

Poe appears to take this translation almost verbatim, as he did with the description of Maria Malibran's performance from the memoirs. As in that previous example, he makes a few key changes that reveal more than they conceal. The first excerpt remains essentially identical to the source that I propose. In the second excerpt from Plato, however, Poe's "Rhythm and Harmony *penetrate* most *intimately* into the soul," whereas the anonymous original writer posits "Rhythm and Harmony to *settle* most *deeply* into the *inner* soul" (italics mine). Poe then changes the "comely" from the original article to the "beautiful," a change to which his own emphases draw attention. Crucially, Poe then deletes every reference in the original source to the importance of a "just aversion" to the "faults and imperfections in art or nature" or to the need to "censure and hate deformity."

Poe writes elsewhere that the "pure imagination chooses, *from either beauty or deformity*, only the most combinable things hitherto uncombined; [. . .] Even out of deformities it fabricates that *beauty* which is at once its sole object and inevitable test."[20] For Poe, there is only the deepest, most intimate connection between higher forms of music, Rhythm, Harmony, the soul, and the beautiful, and none of these require an aversion to perversity, to deformity, or to imperfection. Certainly, this has some connection with μουσικη, which the article in *The American Eclectic* introduces with this insight: "We are thus brought to the inquiry, whether there is any thing in the system which we possess corresponding to the μουσικη of the ancients [. . .]? Music, in our own more limited sense of the word, we do not cultivate as the ancients did."[21] Indeed, for Poe, perversity, deformity, faults, and imperfections are part and parcel of this "limited sense of the word" in which we, in our modern condition, can only comprehend it.

Poe discusses the term once again in his "Marginalia." He writes:

> The phrase of which our poets, and more especially our orators, are so fond—the phrase "music of the spheres"—has arisen simply from a misconception of the Platonic word μουσικη—which, with the Athenians, included not merely the harmonies of tune and time, but *proportion* generally. [. . .] By the "music of the spheres" is meant the agreements—the adaptations—in a word, the proportions—developed in the astronomical laws. He [Plato] had *no* allusion to music in *our* understanding of the term.[22]

The "music of the spheres" is inextricable from μουσικη here, both of which for Poe indicate an ancient unification of music and poetry, of words and song, as well as of an ancient universal harmony. However, this "music of the spheres" reveals only that music in which, in *"our* understanding," we cannot participate. Tying the history of the idea of the music of the spheres into the historical development of the concept of absolute music, Daniel Chua argues that what "the Romantics discovered as absolute music was a mere shadow of what Pythagoras formulated two thousand years earlier, for the absolute music he bequeathed to humanity was not so much a music to be composed as a music that composed the world."[23] Chua elaborates:

> In Plato's account of creation, music tunes the cosmos according to the Pythagorean ratios [. . .], and scales the human soul to the same proportions. This enabled the inaudible sounds of the heavens to vibrate within the earthly soul, and, conversely, for the audible tones of human music to reflect the celestial spheres, so that heaven and earth could be harmonized within the unity of a well-tuned scale. [. . .] So music, as the invisible and inaudible harmony of the spheres, imposed a unity over creation, linking everything along the entire chain of being.[24]

The ancient image of music acting like "a 'taut string' stretched between heaven and earth, [. . .] able to conceptualise the unitary structure of the entire cosmos" gives rise to Poe's idea of "a strange sound, as of a harp-string broken / T'awake us—'Tis a symbol and a token / Of what in other worlds shall be."[25] That Pythagorean notion of the "taut string" turns into "a strange sound, as of a harp-string broken," and the music of the spheres degenerates into a "mere shadow," as Chua posits, of its former self, silent and wholly separated from the fallen modern condition. More than the Romantics, however, for whom "the absolute was an 'infinite yearning' for the 'spirit realm,'"[26] Poe recognizes in his yearning the totality of separation between the earth and the ethereal, the present and the mythological past, music and words.

Thus, returning to Peter Dayan's point that in the works of Mallarmé one can find a "rigorous and rigid distinction between two types of music: the audible kind, that exists in physically present sound [. . .] and the silent kind, which may be produced by poetry," one can find a similar distinction arising in Poe, with a number of consequences.[27] In his tales, the real-world music discussed at the very beginning of this book highlights the ways words and utterance are continually related as failed renderings of once-performed audible music; audible public performances of music associated with madness and gore become harsh, dissonant, and protracted; and liminal music oscillates between the audible sound and the inaudible music. Poe's poetry, while drawing on similar themes, does not take up real-world music, does not describe that which can be described as harsh and dissonant, but moves toward attempting to convey a kind of silent music.

Returning to "Tamerlane," that "music of so strange a sound" that "bindest life around" cannot fall under the "audible kind" of music. It is neither "physically present sound, created, for example, by the instruments of the orchestra," nor is it definably related to the "audible qualities of verse," to adopt Peter Dayan's phrase.[28] This "music" in "Tamerlane" "has no physical existence accessible to any of the five senses" because it remains unarticulated and synesthetic.[29] That the "sound" is "strange" is complicated by the idea of the "music" "bind[ing] life around," approaching the idea of silent music.

Similarly, in "The Sleeper," the setting of the poem is "midnight" in a "universal valley" into which an "opiate vapour" "steals [. . .] musically."[30] The "universal valley" houses Irenë, "The Sleeper," or "the fair lady who will never awaken."[31] As in "Tamerlane," Poe sets the poem on the cusp of life and death, in this case also in a liminal space representing the meeting point of the earthly and the otherworldly. An earthly "valley" becomes "universal," and the speaker calls for a "chamber changed for one more holy" as Irenë would "lie / Forever with unopened eye, / While the pale sheeted ghosts go by!", bringing together her material existence on earth with her possible spiritual existence beyond, resulting in a haunted otherworldly landscape reminiscent of "Ulalume."[32] The poem opens:

> At midnight, in the month of June,
> I stand beneath the mystic moon.
> An opiate vapour, dewy, dim,
> Exhales from out her golden rim,
> And, softly dripping, drop by drop,
> Upon the quiet mountain top,
> Steals drowsily and musically
> Into the universal valley.[33]

As in "Tamerlane," the word "musically" does not describe audible, articulated music. In fact, in the following stanza, the speaker describes the scene as "all solemn silentness," detaching any sound from the image of the "musically" moving "vapour" altogether.[34] It also draws upon that context of "solemn music" described in the context of "Fanny," that which resonates with the "music of the spheres," the "learned-contemplative" models of music as opposed to the "common-active" models.[35]

William Hunter argued that the "opiate vapour" references *Macbeth*, becoming a *"virus lunare."*[36] Mabbott responds by explaining that "the drop is thought of as very powerful and beneficent (though witches might seek it for bad uses) and that the irony of Poe's poem depends on the idea the drop came too late for the lady."[37] The moon "exhales" from its "golden rim" this powerful and enchanting "opiate vapour," again tying in breath with unarticulated meaning, at an ineffectual moment for Irenë. Indeed, the "opiate vapour" is a failure, and "steals" to the valley "musically" as a failed rendering of a heavenly promise. This "musically" moving "opiate vapour" reflects the "Idea! which bindest life around / With music of so strange a sound" in "Tamerlane," in that the music points toward an undefined heavenly promise or ideal that fails on earth. Yet this failed rendering still points heavenward by continually referring to an undefined, enchanting, and divine otherworldly idea. This idea of the failed rendering that still points heavenward relates back to Poe's use of Plato and the "music of the spheres." Poe excises from the translation of Plato anything that finds fault with deformity, with the perverse. Instead, Poe embraces the concept of the inherent failure of earth and harnesses it. In this way, music in Poe's poetry approaches silence such that it communicates an inherent inability to be assimilated to any ancient understanding of the "music of the spheres"; still, the further references to music move toward attempting to convey Music, the less related to the audible and the more silent they become.

"AL AARAAF": MUSIC OF THE PASSION-HEARTED

Tying together the Platonic, music, and ideals, Maurice Bennett explains the central images of Poe's "Al Aaraaf":

> Objectively, poetry is a Platonic ideal beyond the reach of mortals. This inaccessibility is expressed in the figure of the star [. . .]. To contemplate this star is to arouse those vague and inexpressible longings that most resemble the reaction to music. Considered as a syllogism, music, the star, and a beautiful woman become nearly equivalent metaphors. Unable to define the inexpressible, Poe becomes subjective, and he redefines poetry as effect, as that which most intensely arouses man's metaphysical aspirations.[38]

Bennett sees poetry and music interlinking in Poe's work. If poetry is a "Platonic ideal beyond the reach of mortals" whose power of inaccessibility resembles a "reaction to music," then music and poetry are both an "effect" and as well as the expression of the longing for themselves. Music is both the medium for transcendence and, in a way, the description of that transcendence itself. Much as I argue, Bennett interprets poetry's relationship to music as that which is "beyond the reach of mortals," but I think that his positioning "Al Aaraaf" as the star that parallels a Platonic ideal proves false.

Like other poems of Poe's, "Al Aaraaf" takes place in an explicitly otherworldly landscape, but unlike those poems, "Al Aaraaf" is the only one that overtly takes place in a spiritual limbo. Poe claims to have taken the setting from "the Al Aaraaf of the Arabians, a medium between Heaven and Hell where men suffer no punishment, but yet do not attain that tranquil and even happiness which they suppose to be the characteristic of heavenly enjoyment."[39] Al Aaraaf falls between earth and the divine, if placed on an imagined continuum between them. As Floyd Stovall explains:

> The underlying plan of *Al Aaraaf* might be illustrated by a chart of the stellar universe, with three slight modifications: increasing the relative size of the Earth, adding a prominent star [. . .], and localizing God and Heaven in the region without and above the material universe, visible but unapproachable. Through the added star, which is Al Aaraaf, rays of influence flow from God to all parts of the cosmos. The poem is thus a representation, mainly pictorial, of the relation of God to the whole universe, but to the inhabitants of Earth and Al Aaraaf in particular.[40]

Earth, if imagined as fallen and thus as furthest from God, is far more distant from Al Aaraaf than heaven. When critics such as Daniel Hoffman argue that Al Aaraaf is the "evanescent terrain of the ideal, and the only resemblance to human life on Al Aaraaf is the presence, among certain inhabitants, of that impure passion, love," they are not considering that, although nearer to the divine than the earth, Al Aaraaf is simultaneously separated from the ideal, as well.[41] Al Aaraaf then truly cannot be "a breathing-into-being of a realm of the ideal," as Hoffman argues.[42] As Hoffman himself later points out, those who "pass for persons" on the star, Michelangelo (Angelo) and Ianthe, "are, on that distant star, doomed not to know true Heaven because they love one another."[43] "Doomed" lovers, Angelo and Ianthe are more divinely fallen than those on earth, closer on a continuum toward the ideal, but they are not in heaven. A setting at once real and mythological, Al Aaraaf (as Poe himself notes) is a "star [that] was discovered by Tycho Brahe which appeared suddenly in the heavens—attained, in a few days, a brilliancy surpassing that of Jupiter—then as suddenly disappeared, and has never been seen since."[44] Just as we live tenuous earthly lives, this more heavenly world presents the looming danger of mortality. Poe wrote, "those who make choice of the star as their residence do not enjoy immortality—but, after a second life of high excitement, sink into forgetfulness and death—."[45]

Forgetfulness and death do not foreground the poem, however. Rather, in the first part of the poem, Poe describes the star as a kind of fairy-tale realm. As he introduces Nesace, the "presiding spirit of a star," he sets the scene:[46]

> O! nothing earthly save the thrill
> Of melody in woodland rill—
> Or (music of the passion-hearted)
> Joy's voice so peacefully departed
> That like the murmur in the shell,
> Its echo dwelleth and will dwell—
> [...]
> Adorn yon world afar, afar—
> The wandering star.[47]

Immediately we see that "nothing earthly" adorns Al Aaraaf, apart from what the speaker expresses in two distinct musical images. The first is the "thrill" of "melody," but not the "melody" itself, that stems from a stream, or "woodland rill." Attached not to utterance, but to the natural landscape as a heard sound of unarticulated pitch, this image uses the "melody of woodland rill" as a distant metaphor for an undefined "thrill" on the star. The second is the "music" compared to the departure of "Joy's voice," existing only by its absence. In other words, rather than relating the "voice" or the "music," the speaker conveys their absence, comparing "Joy's voice," and "music" in turn, with the "murmur in the shell" that seemingly has no origin apart from the symbolic notion of it as the voice of the sea, echoing those distant notions of madness introduced in the first part of this book. The "echo" moves the shell's "murmur" further and further away from any originating sound, a murmur that in turn characterizes the departure of "Joy's voice," itself unheard and undefined. No death interrupts this scene, but these murmurs hearken back to those murmurs of "Eleonora," discussed in chapter 3, murmurs that imply an unarticulated meaning, these informing the narrator of ethereal, otherworldly implications of death. Crucially, these two musical images of the "melody of woodland rill" and the "murmur in the shell" describe all that reminds the speaker of the "earthly," revealing the ways in which music still conveys a sense of the beyond, of the impending failure of the present inhabitants of the star to conceive of the ideal beyond them. The echoes, the murmurs, although so distant they almost prove silent, still voice a reminder of mortality.

Similarly, at the beginning of the second part of the poem, the poet describes a temple, which the spirit Nesace enters:

> But what is this?—it cometh—and it brings
> A music with it—'tis the rush of wings—
> A pause—and then a sweeping, falling strain
> And Nesace is in her halls again.[48]

The "music" in this instance is "the rush of wings," an audible sound. Yet this is complicated as the line moves from the compressed image of the "rush of wings" to a "pause," indicating soundlessness, and again to "a sweeping, falling strain" that may relate to the "rush of wings" or to something else entirely, away from the heard and toward the silent. The term "strain" plays upon a musical phrase. By being tied to the "rush of wings," the "strain" might indicate the stress of movement. By being tied to "music," however, the "strain" might indicate a section of music, or a melody, akin to the "dying fall," reminiscent of *Twelfth Night*: "If music be the food of love, play on—/ [. . .] / That strain again! It had a dying fall."[49] As well as this subtle evocation of mortality, of dying, the image of the "strain" ("rush of wings") is also composed of indefinite pitch and undifferentiated rhythm, the strain/rush of wings as music expresses the meeting of the spirit Nesace with the temple of her planet, the "falling strain" representing her fall to her star. In the stanza just following Nesace's arrival to her "halls," Poe elaborates upon the setting:

> Young flowers were whispering in melody
> To happy flowers that night—and tree to tree;
> Fountains were gushing music as they fell
> In many a star-lit grove, or moon-lit dell;
> Yet silence came upon material things—
> Fair flowers, bright waterfalls and angel wings—
> And sound alone that from the spirit sprang
> Bore burthen to the charm the maiden sang:[50]

Melody, that which flowers whisper, as fountains gush music, reflects the beginning of the poem, those images that use music to convey a sense of unarticulated meaning. Subsequent to Nesace's "falling strain," she prepares to sing a "charm," which silences the surrounding landscape, revealing a hierarchy in music: Nesace overtakes the music of the surrounding world. Her voice further complicates the music of the start. Arising in the silence of the surrounding world, "sound alone that from the spirit sprang," Nesace's voice is reminiscent of that relationship between spirit as breath, the soul, and song, or the consideration of the "voice to be articulated and controlled by our inmost soul, the central Spirit located in the heart."[51] Like the "one burden" interpreted by the speaker of "The Raven" as being borne by the songs of some imagined master condensed into the raven's "nevermore," this breathing in song of Nesace "bore burthen" to her charm in some indefinite sense unreachable by the reader.

When the "charm the maiden sang" is printed in the text in the lines following, they arrive already a step removed from the "sound alone that from the spirit sprang"; the fact of the words themselves negates the charm's incarnation. In the charm, Nesace invokes Ligeia. The second stanza begins:

> Ligeia! Ligeia!
> My beautiful one!

> Whose harshest idea
> Will to melody run,
> [...]
> Ligeia! wherever
> Thy image may be,
> No magic shall sever
> Thy music from thee.
> Thou hast bound many eyes
> In a dreamy sleep—
> But the strains still arise
> Which *thy* vigilance keep—
> The sound of the rain
> Which leaps down to the flower,
> And dances again
> In the rhythm of the shower—
> The murmur that springs
> From the growing of grass
> Are the music of things—
> But are modell'd, alas![52] —

This poem was written long before the tale "Ligeia," the only definitive connection between the two Ligeias being their musicality. She presides over the "music of things," which is described in natural imagery. The "sound of the rain" may be a readily imagined sound, but always with indefinite pitch and undifferentiated rhythm, compounded here by the description in this stanza that the "sound of the rain" then "leaps down to the flower, / And dances again" in the "rhythm of the shower." The ideas of sound and image conflate in continuous motion rather than specified sound. The murmur of the "growing of grass" similarly indicates movement as the slightest idea of sound, the murmur, and unarticulated meaning; Poe adds a footnote to this murmur: "I met with this idea in an old English tale, [...] 'The verie essence and, as it were, springeheade and origine of all musiche is the verie pleasaunte sounde which the trees of the forest do make when they growe.'"[53] Possibly invented, his reference has not been discovered, but the implication that the "music of things" approaches silence, the "sounde" that the trees make when they grow, reiterates in the poem that the music of Al Aaraaf, although closer to silent than the music of earth, is still based on heard sound, which inherently indicates falsity, or failure, or death. Ligeia, the presiding spirit of music, still sees "strains" that "arise" in the "music of things," which are "modell'd," on an ideal, or are themselves a failed rendering of the divine, "alas."

Floyd Stovall argues that in "Al Aaraaf":

> The divine harmony [...] descends from God to men not in its original purity, but as made intelligible to the terrestrial senses [...], just as the absolute silence of God's voice is first translated into the material si-

lence of Nesace's spiritual song, and then further translated into the audible music of Ligeia.[54]

Stovall follows the idea discussed in this book that the "absolute silence of God's voice" as the heavenly or the divine does not translate to the fallen realms "in its original purity." Audible music, following this logic, is the most fallen, the most earthly of music, which is "made intelligible to the terrestrial senses." Ligeia's music on Al Aaraaf is not so audible, as Stovall argues her "melody" truly cannot be determined; it does not relate to "real-world" or "heard" earthly "melodies." Instead, Nesace invokes Ligeia in the poem, and Nesace controls the description of Ligeia's melody; Ligeia herself remains absent. Nesace ends her invocation of Ligeia with the plea:

> Go! breathe on their slumber,
> All softly in ear,
> The musical number
> They slumber'd to hear[55] —

Just after describing "the music of things" as "modell'd," Ligeia's invocation calls for a "musical number," reiterating the dual nature of Ligeia's implicitly powerful "music" (later described as a "spell"[56]) and that powerful "music" fallen from its divine ideal. That "musical number" refers to the music of the spheres; the "number" parallels the Pythagorean intervals, those that reflect the ancient image of music acting like "a 'taut string' stretched between heaven and earth, [. . .] able to conceptualise the unitary structure of the entire cosmos."[57] More divine than the music of the earth, yet still fallen from some ideal, this music can be described only in terms of "breath," such that the merest of sounds, the breath alone, dictates this more heavenly music as it moves toward silence.

Even when Poe's literary music directly summons the sense of, it is only to draw attention to music's very failure. After Nesace's "song" within the poem, the speaker asks

> What guilty spirit, in what shrubbery dim,
> Heard not the stirring summons of that hymn?
> But two: they fell: for Heaven no grace imparts
> To those who hear not for their beating hearts.[58]

In a kind of reverse positioning from earlier examples, the higher music is silent to the fallen "guilty" spirits who cannot access it "for their beating hearts." In other instances in the poem, songs that function as hymns are continually unheard, synesthetic, and otherworldly. The speaker addresses "Fair flowers, and fairy! to whose care is given / To bear the Goddess' song, in odors, up to Heaven," rendering a synesthetic image of the "song" that "flowers" and "fairy" "bear" in "odors" to heaven.[59] In speaking of how Poe uses synesthesia, Daniel Hoffman writes:

In "Al Aaraaf" Poe had to depend upon his own imaginative distortions, through synaesthesia, of common objects (like flowers, stars, and meteors) in order to make tangible his wholly imaginary world. So his flowers sing hymns, his silences speak, the twilight murmurs as it falls (II, 40–41) [. . .]. In certain of his later poems, Poe creates a landscape [. . .] so little like *any* sensible objects, because apprehended by no sensations already known to the reader. This is a course at once heroic and hazardous for a poet, since it debars from his art practically all of the experiences of mankind and makes his poetry completely self-defining, self-limiting, solipsistic.[60]

To take Hoffman's argument a step further, perhaps we cannot even say that Poe "creates a landscape" through synaesthesia, but rather that he *attempts* to create a landscape primarily through composites of sound-based images that create a wholly imaginary space. All three common objects Hoffman gives, even if he does not explicitly state it, transform sound in some capacity; they all describe sounds that one cannot hear and that one cannot truly imagine hearing (flowers singing, silences speaking, and twilight murmuring). This inaudible music depends, to return to Peter Dayan's conceptualization of it, "on two things: the presence of reference to music, of an evocation of music which will resonate with the audience; and the careful removal of our ability to be sure of what might have been the sound of that resonating music."[61]

These elements of inaudible music arise also in "The Lake—To —." Mabbott gives the background for "The Lake—To —" as "founded on fact, recording a visit near sunset to a place reputedly haunted by the ghosts of two lovers, neither unfriendly nor truly unhappy. The place is the Lake of the Dismal Swamp."[62] Neither of these "lovers" nor their "ghosts" make their way into Poe's poem, however. Rather, the haunted quality of the poem is implicit in the tension that results between the "tremulous delight" the speaker feels and the "Death" that "was in that poisonous wave" of the lake.[63] This poem, like the others we have analyzed, takes us to the meeting point of the earthly, and the otherworldly. The first stanza describes the speaker's love for the swamp, a love for the "lovely [. . .] loneliness" of the lake.[64] In the second stanza, the tone changes as "Night" arrives:

> But when the Night had thrown her pall
> Upon that spot, as upon all,
> And the mystic wind went by
> Murmuring in melody—
> Then—ah then I would awake
> To the terror of the lone lake.
> Yet that terror was not fright,
> But a tremulous delight—
> A feeling not the jewelled mine
> Could teach or bribe me to define—

Nor Love—although the Love were thine.⁶⁵

That the "mystic wind" would pass by "Murmuring" parallels the "whispering" flowers of "Al Aaraaf," and the two examples together correspond to those from chapter 2 of this book: "The Coliseum" and "The Haunted Palace." "Murmuring," like "whispering," indicates indistinct or faintly audible speech. Once again, "melody" relates an unarticulated meaning, meaning without specified words. Moreover, the combination of the arrival of "Night" and the wind "Murmuring in melody" is what awakens the speaker to a "terror" of "a tremulous delight" that nothing can "teach" or "bribe" him "to define." Although melody works similarly to songs in multiple ways in Poe's poetry, it continually implies unarticulated meaning as well as unarticulated sound. While music itself may be based in sound (whether or not imaginable) or based in silence, and while it may encompass melody, melody lives in whispers, images, prophetic sounds, twangs, and murmurs.

"ISRAFEL": SWEETEST VOICE OF ALL GOD'S CREATURES

Both the themes of the implicitly fallen and the divinely otherworldly arise in "Israfel" in ways that synthesize some of Poe's poetic music. The poem foregrounds its musical setting, beginning "In Heaven a spirit doth dwell / 'Whose heart-strings are a lute.'"⁶⁶ These first two lines establish the lute as a representation of Israfel's heart, rather than a separate musical instrument upon which he plays. This lute-as-heart, the "spirit" Israfel's central organ, creates a complex image when one considers the connections between the lute and the Æolian harp, Psyche and the ventum textilem, the soul and the breath. Daniel Hoffman argues that the "suspended lute is of course an Æolian harp, that favorite image of the Romantics for the songs made by the breath—that is, the spirit—of Nature herself."⁶⁷ In the first part of this argument, Hoffman designates the lute as, "of course," an Æolian harp. In the second, he describes the products of this Æolian harp as "songs," "songs" moreover "made by the breath [. . .] of Nature." In doing so, Hoffman's argument reveals the dual nature of this "favorite image" of the Romantics by inferring that it at once produces real "songs" from an actual Æolian harp itself and that it produces "songs," in some symbolic sense, from the Æolian harp as an idea. Hoffman characterizes the wind used to create these "songs" as the "breath [. . .] of Nature" personified. This accords with the schema Losseff constructs: "The physical means of expelling the voice from the 'soul' is the breath," and the voice itself is "controlled by our inmost soul, the central Spirit located in the heart."⁶⁸ However, this interpretation seemingly implies that the song is a heard musical product, suggesting a duality in Daniel Hoffman's interpretation of Israfel as poet and the "song" as poem: "Israfel's lyre! Poe would, if he could, have always smitten those angelic strings. Poetry, to him, is *song*."⁶⁹ In fact, Poe himself has now become more or less synonymous with Israfel in some critical writings.⁷⁰

By combining the metaphor of the Æolian harp and the "song" as a poem, Hoffman mixes distinct and complex definitions of "song." In the first sense, he approaches the Romantic definition of song already discussed a few times as Kramer describes it, that "the poet hears a song that assumes epiphanic power precisely because it is unintelligible, and often at the very point where it passes the threshold of intelligibility. The poet's imagination is initially aroused by the impulse to insert his own words in the linguistic gap opened by the song."⁷¹ In the second sense, Hoffman approaches what Kramer describes as "song" in "its traditional definition," or as "a form of synthesis. It is the art that reconciles music and poetry."⁷² Both definitions oppose, for instance, the way Burton Pollin approaches Poe as a writer of "songs." By merging the first two descriptions of "song," Hoffman undercuts the second, the one that he otherwise appears to privilege, assuming once the poet's words are in place, they "gradually dissolve like the song's own, leaving the poet mute and transfixed."⁷³

Looking more closely then at these "musical" images, it seems that in the context of the poem it is the angel's "heart-strings" that comprise the lute, and the instrument upon which he plays is not the lute, but the lyre:

> And they say (the starry choir
> And the other listening things)
> That Israfeli's fire
> Is owing to that lyre
> By which he sits and sings—
> The trembling living wire
> Of those unusual strings.⁷⁴

The poet knows of Israfel only because of what "the starry choir and other listening things" "say" to him, reminiscent once more of the departure from the myth of the music of the spheres: "stars no longer sang, and scales no longer laddered the sky."⁷⁵ The image of a played instrument, or the "lyre / By which [Israfel] sits and sings," then approaches "The trembling *living wire* / Of those unusual strings," which refer back to Israfel's "heart-strings," conflating the two such that they are impossible to distinguish from one another (italics mine). Instead of music acting as "a 'taut string' stretched between heaven and earth," Israfel's heart-strings live in silent confusion, separate from the speaker-poet.⁷⁶

Poe altered this section from its first edition in a way that makes Israfel's "lute," heart-strings, and the lyre upon which he plays as indistinguishable as possible. In the first published edition of "Israfel," Poe writes, "That Israfeli's fire / Is owing to that lyre / With those unusual strings."⁷⁷ In the latest edition, however, whether Israfel's "fire" is owed to the instrument "By which" he sings or the actual "living wire" of his heart is impossible to tease out, made even more complex by version [C], in which it is "That trembling living lyre."[78] While both the lute and the lyre may in this case be related to the Æolian harp in its form as an actual musical instrument, they also move into the context described earlier, constructed of "various notions of the soul as an instrument, or the body as the instrument upon which the soul plays, or the soul as the melody or chordal effusion of the body's strings."[79] Rather than representing actual "heard" instruments, these instead construct a complex mutable image; there is no "real-world" equivalent for this combination.

Just as there is no real-world equivalent also to the "starry choir" that listens to Israfel's singing, and therefore the musical image resulting from it is imaginary rather than experiential, the poet does not use the lute and the lyre to refer to a reader's musical experience. The idealized nature of these instruments contorts in their context: "And the giddy stars (so legends tell), / Ceasing their hymns, attend the spell / Of his voice, all mute."[80] The angel Israfel, rather than playing to a mortal or earthly audience, plays to an audience of personified stars that then relate this image of Israfel to the poet. Israfel's playing is thus a few steps removed from that which can be named or defined. While the stars are "mute" and "attend" Israfel's "voice," his "voice" is a "spell," a scene that mirrors the aforementioned image of the Romantic "listener/poet [. . .] mute and transfixed" once "his own words [. . .] gradually dissolve like the song's own."[81] Yet, in doing so, the stars attend the power produced by Israfel's voice, rather than the sound of the "song," per se. Certainly the poet reiterates his posture of listening, but there is nothing that can be defined that he actually hears.

Separately, the speaker addresses Israfel, "With the fervour of thy lute— / Well may the stars be mute!"[82] That the stars must be "mute" and "listening" implies that they await a "heard" song, yet rather than describe a "heard" song, the speaker portrays only the "fervour" that surrounds it. In other words, as in previous examples, there is no "music" and no actual "words" to "dissolve." Steven Frye responds to the "mute" and "listening" stars attending Israfel in terms of a merged literal and metaphorical music:

> "Israfel" speaks of an angel of music whose heart-strings are those of a lute. The poet sings in praise of the angel Israfel's song, which embodies a transcendence intimated by the heart but which is imperfectly rendered in our world, through the dark, refracted murmur of human language. [. . .] Poe knows that the power of the angel's song is beyond the reach of words. But in all of his work, his hope is to still the stars and to lift the soul to reverie.[83]

Frye allows the images presented by the poem, "Israfel," his "heart-strings," the "lute," his "song," to merge, but their imitation in "words" still hold some "hope" for transcendent power for the reader, however rendered through "refracted [. . .] language." I believe instead that Poe's Israfel, if an "angel of music," is an angel of music who does not embody "transcendence," but who represents an ideal form that the human cannot clarify, hear, or define. Although Frye acknowledges a similar division between the "dark, refracted murmur of human language" as the mortal opposite of the angelic music, he does not go far enough to acknowledge its silence. More than being "beyond the reach of words," the "soul" cannot be lifted "to reverie" but is inevitably cut off from this ideal. That notion of "a 'taut string' stretched between heaven and earth" that represented the "unitary structure of the entire cosmos" in the myth of the music of the spheres has broken,[84] leaving an unbridgeable gap between mortality and immortality, but musical terminology voices that unknowable beyond without articulation, in its failure pointing heavenward.

References to the lute and the lyre, to the voice and to song, fuse into a mutable image associated with music, an image that then again resists a traditional musical description. Ultimately, the poem ends with the idea that, should Israfel and the poem's speaker trade places:

> He might not sing so wildly well
> A mortal melody,
> While a bolder note than this might swell
> From my lyre within the sky.[85]

The mortal song as "melody" calls to mind the "lip-begotten words" of "To —."[86] By doing so, it reintroduces division, rather than a "mythical union between a lower reality embodied in language and a higher one embodied in music."[87] A "note" alone will "swell" from the speaker's "lyre within the sky," implying that one note alone is still earthly, but "swells" heavenward, resembling that idea of the "harp string broken" in "[Stanzas]." That is a symbol of what "in other worlds shall be," such that the single note, moving toward silence while still incorporating musical symbolism, conveys the otherworldly in an unarticulated sense. The idea of the "note" as music will continue to be discussed in greater detail and traced through Poe's works in chapter 6 of this book, beginning with "The Bells."

POWER OF WORDS: THE NAIAD VOICE THAT ADDRESSES THEM FROM BELOW

One might see here why such poetic uncertainty does not deter critics, such as Glen Omans, from arguing that the poem "creates the experience in which the reader is made aware of these parallels [the earthly poet to the heavenly singer], 'Israfel' itself may be said to be a poem-symbol that makes possible the perceptual leap from real to ideal, from descendent to transcendent."[88] For Omans, the poem embodies the same power, however undefined, that Israfel's singing does. In fact, he argues that the poem "makes clear" that "the artist's endeavor is to envision the ideal through its symbols and then re-embody the ideal in a work of art. [. . .] As symbol, the work of art has the capacity to lead other, less perceptive viewers to a vision similar to that originally experienced by the artist."[89] Omans maintains a position opposing Frye's; rather than human language being a "refracted murmur" of the power of Israfel's singing, human language can actually "re-embody the ideal in a work of art," thereby allowing the reader to "envision the ideal," however undefined that is, as well.

The same duality arises in another poem that cites "Israfel." In the two years before Poe died, he composed and edited "To —". The poem is more directly personal than some of his others, as he takes the role of the speaker openly, writing:

> Not long ago, the writer of these lines,
> In the mad pride of intellectuality,
> Maintained the "power of words"—denied that ever
> A thought arose within the human brain
> Beyond the utterance of the human tongue;
> And now, as if in mockery of that boast,
> Two words—two foreign soft dissyllables—
> Italian tones made only to be murmured
> By angels dreaming in the moonlit "dew
> That hangs like chains of pearl of Hermon hill" —
> Have stirred from out the abysses of his heart,
> Unthought-like thoughts that are the souls of thought,
> Richer, far wilder, far diviner visions
> Than even the seraph harper, Israfel,
> Who has "the sweetest voice of all God's creatures,"
> Could hope to utter. And I! my spells are broken.[90]

As Mabbott notes, Poe "published a story called 'The Power of Words' in 1845," but the first few lines of this poem may refer instead "to a passage in 'Marginalia,' number 149, published in *Graham's* for March 1846: [. . .] 'so entire is my faith in the *power of words*, that, at times, I have believed it possible to embody even the evanescence of fancies such as I have attempted to describe.'"[91] In that passage, Poe claims that no "thought, properly so called, is out of the reach of language."[92] He reframes thoughts as "fancies," which "are *not* thoughts, and to which, *as yet*, I have found it absolutely impossible to adapt language" and are beyond the reach of words.[93] Originally titled "To Marie Louise," the poem's "two words" may be the name "Marie Louise" itself: "The foreign dissyllables are the lady's personal names, 'Marie Louise,' but these are French, and not 'Italian tones,' as in the version Poe published."[94] Returning to Peter Dayan's argument regarding the Orphic myth, "what we love and sing must remain, in Poe's words, 'Nameless *here* for evermore.' The moment at which Orpheus turns and sees her is the moment [. . .] in which the shade would [. . .] acquire a name; at that same moment, literature would die. To sing well is to avoid that naming."[95] Nowhere than here is it more clear that, not only does "the ordinary use of language" oppose that which is "identified with music," to adopt Peter Dayan's terminology, but also that which cannot be uttered is that which cannot be described in terms of the real, or of "that which can be seen and possessed."[96] In hopes of keeping alive these thoughts he cannot express, he does not define them, but quickly moves them multiple times away from that in which things are named, until they land in the realm of the musical, of Israfel, and beyond. Even with this rapid movement to the liminal, the poet looks at those "Two words" long enough to kill the idea therein: "And I! my spells are broken."

Returning to "Israfel," along the same lines, in some critical responses, the poet's "bolder" note is viewed much more positively than the word alone might signal. Mónica Peláez argues:

> These verses imply that it is the angel's exposure to the "ecstasies above" that enables him to compose such an unequaled song. The earthbound poet, on the other hand, inhabits a "world of sweets and sours." [. . .] The poem [. . .] [suggests] that the forthcoming bliss hinges on the ability to create a higher form of poetry. If the speaker could play the "lyre within the sky," he reasons, his "mortal melody" would be transformed into a "bolder note." This vision of the afterlife as a site of poetic accomplishment complements a tradition that focused above all else on the spiritual qualities of heaven.[97]

Peláez makes an argument for a "sentimental" Poe, a Poe who views death as a solace, a reprieve following mortal struggle. In doing so, she argues that the poet transcended to the afterlife or the poet with the idea of the afterlife in mind may attain a "higher form of poetry" because the "sours" of the world are removed. This still does not answer why Poe's speaker's note may be "bolder" than Israfel's, or what this "bolder" note is, however. In fact, the reverse is implied in Poe's poem, that mortal struggle adds this "boldness" beyond that of the creature who has only experienced perfect bliss.

In his review of Thomas Moore, Poe argues that "Sensitive Plant" and "Undine" are the "finest possible examples of the purely *ideal*."[98] He goes on to argue that this is the case because with

> each note of the lyre is heard a ghostly, and not always a distinct, but an august and soul-exalting *echo*. [. . .] But not so in poems which the world has always persisted in terming *fanciful*. Here the upper current is often exceedingly brilliant and beautiful; but then men *feel* that this upper current *is all*. No Naiad voice addresses them *from below*. The

notes of the air of the song do not tremble with the according tones of the accompaniment.[99]

Burton Pollin ties Poe's "Naiad" to Undine herself, arguing that "Undine is a Teutonic equivalent of a naiad and comes from under the sea" and that she is "accompanied by three of the four elementals which Paracelus and the whole lore of the Kabbala had evolved as mediators between God and man. [. . .] [I]n addition to the fairy Undine, of the wavy element, the reader meets sylphs or spirits of the air and goblins (or kobolds) of the earth."[100] Pollin's positioning of Poe's Naiad interestingly returns us once more to the sea or to water as that hallmark of liminality. Poe's musical metaphor, that with "each note of the lyre is heard a ghostly [. . .] *echo*," resonates only by being lowered to the liminal, but not by being too fallen as to meet with the earthly.

The complication with Poe's musical spectrum that this introduces is the necessity of deformity, failure, perversity, to inversely highlight the ethereal, the more silent and divinely musical. Like that notion introduced in chapter 4, in which Poe describes Art as "'the reproduction of what the Senses perceive in Nature through the veil of the soul,'" there appears to be a continual insistence in Poe's poetry on the liminal as best conveying what the fallen mind can conceive of as the heavenly.[101] The point of paradox best illustrates a higher, more silent form of music, a failed rendering that points heavenward. The murmur, the mixed metaphor of the heart, the spirit, the soul, and the strings moves in between the earthly and the otherworldly, as does the single note, which takes on its own complications in other contexts.

NOTES

1. Poe, "Tamerlane," 1.
2. Ibid., 177–86.
3. Although the influence of Poe on other poets is beyond the scope of this book, it is worth noting that the influence of Poe on Mallarmé continually arises in criticism. Dahlhaus posits that "Poe's 'The Philosophy of Composition' represents to a certain extent the charter of *poésie pure*, and historical influence on Baudelaire and Mallarmé can be traced back to Poe." See Dahlhaus, *Idea of Absolute Music*, 147.
4. Peter Dayan, *Art as Music*, 98–99.
5. Ibid., 99.
6. Ibid., 83.
7. Ibid.
8. Hollander, *Untuning of the Sky*, 28.
9. Ibid.
10. Ibid., 29.
11. Ibid.
12. Poe, "Colloquy of Monos," 608.
13. Ibid., 609.
14. Ibid., 610–11.
15. Ferrari, ed., *Plato: The Republic*, 61.
16. Hollander, *Untuning of the Sky*, 13.

17. Poe, "Colloquy of Monos," 611.
18. Mabbott, *Edgar Allan Poe: Tales*, 1: 607; "Education of the Intellect," 428.
19. Ibid., 437–38.
20. Poe, Rev. of *Prose and Verse*, 278.
21. "Education of the Intellect," 439.
22. Poe, "Marginalia," 1457–58.
23. Chua, *Absolute Music*, 15.
24. Ibid.
25. Chua, *Absolute Music*, 77; Poe, "[Stanzas]," 23–25.
26. Chua, *Absolute Music*, 22.
27. Peter Dayan, *Art as Music*, 98–99.
28. Ibid., 99.
29. Ibid.
30. Poe, "The Sleeper," 8, 3, 7.
31. Mabbott, *Edgar Allan Poe: Complete Poems*, 180.
32. Poe, "The Sleeper," 42–44.
33. Ibid., 1–8.
34. Ibid., 36.
35. Hollander, *Untuning of the Sky*, 256.
36. Hunter, "Poe's 'The Sleeper,'" 57.
37. Mabbott, "Poe's 'The Sleeper' Again," 340.
38. Bennett, "'Madness of Art,'" 2.
39. Poe, "Letter 12," 26.
40. Stovall, "Interpretation of Poe's 'Al Aaraaf,'" 107.
41. Daniel Hoffman, *Poe*, 38.
42. Ibid.
43. Ibid., 42.
44. See Poe, "Al Aaraaf"; See Mabbott, *Edgar Allan Poe: Complete Poems*, 99.
45. Poe, "Letter 12," 27.
46. Mabbott, *Edgar Allan Poe: Complete Poems*, 115.
47. Poe, "Al Aaraaf," Part I: 5–10, 14–15.
48. Ibid., Part II: 48–51.
49. Shakespeare, *Twelfth Night*, 1.1.1–4.
50. Poe, "Al Aaraaf," Part II: 60–67.
51. Losseff, "Voice, the Breath," 7–8.
52. Poe, "Al Aaraaf," II: 100–03, 112–27.
53. Mabbott, *Edgar Allan Poe: Complete Poems*, 110.
54. Stovall, "Interpretation of Poe's 'Al Aaraaf,'" 126.
55. Poe, "Al Aaraaf," II: 144–47.
56. Ibid., 152.
57. Chua, *Absolute Music*, 77.
58. Poe, "Al Aaraaf," II: 174–77.
59. Ibid., 80–81.
60. Daniel Hoffman, *Poe*, 45.
61. Peter Dayan, *Art as Music*, 83.
62. Mabbott, *Edgar Allan Poe: Complete Poems*, 83.
63. Poe, "The Lake—To —," 14, 18.
64. Ibid., 4.
65. Ibid., 7–17.
66. Poe, "Israfel [G]," 1–2. Although Poe frames this phrase as a direct quotation from the Qur'an, it is not: "Poe must have derived his quotation and description from a source or sources other than the Koran, for nothing of the kind can be found in it." See Davidson, *Dictionary of Angels*, 152.
67. Daniel Hoffman, *Poe*, 52.
68. Losseff, "Voice, the Breath," 7–8.
69. Daniel Hoffman, *Poe*, 52.

70. See, for instance, Allen, *Israfel* [sic].
71. Kramer, *Music and Poetry*, 139.
72. Ibid., 125.
73. Ibid., 139.
74. Poe, "Israfel [G]," 16–22.
75. Chua, *Absolute Music*, 21.
76. Ibid., 77.
77. Poe, "Israfel [A]," 14–16.
78. Poe, "Israfel [C]," 21.
79. Hollander, *Untuning of the Sky*, 268.
80. Poe, "Israfel [G]," 5–7.
81. Kramer, *Music and Poetry*, 139.
82. Poe, "Israfel [G]," 38–39.
83. Frye, ed., *Critical Insights*, 7.
84. Chua, *Absolute Music*, 77.
85. Poe, "Israfel [G]," 48–51.
86. Poe, "To —," 4.
87. Kramer, *Music and Poetry*, 2.
88. Omans, "Poe and Washington Allston," 5.
89. Ibid.
90. Poe, "To —," 1–16.
91. Mabbott, *Edgar Allan Poe: Complete Poems*, 408.
92. Poe, "Marginalia," 1383.
93. Ibid.
94. Ibid., 406, 408.
95. Peter Dayan, *Music Writing Poetry*, 97.
96. Ibid., 98–99.
97. Peláez, "Sentimental Poe," 80.
98. Edgar Allan Poe, Rev. of *Alciphron*, 337.
99. Ibid., 337–38.
100. Ibid.
101. Poe, "Marginalia," 1458.

SIX
But Gradually My Songs They Ceased

> In an aeolian romanticism Beauty will be known only like Wordsworth's Lucy, in forms of an absent presence [. . .] Poe is closer—always—to [...] the commanding spirit Shelley prays to be in the "Ode to the West Wind." Poe becomes that spirit—a lucid lutanist, like Blake's devil, "a harper [singing] to the harp" in a netherworld he chooses to inhabit in order to transform. Becoming the artist of the death of Beauty, Poe makes all things possible.
>
> —Jerome McGann

While chapter 4 of this book revealed that typically only birds sing songs in Poe's poetry, drawing upon Lawrence Kramer's argument that, in certain nineteenth-century poetry, "the singer in these poems is usually either a bird [...], or a girl," in this chapter we will explore a singularity in Poe's poetry, one that reveals a completely different type of singer.[1] When Poe finally discloses his only human singer in a poem in his "Eldorado," that singer takes the form of a man. This singularity in Poe's works, the only of Poe's poems in which a song is sung by a human, also evinces this dual level of what Poe calls the "upper current" and the voice "*from below*,"[2] or what we have interpreted as a kind of dark liminality:

> Gaily bedight,
> A gallant knight,
> In sunshine and in shadow,
> Had journeyed long,
> Singing a song,
> In search of Eldorado.
>
> But he grew old—
> This knight so bold—
> And o'er his heart a shadow
> Fell, as he found

> No spot of ground
> That looked like Eldorado.[3]

What at first glance appears to be a straightforward example of a knight "singing a song" in the fullest sense of real-world music quickly unravels as something more complex. The "shadow" of the initial journey "In sunshine and in shadow" does not appear to take on any deep significance; this is earthly shadow, or that which is encountered every day. But as the knight "grew old," the "shadow" that fell "o'er his heart" prefigures another kind of shadow altogether. He journeys on to speak to "a pilgrim shadow—," who informs the knight that he must ride "Down the Valley of the Shadow," layering the levels of the knight's dark liminality in ways reminiscent of the death associated with the protagonists of Poe's ballads.[4] This twofold shadow also recalls another of Poe's poems, "Sonnet—Silence":

> There are some qualities—some incorporate things,
> That have a double life, which thus is made
> A type of twin entity which springs
> From matter and light, evinced in solid and shade.
> There is 6a two-fold *Silence*—sea and shore—
> Body and Soul. One dwells in lonely places,
> Newly with grass o'ergrown; some solemn graces,
> Some human memories and tearful lore,
> Render him terrorless: his name's "No more."
> He is the corporate Silence: dread him not!
> No power hath he of evil in himself;
> But should some urgent fate (untimely lot!)
> Bring thee to meet his shadow (nameless elf,
> That haunteth the lone regions where hath trod
> No foot of man,) commend thyself to God![5]

We can find in this poem a series of tropes that I have been continually culling from Poe's works and reassembling in this book in terms of their relationship to Poe's musical vocabulary. The first of these is the "double life" or "twin entity" of the earthly and the otherworldly, that which "springs / From matter and light" and becomes "solid and shade." The second of these is the parallel "two-fold *Silence*" of "sea and shore" or "body and soul"; there is earthly silence, "corporate" death that is both natural and inescapable, and there is another kind of silence, the "shadow" of the "corporate" incarnation, that "haunteth the lone regions where hath trod / No foot of man." Crucially, the "corporate," earthly silence has a name, "No more," while "his shadow" is a "nameless elf" that, like Lenore, is "nameless *here* for evermore."[6]

Silence and shadow interweave in ways intimately connected to the terrifying unknown of death. In "Eldorado," the repetition of the word "shadow" evinces this shift in meaning, from earthly shadow and the body's death, to otherworldly shadow and the destination of the soul.

Burton Pollin explores the repetition of "Eldorado" and "shadow," writing:

> In "Eldorado" there is even a trace of a technique used in "The Raven"—the shifting significance of the evocative word "nevermore." The word "Eldorado" provides a repetend in a changing last line context. Moreover, in the rhyming third line of each stanza, Poe ingeniously tries to accomplish the same feat with "shadow," for which he furnishes a varying context and meaning: the opposite of sunshine, a dark mood, a phantom, and death.[7]

As it turns out, the "song" the knight "sings" is not heard, seen, or defined in a way that aligns itself with real-world music so that the "song" itself becomes of "varying context and meaning," impossible to pin down, just as "shadow" does in this poem. The "song" in "Eldorado," a word dropped after the first stanza, becomes another element of Poe's "indistinct" themes:

> Poe peopled his stage with veiled, shadowy figures, with troops of Echoes and "evil things, in robes of sorrow" ("The Haunted Palace"), with ill angels and ghouls ("Dream-Land"), and with dim "nothings which were real" ("Tamerlane"). Even his protagonists or featured characters remain indistinct, like the gallant knight seeking Eldorado. All we know of him is that he started out "gaily bedight"; and all we know of the one person he encountered on his way is that he was a pilgrim Shadow.[8]

Even if the knight "sings a song," he is himself "indistinct," parallel, in Fagin's response, to the aforementioned "Echoes" and "ghouls," or to the "terrorless" "shade" of "Sonnet—Silence," a corporeal representation of earthly death. His "song," in turn, comes to life as an inarticulate notion from an indistinct character, and its twin, as a product of the other, the incorporeal Shadow, remains absent from the poem.

This is the only one of Poe's poems that explicitly takes up the human singing a song as a subject, and its unarticulated association with shadow in both senses reimagines one of Poe's tales, "Shadow.—A Parable." As in "Eldorado," references to shadows in various forms inundate the text, beginning with the epigraph ("Yea! though I walk through the valley of the *Shadow*"[9]) and in the first line, "Ye who read are still among the living; but I who write shall have long since gone my way into the region of shadows."[10] This tale of terror and "Pestilence," that reminder in disease of death-in-life, is told by Oinos, who sits in a "company of seven" in a circumscribed chamber:

> Black draperies, likewise, in the gloomy room, shut out from our view the moon, the lurid stars, and the peopleless streets—but the boding and the memory of Evil, they would not be so excluded. There were things around us and about of which I can render no distinct account— things material and spiritual—heaviness in the atmosphere—a sense of

suffocation—anxiety—and, above all, that terrible state of existence which the nervous experience when the senses are keenly living and awake, and meanwhile the powers of thought lie dormant.[11]

The room contains a kind of liminal space then, that which does not give a clear sense of death or life, all within moving from life to death without clearly arriving there. With no view of people or the natural world outside the room, the room itself becomes a darkened dreamlike landscape of which Oinos can "render no distinct account" apart from the feeling of limbo in having both heightened senses and dormant thought. Despite the "terrible state of existence" in which the narrator and his companions are kept, Oinos writes:

> Yet we laughed and were merry in our proper way—which was hysterical; and sang the songs of Anacreon—which were madness; and drank deeply—although the purple wine reminded us of blood. For there was yet another tenant of our chamber in the person of young Zoilus. Dead, and at full length he lay, enshrouded;—the genius and the demon of the scene.[12]

Oinos tells us that the songs "were madness," weaving in this theme that has been occurring again and again in the tales. As Michael Williams argues, "although the songs were 'those of the son of Teios,' which epitomize the denial of time, his effort is undercut first by the simple fact that they are not his own songs—his voice can only echo those already sung by a man long dead."[13] There is also another layer to the songs of Anacreon and the inescapability of time, which John Hollander hints at in a separate context by arguing that the "Anacreontic [. . .] complains of its author's lyre and how it could only play songs of love, despite his desire to sing epic."[14] Like the tales described in the first part of this book that use madness to foreground music's removal from an original source, a mythological origin that unifies words and music, this tale describes the "songs of Anacreon" as madness because they convey the futile attempt to celebrate life as they sit before a corpse that becomes a "demon" and perversely a "genius." This corpse, corporate silence, provides the antithesis to the shadow, the "nameless elf." In another way, the corpse represents life turning to death, and the shadow represents death turning to life. Acting in opposition to one another, "Whereas the corpse [. . .] offered a recognizably human form onto which the narrator could project 'expression' and significance, the shadow is just shadow, silent and unmotivated," and darkly absolute.[15]

As Oinos goes into detail about the singing, something other than the human fear or celebration of life in rejection of bodily death emerges:

> But although I, Oinos, felt that the eyes of the departed were upon me, still I forced myself not to perceive the bitterness of their expression, and, gazing down steadily into the depths of the ebony mirror, sang with a loud and sonorous voice the songs of the son of Teios. But

gradually my songs they ceased, and their echoes, rolling afar off among the sable draperies of the chamber, became weak, and undistinguishable, and so faded away. And lo! from among those sable draperies where the sounds of the song departed, there came forth a dark and undefined shadow—a shadow such as the moon, when low in heaven, might fashion from the figure of a man: but it was the shadow neither of man, nor of God, nor of any familiar thing.[16]

The "echoes" of the "songs" continue until they "faded away," but the departure of the "sounds of the song" gives rise to the "dark and undefined shadow." Whereas "song" in Poe's poetry is undefined, not necessarily ever sung at all in a way that can be described in terms of real-world music, this "song" is more connected to real-world music by being compared to Anacreon. As in the other examples in this book, those songs are not musically scored, such that Oinos's songs, once moving into performance in the real-world sense, become associated with utterance. However, like in Poe's poetry, the departure of this specific, worldly, "loud and sonorous" song, continued through its "echoes," leads to the emergence of something undefined and otherworldly.

Douglas Anderson explains this scene of Oinos and his peers:

> awaiting their own grim fate as they watch over the corpse, attempting in vain to bolster their spirits by singing as loudly as possible "the songs of the son of Teios," Anacreontic hymns to pleasure and to resignation. Oinos himself almost perversely directs his voice toward the table's glossy surface, producing a crowd of weakening echoes to which only his dead friend appears to be listening, until a shadow [. . .] emerges from the same draperies which consumed his last notes.[17]

Anderson also interprets the Shadow's response as resembling in "composite speech" the "plural echoes that had accompanied Oinos's desperate song [. . .]. Its 'cadences' are [. . .] the aggregate utterance of a human multitude: an audible census of the dead that gives voice to the 'dead weight' of sensory life."[18] A certain link between musicality and the aggregate voice of a multitude is indeed embedded in Poe's assertion that the "tones in the voice of the shadow were not the tones of any one being, but of a multitude of beings, and, varying in their cadences from syllable to syllable, fell duskily upon our ears in the well remembered and familiar accents of many thousand departed friends."[19] The multitudinous tones add to the terror in the scene, and he uses this more than once in his tales, as mentioned in chapter 3 in terms of "The Fall of the House of Usher" and "The Black Cat."

In "A Tale of the Ragged Mountains," the protagonist, Bedloe, describes a similar soundscape, which precedes the transformation of the landscape: "a low, continuous murmur, like that arising from a full, but gently-flowing river, came to my ears, intermingled with the peculiar hum of multitudinous human voices. While I listened in an extremity of astonishment—[. . .] a strong and brief gust of wind bore off the incumbent fog as if by the wand of an enchanter."[20] In this case, the murmur and the low sounds arising from the natural world are the earthly opposition to the multiple familiar tones of the "thousand departed friends" that arose in "Shadow.—A Parable." In "The Conversation of Eiros and Charmion," the connection between death and the indeterminate, multitudinous, breathy sound is made even more distinct in that Eiros no longer hears after he dies "that mad, rushing, horrible sound, like the 'voice of many waters.'"[21] That "voice of many waters," when tied not to the natural world, as in "A Tale of the Ragged Mountains," but rather to the dark unknown, as in "The Fall of the House of Usher," is associated with the "mad," with the "horrible," with that which voices the terrifying question of what happens not to the body, but to the soul after death.

Returning then to "Shadow.—A Parable," as Michael Williams argues, "Confronted by his unmotivated shadow-text, Oinos attempts to place it [. . .]. He hopes that it will speak with a single authoritative voice that will give it unity, but it does not [. . .]. At this moment of Oinos's discovery [. . .], the tale abruptly ceases."[22] In this text, the figure of the shadow itself is an attempt "to give substance to the unknowable—the moment of biological death that is either terminal point or threshold to another condition that is feared, or longed for, or both. To the living, Shadow both marks an absolute secret and, in itself, is indefinite and unknowable."[23] It is only the fact of the Shadow's existence as an "absolute secret" that allows it to be born from the echoes of Oinos's song. Returning to Peter Dayan's argument regarding Orpheus, literature "identified with music" is what "allows us to lead that which we love out of obscurity; but only for so long as we continue not to name it, not to look at it."[24] Yet, in Poe's case, that "which we love" and which we lead "out of obscurity" transforms as well and more powerfully into that which we fear, so long as it represents what one "cannot see, of a ghost, of one who returns, of a 'revenant.'"[25]

"THE CASK OF AMONTILLADO": THE CONICAL CAP AND BELLS

"The Cask of Amontillado" is also a tale of doubling, as many critics have effectively argued in varying ways.[26] The narrator, Montresor, parallels his nemesis, Fortunato: "Mon*tresor*. *Fortun*ato. Are these not synonymous? [. . .] But has not Montresor walled up himself in this revenge?"[27] The story also takes place on "one evening during the supreme madness of the carnival season."[28] As Peter Burke explains, "Carnival was an enactment of 'the world turned upside down' [. . .]. There was physical reversal [. . .]. Also represented was the reversal of the relations between man and man, whether age reversal, sex reversal, or other inversion of status."[29] The image of the "world turned upside down" positions this tale; Montresor tells us that Fortunato "was a man to be respected and even feared," but when Montresor meets him on the night of his revenge during carnival, "the man wore motley. He had on a tight-fitting parti-striped dress, and his head was surmounted by the conical cap and bells."[30]

Indeed, the only real characterization of Fortunato is as a fool for the entirety of the tale, a characterization that hinges upon the bells of his costume. Rodriquez points out, "The sounding bells of Fortunato's cap will recur many times throughout the pilgrimage to his immolation, as a reminder of mortal and contrapuntal parodic accompaniment."[31] As they make their way into the catacombs, Montresor realizes that "the bells upon [Fortunato's] cap jingled as he strode," and when Fortunato stops to drink some wine, he "paused and nodded to [Montresor] familiarly, while his bells jingled," and the "wine sparkled in his eyes and the bells jingled."[32]

Returning once again to Foucault, there is another kind of madman he describes: "the character of the Madman, the Fool, or the Simpleton assumes more and more importance. [. . .] [H]e stands center stage as the guardian of truth—[. . .]. If folly leads each man into a blindness where he is lost, the madman, on the contrary, reminds each man of his truth."[33] That truth ultimately deals with the "theme of death," shifting it from the notion of that "from which nothing escapes" to "mockery of madness [that] replaces death and its solemnity."[34] From here on, "Death's annihilation is no longer anything because it was already everything, because life itself was only futility, vain words, a squabble of cap and bells. Madness is the *déjà-là* of death."[35] What "death unmasks was never more than a mask [. . .]. [W]hen the madman laughs, he already laughs with the laugh of death; the lunatic, anticipating the macabre, has disarmed it."[36] This is a madness closely akin to that explored throughout this book, a madness that expresses the underside of the world, the tomb or the dark absolute; through the recognition that bodily death "is no longer anything because it was already everything," this madness, the "*déjà-là* of death," surpasses the corporeal and terrifyingly echoes the fears of "The Shadow.—A Parable" in that it is one in which ordinary language does not suffice to voice the unknown counterpart of death, and instead the bell takes its place.

Although Foucault claims that "life itself was only futility, vain words, a squabble of cap and bells," surely if the madman "already laughs with the laugh of death," if he has "disarmed it," then his bells voice a more absolute, Deathly theme. Returning to "The Cask of Amontillado," the story's denouement that rests upon Fortunato's sad jest, his characterization as fool, unfolds the permutations of the bells in telling ways. Once Fortunato has been entombed, Montresor describes his reaction:

But now there came from out the niche a low laugh that erected the hairs upon my head. It was succeeded by a sad voice, which I had difficulty in recognising as that of the noble Fortunato.

The voice said—"Ha! ha! ha!—he! he!—a very good joke indeed—an excellent jest. We will have many a rich laugh about it at the palazzo—he! he! he!—over our wine—he! he! he! [. . .] Let us be gone."

"Yes," I said, "let us be gone."

"For the love of God, Montresor!"

"Yes," I said, "for the love of God!"

But to these words I hearkened in vain for a reply. I grew impatient. I called aloud—"Fortunato!" No answer. I called again—"Fortunato!" No answer still. I thrust a torch through the remaining aperture and let it fall within. There came forth in return only a jingling of the bells. My heart grew sick—on account of the dampness of the catacombs. [. . .] *In páce recquiescat!*[37]

As in "Eldorado," in which the repetition of the word "shadow" develops the earthly shadow to the notion of age and bodily death and finally to the incorporeal, terrifying, unknown of the soul's death, the repetition of the bells in this story marks a similar transition. The bells represent an extreme case in the spectrum of types of music in Poe's work, as they most capably voice the unknown of death. In this case, the bells work as counterparts to the associations of folly and jest, throwing back onto Montresor all the qualities he tries to impose on Fortunato. To reiterate Foucault's point, "Death's annihilation is no longer anything because it was already everything, because life itself was only futility, vain words, a squabble of cap and bells. Madness is the *déjà-là* of death."[38] Fortunato's body dies, but his physical immolation, although horrifying, does not point to the unknown terror of the beyond. His bells, rather, answering Montresor's final act, respond with the notion that physical "Death's annihilation is no longer anything because it was always everything," and they in turn voice the question of what happens, perversely, to both characters' souls in that final scene. The terror of the tale arises as the possibility of nonphysical death arises in ways that can no longer be articulated with words, the narrator "hearkened in vain for a reply," and at the moment of Fortunato's immolation, only a "jingling of the bells" returns to him; Fortunato's physical death was "always everything" and so is "no longer anything," but deeper, darker, and unarticulated questions arise from the bells that point back to Montresor himself.

Bells are continually associated with the meeting of the earthly and the otherworldly, persistently ending in the reminder of death and the unknown in Poe's works. In his description of the dying process in "The Colloquy of Monos and Una," Monos "became possessed by a vague uneasiness—an anxiety such as the sleeper feels when sad real sounds fall continuously within his ear—low distant bell-tones, solemn, at long but equal intervals, and commingling with melancholy dreams."[39] The illustration that the "bell-tones" fall at "long but equal intervals" heightens the traditionally human musical element of the sound through similarity to the rhythm of a song, but that does not disguise the fact that the bell-tones do not appear to make any different tonal impression on the listener. They work as music, however, because of the description of their effect, that they possess Monos with "a vague uneasiness," which describes the effect of the impending other. The sound imparts a subtle, if evanescent, implication that leaves the listener with a sense of the undefined beyond. The sound creates the liminal space between earth and otherworldly that allows Poe to write with his trademark ubiquitous feeling of madness.

Monos conveys his heightened senses associated with the process of death, describing his awareness that "issuing from the flame of each lamp, (for there were many,) there flowed unbrokenly into [his] ears a train of melodious monotone."[40] The concept of a "melodious monotone" would seem more like an oxymoron than a useful descriptor. However, its place is clear enough in the spectrum of Poe's music, between melody and the single note. The melodious monotone takes us further along the musical scale toward the idea of death, as it does not necessitate either rhythm or change in note as in a traditional song; it moves toward silence. Monos describes the process of dying, telling Una: "Thus your wild sobs floated into my ear with all their mournful cadences, and were appreciated in their every variation of sad tone; but they were soft musical sounds and no more."[41] Monos goes on to describe the "wild sobs" as issuing "gaspingly, with loud cries" in the real world, but that he perceived them as having "floated" into his ear, of "every variation of sad tone," and as "soft musical sounds and no more." As he dies, the theme that has been recurring in Poe's works is reversed. Rather than the "musical sounds" importing something otherworldly, they are earthbound, imparting no meaning to the dead. Indeed, Monos describes his reason at this point as "extinct" as he moves from the realm of the rational to the realm of the irrational, or the supernatural. As Monos moves closer to death, the musicality of Una's sobs imparts even less anxiety for comprehension; they simply *are*.

"THE BELLS": *WHAT* A WORLD OF SOLEMN THOUGHT THEIR MONODY COMPELS

In "The Pit and the Pendulum," the narrator also describes that "there stole into [his] fancy, like a rich musical note, the thought of what sweet rest there must be in the grave."[42] The "sweet rest" of the "grave" is compared to the movement into one's mind of "a rich musical note." The sound of this "musical note" is not evoked, but the idea of a single "musical note" is always allied with the idea of death. Nowhere is that more clearly indicated than in "The Bells" itself. The poem begins:

> Hear the sledges with the bells—
> Silver bells!
> *What* a world of merriment their melody foretells!
> How they tinkle, tinkle, tinkle,
> In the icy air of night!
> While the stars that oversprinkle
> All the Heavens, seem to twinkle
> With a crystalline delight;
> Keeping time, time, time,
> In a sort of Runic rhyme,
> To the tintinnabulation that so musically wells
> From the bells, bells, bells, bells,
> Bells, bells, bells—
> From the jingling and the tinkling of the bells.[43]

The poem begins with the speaker demanding the reader to "Hear," to "hear" the silver bells that typically decorate the front of a sleigh, or sledge. Of course, the reader cannot hear the bells, but can certainly imagine the real-world sound of sleigh bells. Returning once more to Leppert's terminology of real-world music, the first two lines fall along a description closely aligned to it. They denote a sound that is called upon to be experienced as "sound via the sense of hearing" and that has a visible source and the potential of being notated.[44] Musical terminology does not infiltrate these first two lines, however, and as the stanza progresses it becomes more complex. The third line introduces a refrain that recurs and changes throughout the poem: "*What* a world of merriment their melody foretells!" This real-world sound of the first two lines takes a sudden shift into the imagined interpretation of the narrator. First, the speaker emphasizes the "*what*" of the phrase, questioning the parameters of the "world of merriment" foretold. Second, in doing so, he interprets their sound as "melody," and it is that interpretation of the sound in musical terminology that leads to the world of merriment foretold. Mirroring the melody of the bells is the twinkling of the stars above, whose twinkling is compared to a "Runic rhyme," or a kind of incantation or spell, that backs the "tintinnabulation that so musically wells" from the bells, which themselves jingle and tinkle. Ultimately, this means that as the stanza continues, it reflects real-world music less and less. The music and the melody of the bells stem from their association with an unknown world of merriment foretold; the undeciphered twinkling of the stars in the sky represents that earthly separation from the music of the spheres.

Similarly, the second stanza continues with the same themes, building upon them as it progresses to the crucial third stanza:

> Hear the mellow wedding bells —
> Golden bells!
> *What* a world of happiness their harmony foretells!
> Through the balmy air of night
> How they ring out their delight! —
> From the molten-golden notes
> And all in tune,
> What a liquid ditty floats
> To the turtle-dove that listens while she gloats
> On the moon!
> Oh, from out the sounding cells
> *What* a gush of euphony voluminously wells!
> How it swells!
> How it dwells
> On the Future! — how it tells
> Of the rapture that impels
> To the swinging and the ringing
> Of the bells, bells, bells! —
> Of the bells, bells, bells, bells,
> Bells, bells, bells —
> To the rhyming and the chiming of the bells![45]

Whereas the speaker interprets the silver bells as melody, he interprets the golden bells as "harmony," which foretell of a "world of happiness" that is similarly questioned. Rather than describe this "world of happiness," the speaker asks and exclaims "*What*" a world they foretell. Like the bells of the first stanza, the golden bells themselves fit into the framework of real-world music, which immediately changes to something else after the third line. They ring a "delight," rather than a tune, their "ditty" is "liquid" and moves to a turtle-dove who gloats on the moon. They build, then, to a "gush of euphony," which cannot be defined, a euphony that dwells on the future, continuing its indefinite image as it builds. That which they foretell seems timeless, outside of the realm of the present, a circumscribed otherworldly bliss to which we have no access. As Paul Williams suggests, "the third line in each of these stanzas reads that a *world* of merriment and a *world* of happiness is *foretold*. In the third stanza, however, line three brings the terror of the alarm bells into the present world and time. The despair and horror is immediate."[46] The stanza he refers to proceeds as follows:

> Hear the loud alarum bells —

> Brazen bells!
> *What* tale of terror, now, their turbulency tells!
> In the startled ear of Night
> How they scream out their affright!
> Too much horrified to speak,
> They can only shriek, shriek,
> Out of tune,
> [...]
> What a tale their terror tells
> Of despair!
> How they clang and clash and roar!
> What a horror they outpour
> In the bosom of the palpitating air![47]

The stanza expands and reintroduces themes discussed continually throughout this book. The "loud alarum bells" describe a real-world sound, which mutates in the speaker's mind not to music but to the "shriek," and the listener is not a human, but the "Night." As in the first part of this book, the "shriek" voices that which cannot be articulated, as these bells are "too horrified to speak." They are described as doing so "out of tune," or discordantly, to return to that idea of bells "jangled out of time and harsh." In this case, however, like the shriek of the black cat, they speak to the material and the demonic earthly components of death, or to the physical horror of death.

This mutates to the death associated with the shadow, the death of the unknown, the underside of the world in the next stanza, in which "the merriment and happiness foretold in stanzas one and two are fulfilled in the poem as that of the king of the Ghouls and his followers. May not the poem be said to state, therefore, that the existence of life foretells the triumph of death, which undercuts mankind's moments of purest apparent joy?"[48] The poem unfolds as follows:

> Hear the tolling of the bells—
> Iron bells!
> *What* a world of solemn thought their monody compels!
> In the silence of the night
> How we shiver with affright
> At the melancholy meaning of the tone!
> For every sound that floats
> From the rust within their throats
> Is a groan.
> And the people—ah, the people
> They that dwell up in the steeple
> All alone,
> And who, tolling, tolling, tolling,
> In that muffled monotone,
> Feel a glory in so rolling
> On the human heart a stone—

> They are neither man nor woman—
> They are neither brute nor human,
> They are Ghouls: —⁴⁹

The descriptions now mutate, bringing in language used in Poe's ballads. The stanza begins just like the other three, with a call to "Hear" the bells, but now they do not "foretell," but they "compel" a "world of solemn thought," forcing their resonance onto the present. That which compels this solemnity is, moreover, described as "monody" and the "meaning" is found in their "tone," which is in turn compared to the "groan," replicating the sound of the speaker's heart in "Ulalume." The groaning, the monody, and the single tone betoken and call out to the kind of music that lies in between the real world and the otherworldly, to the powerfully liminal. In positioning the iron bells in this way, the final stanza becomes instantly haunted, like the landscape of "Ulalume," with ghouls:

> And their king it is who tolls:—
> And he rolls, rolls, rolls, rolls
> A Pæan from the bells!
> And his merry bosom swells
> With the Pæan of the bells!
> And he dances and he yells;
> Keeping time, time, time,
> In a sort of Runic rhyme,
> To the Pæan of the bells—
> Of the bells: —⁵⁰

As Paul Williams observes, "the sound of the iron bells is three times called a *paean*, a song of triumph, which in the poem could only be sung in praise of death. The 'Runic rhyme' of stanza one reappears twice in the final stanza, and is described as 'happy,' as though its meaning is quite clear to the dancing figures of death."⁵¹ This brings up a crucial connection to another of Poe's poems, "A Pæan," which more clearly illustrates the resonances of this "song of triumph" being invoked in the context of death.

"A Pæan": The Requiem for the Loveliest Dead

"A Pæan," which transforms later into the poem "Lenore," is often considered "a steppingstone to 'The Raven,'" first published in 1845, in which Lenore is also a character.⁵² As with the other poems mentioned, death is a theme, and the words from a musical vocabulary arise in the consideration of the meeting point of the earthly and the otherworldly. The early version of the poem has a speaker describing the events leading up to the funeral of his beloved, "Helen." The poem begins:

> How shall the burial rite be read?
> The solemn song be sung?

> The requiem for the loveliest dead,
> That ever died so young?⁵³

The question at the center of this poem's beginning is constructed in a series of parallels, which draw into the notion of the "requiem" the questions "how shall" a "burial rite be read" and a "solemn song be sung." This instantly confuses the idea of reading and singing while pulling from "solemn music" as discussed in the contexts of "Fanny" and "The Sleeper"—that which associates solemnity with "learned-contemplative" models of music as opposed to the "common-active" models.⁵⁴ This divide between what defines the "common" and what defines the "contemplative" forms the thrust of the poem. The title adds to this confusion in that a "pæan" differs from any other form of song and is often attributed to "thanksgiving for deliverance, victory in battle, [. . .] (hence also) a war song invoking such victory" tied to mythology.⁵⁵ There is then also a dual notion of the "requiem" and the "pæan" as opposing in remembering death and victory. Crucially, the pæan, in being part of a specifically mythological history, is not anything Poe's readers will have heard. These connotations to the term illuminate the first few lines of the poem; the title of the poem either asks for or celebrates victory via a communication between earth and the gods, while the first few lines refer to the earthly song in a specifically Christian tradition.

> The poem continues:
> They loved her for her wealth—
> And they hated her for her pride—
> But she grew in feeble health,
> And they *love* her—that she died.
> They tell me (while they speak
> Of her "costly broider'd pall")
> That my voice is growing weak—
> That I should not sing at all—
> Or that my tone should be
> Tun'd to such solemn song
> So mournfully—so mournfully,
> That the dead may feel no wrong.⁵⁶

The speaker places himself as the defender of the woman who has died, claiming that her friends "*love* her—that she died." These implicitly false "friends" of the deceased argue that the narrator "should not sing at all" but that if he does sing, the narrator's "tone" should be "tun'd to such solemn song" that the "dead may feel no wrong." They do not name a song he must sing, but rather argue what the speaker's "tone" must be, implying he should take up the mournful tone of the requiem. The narrator knows, however, that his "tone" cannot truly be "tun'd" to "solemn song": it engenders in the crass, "common-active" mode of heard music the implications of the unheard, "learned-contemplative" prayer, to adopt Hollander's terms.[57] Instead, the narrator rejects the problematic "mournful" "requiem," and he decides "I will no requiem raise, / But waft thee on thy flight, / With a Pæan of old days."[58] Dismissing the requiem, representative of the modern, readily imagined Christian funeral, the speaker adopts the mythological pæan. Rather than sing "Of the dead — dead — who lies / All motionless," the speaker "waft[s]" her to heaven with a "Pæan."

When the poem becomes "Lenore" in a later incarnation, these ideas remain and develop ever more strongly, even though the shape of the poem itself changes. In this instance, the poem begins:

> Ah, broken is the golden bowl! — the spirit flown forever!
> Let the bell toll! — a saintly soul floats on the Stygian river: —
> [...]
> Come, let the burial rite be read — the funeral song be sung! —
> An anthem for the queenliest dead that ever died so young —
> A dirge for her the doubly dead in that she died so young.[59]

Beginning in the voice of the false friends of Lenore, this version has them directly and immediately call for the "burial rite" to be read and the "funeral song" to be sung, both iterations of audible and real-world music associated with utterance. More importantly, they call for the "bell" to "toll" for her, as her "soul floats on the Stygian river." Then the lines that began the earlier version of the poem transform here. The speaker of the earlier version of the poem is now the third person, Guy de Vere.[60] He directly responds to the poem's initial speakers:

> "Wretches! ye loved her for her wealth and ye hated her for her pride;
> And, when she fell in feeble health, ye blessed her — that she died: —
> How *shall* the ritual then be read — the requiem how be sung
> By you — by yours, the evil eye — by yours the slanderous tongue
> That did to death the innocence that died and died so young?"
> [...]
> "Avaunt! — avaunt! to friends from fiends the indignant ghost is riven —
> From Hell unto a high estate within the utmost Heaven —
> From moan and groan to a golden throne beside the King of Heaven —
> Let *no* bell toll, then, lest her soul, amid its hallowed mirth
> Should catch the note as it doth float from up the damnéd Earth!
> And I — tonight my heart is light: — no dirge will I upraise,
> But waft the angel on her flight with a Pæan of old days!"[61]

More than a too wordy, too material, too earthly insult to Lenore's spirit, the "song" that Lenore's false friends suggest becomes associated with that which actually impedes her from transcendence. These false friends are "fiends" who control Lenore's "indignant ghost," which once freed by Guy de Vere makes the transit from "moan and groan" to "Heaven," which is conspicuously absent of sound descriptors. The note carries a power in that liminal space that Lenore must pass through; the bell that tolls the single note could be something that Lenore's "soul" could "catch" in ways that pull her back toward "the damnéd Earth," a concept that the "wretches" to whom he responds clearly do not understand. Indeed, the narrator has already decided that a return to a more ancient hymn, a "pæan" to Apollo, is the only acceptable memorial for her because its musical signifiers of the "pæan" are also chosen without any sound-based, heard, or traditionally "musical" signification, more directly relating to an ancient idea of the relationship between music and poetry.

This association between the single note and death has reverberations in "The Bells," as well. Returning to that poem, it ends:

> Keeping time, time, time,
> In a sort of Runic rhyme,
> To the throbbing of the bells—
> Of the bells, bells, bells—
> To the sobbing of the bells:—
> Keeping time, time, time,
> As he knells, knells, knells,
> In a happy Runic rhyme,
> To the rolling of the bells—
> Of the bells, bells, bells:—
> To the tolling of the bells—
> Of the bells, bells, bells, bells,
> Bells, bells, bells—
> To the moaning and the groaning of the bells.[62]

Martin Roth writes about the "peculiar music" of the spondee in Poe's poetry.[63] Roth says that for Poe, meter "continues to develop as a result of the principle of equality and monotony, insuring beauty's continued existence in and through a fallen world. The development of metrics is both angelic and perverse, as all poetic acts are in Poe."[64] For Roth, Poe believes that humans are so fallen that they cannot perceive the original, more pure "simple equality" of monotony, and thus must invent rhythm to allow their fallen ears to perceive beauty at all, but such an act is necessarily a "perversion" from an ideal. Poe's "poetry represents a wild fling into decadence; it is an expression of the diseased nature of the poet in the present," such that due to their "music," his works' poetic effect is accessible to the reader, but is by nature representative of our fallen state.[65] This is true not just of the spondee but also of the subject itself of the single note in Poe's works. John Minahan describes a parallel use of bells in Keats's sonnet "Written in Disgust of Vulgar Superstition":

> The music of vulgar superstition—the melancholy tolling, the sermon's horrid sound—is unusual but ordinary; it exists specifically an other thing, exclusive of the usual form of ordinary life outside the church. By repeating "some other" and "more," Keats hammers home that sense of not-this-ness. He also demonstrates thereby that this music

involves repetition but no finer tone: again and again the bells toll, but they lead only to "more dreadful cares." This music is the basest rhetoric: like the horrid sermon, the bells are organized sounds calculated to have a particular effect. In this case the effect is not pleasure but its opposite, which perhaps becomes, for those who heed the tolling of the bells, a perverse kind of pleasure.[66]

In Poe, the bells indeed represent a kind of otherness, what Minahan calls a "not-this-ness," which act like a "horrid sermon" that reminds one of the unknown of the nonmaterial aspects of death. However, in Poe, more than a "perverse kind of pleasure," the bells are a perversion that speaks both of damnation and the ideal from which it falls. They convey a sense of the other, but they do so in an earthly fashion, for if one attempts to ascend to the ideal, as Lenore does, the single note can only pull one back to that sense of terror. Nowhere is this hierarchy more evident than in "The Masque of the Red Death."

"THE MASQUE OF THE RED DEATH": THE MUSIC SWELLS, AND THE DREAMS LIVE AND WRITHE

Poe sets the scene in ways analogous to "The Cask of Amontillado": "There were buffoons, there were improvisatori, there were ballet-dancers, there were musicians, there was Beauty, there was wine. All these and security were within. Without was the 'Red Death.'"[67] Similar to "The Shadow.—A Parable." in setting, instead of a corpse and the songs of Anacreon, there are "musicians" and "Beauty," "improvisatori" and "ballet-dancers." The main object of the story is a clock whose:

> pendulum swung to and fro with a dull, heavy, and monotonous clang; and [. . .] there came from the brazen lungs of the clock a sound which was clear and loud and deep and exceedingly musical, but of so peculiar a note and emphasis that, at each lapse of an hour, the musicians of the orchestra were constrained to pause, momentarily, in their performance, to harken to the sound; and thus the waltzers perforce ceased their evolutions; and there was a brief disconcert of the whole gay company; and, while the chimes of the clock yet rang, it was observed that the giddiest grew pale, and the more aged and sedate passed their hands over their brows as if in confused revery or meditation. But when the echoes had fully ceased, a light laughter at once pervaded the assembly; the musicians looked at each other and smiled as if at their own nervousness and folly, and made whispering vows, each to the other, that the next chiming of the clock should produce in them no similar emotion; and then, after the lapse of sixty minutes, (which embrace three thousand and six hundred seconds of the Time that flies,) there came yet another chiming of the clock, and then were the same disconcert and tremulousness and meditation as before.[68]

The human-created, earthly sounds of the orchestra must pause to the "exceedingly musical" sound of the clock, that single note that literally "exceeds" music. The clock provides an extreme version of personified sound that allows for a cursory glimpse into the beyond; although the partygoers are aware of the plague outwith the palace, the clock's note points to another lurking form of death. The sound is no longer simply rendered through the filtration of a narrator, but can be conveyed only in terms of its effect upon the souls of the company at large. Just as Poe uses breath-like qualities in his other stories to voice that which remains elusive to utterance, Poe here personifies the clock with "brazen lungs." With that small personification, the clock seems to impart unarticulated meaning to its audience, but the delineation or meaning of that sound remains absent, inferring that the sound exists for its own sake in its definition as a reference to a supernal ideal, in this case, Death. To return once more to the division between the music of the ancients and modern music, such that "modernity, by disenchanting the world, divides it" and thus modern "music is therefore divided."[69] To continue: "In the enchanted world of the ancients, music was an airy substance, it did not occupy space, it was its very essence."[70] As one looks toward that idealized past, represented as linked to the otherworldly, music intrinsically encompasses ether, atmosphere, and breath, which in this case, become darkly liminal in the clock's "brazen lungs."

This dark iteration of "music" as "an airy substance," the single note breathed from the ebony clock, takes a hierarchical place over the music of the orchestra in the scene. As Douglas Anderson notes:

> [at] first the suite seems to echo the seven unique tones of the musical scale, but "disconcert" rather than harmony arises from its design whenever the gigantic ebony clock in the black apartment begins to strike. Confronted with this fatal sign of the "stricken" hour not even Prospero's orchestra can maintain its playing. The clock's note tolerates no competitor for human attention, much as the layout of the entire suite precludes a comprehensive survey of its extent.[71]

Poe makes the image even more pointed as he continues:

> To and fro in the seven chambers there stalked, in fact, a multitude of dreams. And these —the dreams—writhed in and about, taking hue from the rooms, and causing the wild music of the orchestra to seem as the echo of their steps. And, anon, there strikes the ebony clock which stands in the hall of the velvet. And then, for a moment, all is still, and all is silent save the voice of the clock. The dreams are stiff-frozen as they stand. But the echoes of the chime die away—they have endured but an instant—and a light, half-subdued laughter floats after them as they depart. And now again the music swells, and the dreams live, and writhe to and fro more merrily than ever.[72]

Poe continues to create part of the eeriness of this passage through the subtle use of breath. The ball-goers, likened to "dreams" in a way reminiscent of the "luxury of dream" inextricably connected with "indefinitiveness" in Poe's "Marginalia," take on perversely wormlike attributes as they "stalked" and "writhed" and became "stiff-frozen" as the clock chimed.[73] The worm, an agent of death and decay, renders the "dreams," the waltzers, symbolic of death, darkness, and decay themselves as they "writhe" to the orchestra's music. The breath of the passage, voicing the unarticulated meaning that controls them all, grows from the "voice of the clock" itself, and the only other example of breath in the passage, the "half-subdued laughter," remains carefully unattributed as it floats after "them," the chimes and the dreams, as though existing as an aftereffect of the clock's voice, a partial meaning injected into the scene by the clock itself. Although there can be more than one interpretation of what the "dreams" represent, the chiming of the voice of the clock not only reminds the dancers of their fate, Death, but reinforces the hierarchy of music established in this book and the association of Death with the indefinite meaning of such sounds. That the "wild music of the orchestra" seems as the "echo of their steps" reveals the humans' entrenchment with the worldly, that they cannot escape their own frail humanity that drives their every action. That the human orchestra creates sounds that are "wild" pushes it further away from idealized sound than even the breathy voice of the clock that works in a way that creates an undefined spiritual effect upon its listeners. The human orchestra thus symbolizes the imperfect or sinful humans and their inherent loss of divinity. The dreams, "stiff-frozen as they stand," symbolically die a bit every time the clock chimes, and they are even described with the same language as Poe's "The Conqueror Worm."

The poem, consisting of five stanzas, is generally interpreted as corresponding to five acts of a play.[74] In this framework, it inverts the "*theatrum mundi* by the Elizabeth and Jacobean poetic imagination."[75] In it, the "world was viewed as a theater, the earth as a stage, life as a play from womb to tomb."[76] And then again, "the world as a stage had been filled with the Elizabethan scheme of creation from top to middle: God, the angels, man," turns upside down in Poe's poem.[77] Instead, "the implied scale is destroyed [. . .]. The angels retain their customary seats but lose their guardian function. The great chain is disrupted, its links are rearranged."[78] The poem begins:

> Lo! 'tis a gala night
> Within the lonesome latter years!
> An angel throng, bewinged, bedight
> In veils, and drowned in tears,
> Sit in a theatre, to see
> A play of hopes and fears,
> While the orchestra breathes fitfully

The music of the spheres.[79]

The "angel throng" is "bedight / In veils," as though the "gala night" is but a funeral. Moreover, the "veils" hark back to the notion introduced in chapter 4, that Poe calls "'Art,' [. . .] 'the reproduction of what the Senses perceive in Nature through the veil of the soul.' [. . .] The naked Senses sometimes see too little—but then *always* they see too much."[80] The idea of Art in an ideal, rather than a practical sense, returns along with the soul taking on a dual incarnation as breath. Thus, when the "orchestra breathes fitfully," there is a problematized mutable image of the angels interpreting the world through the "veils" of the soul, an interpretation reflected in the fitful breath that does not articulate, but informs or voices struggle. That this fitful breathing is tied to the notion of the music of the spheres resonates with failure of universal proportions. The orchestra, outside the world's stage, is reciprocally affected by the broken connection to the world, by the earth's failure. Whereas all the other examples of this book that connect to the notion of the music of the spheres focus on the earthly viewpoint, this speaks of the celestial suffering, as well.

NOTES

1. Kramer, *Music and Poetry*, 139.
2. Poe, Rev. of *Alciphron*, 337.
3. Poe, "Eldorado," 1–12.
4. Ibid., 15, 21.
5. Poe, "Sonnet—Silence," 1–15.
6. Poe, "The Raven," 11–12.
7. Pollin, "Poe's 'Eldorado,'" 234.
8. Fagin, *Histrionic Mr. Poe*, 153.
9. Poe, "Shadow," 188.
10. Ibid.
11. Ibid., 189.
12. Ibid., 190.
13. Michael Williams, *World of Words*, 58.
14. Hollander, *Untuning of the Sky*, 129.
15. Michael Williams, *World of Words*, 58.
16. Poe, "Shadow," 190.
17. Douglas Anderson, *Pictures of Ascent*, 36.
18. Ibid., 37.
19. Poe, "Shadow," 191.
20. Poe, "Tale of the Ragged Mountains," 944.
21. Poe, "Conversation of Eiros," 456.
22. Michael Williams, *World of Words*, 59.
23. Ibid., 55.
24. Peter Dayan, *Music Writing Literature*, 98.
25. Ibid., 97.
26. See Daniel Hoffman, *Poe*; Rodriguez, "Parody and Language"; Sweet, "Retapping."
27. Daniel Hoffman, *Poe*, 218–19.
28. Poe, "Cask of Amontillado," 1257.
29. Burke, *Popular Culture*, 268.

30. Poe, "Cask of Amontillado," 1257.
31. Rodriguez, "Parody and Language," 44.
32. Poe, "Cask of Amontillado," 1258–60.
33. Foucault, *Madness and Civilization*, 14.
34. Ibid., 15.
35. Ibid., 16.
36. Ibid.
37. Poe, "Cask of Amontillado," 1263.
38. Foucault, *Madness and Civilization*, 16.
39. Poe, "Colloquy of Monos," 614.
40. Ibid. See also Poe's "Marginalia," 1322, in which Poe writes, "The orange ray of the spectrum and the buzz of the gnat (which never rises above the second A), affect me with nearly similar sensations. In hearing the gnat, I perceive the color. In perceiving the color, I seem to hear the gnat."
41. Ibid., 613–14.
42. Poe, "Pit and the Pendulum," 682.
43. Poe, "Bells," 1–14.
44. Leppert, *Sight of Sound*, 64.
45. Poe, "Bells," 15–35.
46. Paul Williams, "A Reading," 24.
47. Poe, "Bells," 36–43, 52–56.
48. Paul Williams, "A Reading," 25.
49. Poe, "Bells," 70–87.
50. Ibid., 88–97.
51. Paul Williams, "A Reading," 25.
52. Mabbott, *Edgar Allan Poe: Complete Poems*, 330.
53. Poe, "A Pæan," 1–4.
54. Hollander, *Untuning of the Sky*, 256.
55. "Pæan," n. *Oxford English Dictionary*.
56. Poe, "A Pæan," 9–20.
57. Hollander, *Untuning of the Sky*, 256.
58. Poe, "A Pæan," 38–40.
59. Poe, "Lenore," 1–2, 5–7.
60. Ibid., 3.
61. Ibid., 5–9, 20–26.
62. Poe, "The Bells," 98–112.
63. Martin Roth, "Poe's Divine Spondee," 16.
64. Ibid., 15.
65. Ibid., 16.
66. Minahan, *Word Like a Bell*, 52.
67. Poe, "Masque of the Red Death," 671.
68. Ibid. 672–73.
69. Chua, *Absolute Music*, 23.
70. Ibid., 52.
71. Douglas Anderson, *Pictures of Ascent*, 151.
72. Poe, "Masque of the Red Death," 673–74.
73. Poe, "Marginalia," 1331.
74. Lubbers, "Poe's 'The Conqueror Worm,'" 375.
75. Ibid., 377.
76. Ibid.
77. Ibid., 378.
78. Ibid.
79. Poe, "Conqueror Worm," 1–8.
80. Poe, "Marginalia," 1458.

Conclusion

> Regarding, then, Beauty as my province, my next question referred to the *tone* of its highest manifestation—and all experience has shown that this tone is one of *sadness*. Beauty of whatever kind, in its supreme development, invariably excites the sensitive soul to tears. Melancholy is thus the most legitimate of all the poetical tones.
> —Edgar Allan Poe, "Philosophy of Composition"

Harold Bloom, famously critical of Poe in varying ways, concedes this: Poe is "inescapable [. . .]: he dreamed universal nightmares."[1] I believe that we never see Poe's universal nightmare in such exquisite detail as when we look at his use of music. By untangling the musical spectrum in Poe's works, one framed upon a hierarchy of divinity, we see Poe's vast network of hopes and fears.

At the base of this hierarchy is real-world music, defined in this book through Richard Leppert's terms as "experienced as sound via the sense of hearing," as that which "refers to notated 'instructions' for producing such sounds," and as that which "is a sight, a richly semantic visual representation."[2] Real-world music transforms in Poe's works into words, into utterance. When that which is best described as akin to real-world music appears without the theme of madness, it is only in earthly love stories, such as in "The Spectacles" and Poe's poetic "songs" "Eulalie" and "Song." When that which is best described as akin to real-world music appears with the theme of madness, as in "The System of Doctor Tarr and Professor Fether" and "Four Beasts in One," music maintains its association with words, but also becomes harsh, discordant, and representative of the "animal in man" that "no longer has any value as a sign of a Beyond."[3] Liminal music, however, separates words from music. While yearning for an ancient mythological past that unified the two, Poe's liminal protagonists can move beyond the too earthly implications of real-world music only by separating utterance from that which is musically voiced. As they move further and further away from real-world music, utterance begins to dissipate, and the reader is left with only a narrative interpretation of that which is enigmatically musically communicated. In doing so, that which is musically voiced becomes less and less describable in terms of the audible; music becomes more and more silent. Yet Poe's characters cannot continue to indefinitely ascend along this hierarchy toward the Silent, the Musical, in terms of that ancient chain of being that moved from earth to God. Humans are fallen, the chain has broken, and as we ascend we are less able to perceive Silence in our states; instead, that which incorporates deformity and darkness, a more liminal and fallen music, becomes a perversity that still points heavenward.

In his "Marginalia," Poe alludes to music in the real-world sense as being distinguished from the other types of music this book explores: "In speaking of song-writing, I mean, of course, the composition of brief poems with an eye to their adaptation for music in the vulgar sense."[4] This quotation leads into one of the passages that convince those like Burton Pollin to believe that Poe wrote his poems to be adapted to music in the real-world sense, but the ways in which Poe transforms the term "music" are inherent in this single line. Music "in the vulgar sense" is that which is associated with the real-world, the heard, the playable, or all that which is allied with this book's definition of it via Leppert. A similar divide between music "in the vulgar sense" and other forms of music arises in Poe's reviews in ways that reflect the themes tied to real-world music in this book. In one of his reviews of others' poetry, Poe argues that "the 'thunder-drum of Heaven' is bathetic and grotesque in the highest degree—a commingling of the most sublime music of Heaven with the most utterly contemptible and common-place of Earth."[5] That "thunder-drum" cannot represent the heavenly because it is too associated with the real world, with the force of sound, whereas Poe's conceptualization of "the most sublime music of Heaven" must remain inaudible. Poe uses a similar comparison between the "lewd fiddling minstrels" and a higher kind of musician in his "Marginalia," in claiming that "indefinitiveness [is] recognized by every musician who is not a mere fiddler, as an important point in the philosophy of his science—as the *soul*, indeed, of the sensations derivable from its practice—sensations which bewilder while they enthrall—and which would *not* so enthrall if they did not so bewilder."[6]

In this way, liminality presents a more complex case in Poe. Moving beyond the notion of real-world music as the base of Poe's musical hierarchy, or "music in the vulgar sense," that music that arises in narratives in which madness represents "strange knowledge, from that fantastic plain, from the underside of the world," or in which characters are caught between the earthly and the heavenly as a divine unknown, takes on paradoxical status that points toward the divine.[7] Returning to the anecdote of Maria Malibran singing for a patient, the complexities that arise when music in Poe's works is less representative of real-world music are formulated in the story:

> Madame Malibran approached a piano which stood in the chamber, and ran her fingers over the keys. In an instant the poor maniac was all attention. She sang the romance in Otello. "Is this divine?" exclaimed the young man, and he appeared violently excited. "No," he added,

"this is the voice of a woman": then bursting into tears, he threw himself into a chair and sobbed aloud.[8]

This story resonates deeply with Poe's notion that "when music affects us to tears, seemingly causeless, we weep *not*, as Gravina supposes, from 'excess of pleasure' but through excess of an impatient, petulant sorrow that, as mere mortals, we are as yet in no condition to banquet upon those supernal ecstasies of which the music affords us merely a suggestive and indefinite glimpse."[9] Thus, in stories, such as "The Fall of the House of Usher," or in poems, such as "Tamerlane," Poe complicates and obscures music, rendering it less allied with real-world music, to voice without articulation the divine that "mere mortals" cannot access. This inaccessible beyond constructs itself with both demonic and heavenly implications: the beyond is both the terrifying unknown associated with death and the hope of the heavenly hereafter.

The mystery of the otherworldly arises from the context of the music of the spheres. That, in Daniel Chua's terms, what "the Romantics discovered as absolute music was a mere shadow of what Pythagoras formulated two thousand years earlier, for the absolute music he bequeathed to humanity was not so much a music to be composed as a music that composed the world."[10] The "'taut string' stretched between heaven and earth, [. . .] able to conceptualise the unitary structure of the entire cosmos" has broken in Poe's oeuvre, a rupture that paradoxically gives birth to a number of tropes that, in their failure, point to the beyond, such as bells, breath, and the single note.[11] In this way, when Baudelaire described Poe as having "uttered the ardent sighs of *the fallen angel who remembers heaven*," his description of Poe's utterance as "ardent sighs" alone in the context of "fallen angel who remembers heaven" reflexively ties together the absence of articulation in the stead of breath, which itself voices a failure that paradoxically points heavenward.[12] Rather than the music of the spheres being silent to human ears due to their continual drone, the music of the spheres has been Silenced, forced into a separate realm of the Timeless, the Divine, or the Musical. Separately, the earthly has been made more audible, recircumscribed into its own realm of time, the fallen, and the vulgarly musical.

Despite its failings, the presence of Music as an idea becomes Poe's tool most closely allied with his conception of higher art literature. Returning to Peter Dayan's notion of the Barthesian Orphic myth, the literary is closely associated to the Musical, as that the "moment at which Orpheus turns and sees her is the moment [. . .] in which the shade would [. . .] acquire a name; at that moment, literature would die. To sing well is to avoid that naming."[13] For Poe, poetry becomes a kind of metonym for literature in its highest form. Poe writes,

> Poetry has never been defined to the satisfaction of all parties. Perhaps, in the present condition of language it never will be. Words cannot

hem it in. Its intangible and purely spiritual nature refuses to be bound down within the widest horizon of mere sounds. But it is not, therefore, misunderstood — at least, not by all men is it misunderstood. Very far from it. If, indeed, there be any one circle of thought distinctly and palpably marked out from amid the jarring and tumultuous chaos of human intelligence, it is the evergreen and radiant Paradise which the true poet knows, and knows alone, as the limited realm of his authority — as the circumscribed Eden of his dreams.[14]

This description of poetry is closely allied to those qualities of the Musical described throughout this book. The additional notion that Poe reveals in this quotation is key to understanding why; Poe argues that there is a "circumscribed Eden" of the poet's "dreams," an "evergreen and radiant Paradise which the true poet knows, and knows alone." Poe never describes the poet conveying this "circumscribed Eden" in words, but rather couches it in a description of poetry that refuses to "be bound down within the widest horizon of mere sounds." Indeed, the sounds themselves would engender a failure. This mirrors another interpretation of Music in terms of this Orphic myth, as Peter Dayan posits: "True love is the love of a shadow that is always only in the process of coming to life, and can never be named; music, the discourse which cannot name, is the proof of its possibility. Literature, although the musical analogy permits its existence as an art, is always threatened by the possibility of naming."[15] Going on to quote and translate Barthes, Dayan elaborates:

> "This Mallarmean language is Orpheus who can only save what he loves by renouncing it, and who nonetheless turns round just a little; it is Literature brought to the gates of the Promised Land, which is to say the gates of a world without literature, to which it would nonetheless be the duty of writers to bear witness." Why should the promised land be a land without literature? Because [. . .] it would be a land of full and immediate presence; the truth would be there, before us; it would need no translators or interpreters. In this land, each name would be perfectly adequate and transparent to its sense. [. . .] Literature uses music to prove the possibility of a discourse that signifies without naming; music needs literature to articulate that proof, without which (as was generally the case before the nineteenth century) listeners might happily allow themselves to believe that music did indeed convey a meaning. Between them is "le chant": the voice not as a vehicle for communicating a message, but as the material presence of the signifying process itself.[16]

Just as Dayan argues in this context that true "love is the love of a shadow that is always only in the process of coming to life," that which moves beyond into the realm of the otherworldly, either through death or through a failure from an ancient unity, becomes a "shadow" or a shade that can take up either demonic or heavenly associations. Moreover, it becomes that which is "always only in the process of coming to life" through Music as a signification "without naming," much in the same way that Poe argues that the *"indefinite* is an element in the true ποιησις,"[17] or "'making' that which *is not yet*; what is 'made' is not the poetized."[18] Thus, when Poe directly ties the indefinite to the Musical, asking, "Why do some persons fatigue themselves in attempts to unravel such fantasy-pieces as the 'Lady of Shalott?' As well unweave the *'ventum textilem.'* [. . .] I *know* that indefinitiveness is an element of the true music—I mean of the true musical expression," he ties together a continual sense of "making."[19] Just as in Dayan's context "love is the love of a shadow that is always only in the process of coming into life," in Poe's works, Music continually "makes" the sense of the "shadow," the beyond, the Silent otherworldly that can never be fully brought into definitive being. The weaving of the *"ventum textilem,"* the woven air that conflates notions of the soul, the breath, the spirit, with Music, the music of the spheres, becomes so central to Poe because it symbolizes the continual "process of coming into life" of that which cannot be understood by any of the five senses, that which cannot be definitively pinned to the real world.

NOTES

1. Bloom, *Bloom's Classic*, xi.
2. Leppert, *Sight of Sound*, 64.
3. Foucault, *Madness and Civilization*, 73.
4. Poe, "Marginalia," 1435.
5. Poe, Rev. of *The Culprit Fay*, 529.
6. Poe, "Marginalia," 1435.
7. Foucault, *Madness and Civilization*, 12.
8. Merlin and Malibran, *Memoirs and Letters*, 1: 214.
9. Poe, "Marginalia," 1313.
10. Chua, *Absolute Music*, 15.
11. Ibid., 77.
12. Baudelaire, *Baudelaire on Poe*, 126.
13. Peter Dayan, *Music Writing Literature*, 97.
14. Poe, Rev. of *The Culprit Fay*, 509.
15. Peter Dayan, *Music Writing Literature*, 98.
16. Ibid., 99.
17. Poe, "Marginalia," 1331.
18. Heidegger, *The Event*, 279.
19. Poe, "Marginalia," 1331.

Appendix

> The great variety of melodious expression which is given out from the keys of a piano, might be made, in proper hands, the basis of an excellent fairy-tale. Let the poet press his finger steadily upon each key, keeping it down, and imagine each prolonged series of undulations the history, of joy or of sorrow, related by a good or evil spirit imprisoned within. There are some of the notes which almost tell, of their own accord, true and intelligible histories.
> —Edgar Allan Poe, "Chapter of Suggestions"

As discussed in the introduction and chapter 1 of this book, Poe rarely cites real-world music. Apart from Poe's possible allusions to Maria Malibran and Henriette Lalande, discussed in chapter 1, Poe cites only one other singer in all of his creative works. In "The Purloined Letter," Dupin describes the Minister's downfall with the metaphor "in all kinds of climbing, as Catalini [sic] said of singing, it is far more easy to get up than to come down."[1] In "A Decided Loss," he puns that "two cats [. . .] leapt up simultaneously with a flourish a la Catalani."[2] (One endearing trait of Poe's is his apparent fondness for cat puns. Mary Louise Shew reminisced of Poe's cat: "He called her 'Catarina': she seemed possessed. I was nervous and almost afraid of his wonderful cat.")[3] In "Von Jung, the Mystific," the narrator claims, "I have seen Sontag received with hisses, and a hurdy-gurdy with sighs."[4]

As with Malibran, Poe would not have seen Catalani perform; she never performed in the United States, and he would have just missed her presence in London when he was there as a child. An article entitled "Madame Catalani" from an 1849 edition of *Chambers's Edinburgh Journal* cites her travels: "Madame Catalani arrived in London in December 1806," and she "came to Paris in 1814."[5] The Poe family did not arrive in Great Britain until 1815.[6] Malibran's memoirs also mention Catalani,[7] but the memoirs were not published until 1840 and "A Decided Loss" was published in 1832. So Poe must have discovered Catalani in another source. Certainly, neither reference relies upon personal experience of Catalani's performances: the first pun plays on Catalani's attributed words, rather than her music. The same is true of Sontag in that she never performed in the United States and her London performances occurred long after Poe was there, but she was also so famous "that the term 'Sontag fever' gained general currency, and she was similarly idolized everywhere."[8] These pieces of information begin to reveal that, although we know Poe has some interest in music, pinning down his real knowledge and experience of it is very difficult, indeed.

AN INHERITED MUSICAL TALENT

Yet the idea that Poe was musically inclined, or that musical influences surrounded him in one way or another, often informs critical analyses of Poe's literary connection to music. Charmenz Lenhart begins her chapter on Poe in her book *Musical Influence on American Poetry* with the claim that "Poe is one of the most musical poets America has produced," and she goes on to argue that "Poe's personal interest in and talent for music were hereditary."[9] Edgar was just "nearly three" years old at the time of his mother's death,[10] but Lenhart posits that Poe's musicality is genetic, or that he "inherited [. . .] musical talent" from his mother.[11] Lenhart justifies her claim that Poe "inherited" his "musical talent" with evidence showing that "he was something of a flutist,"[12] an idea propagated to the present day that, when traced, seems farfetched.[13]

When biographers write about Poe playing the flute, they reflect the story that Poe would accompany his childhood friend Elmira Royster as she played the piano.[14] Hervey Allen writes, "during the Summer and Fall of 1825," Poe would "slip over to the Royster House nearby and [. . .] spend long hours in the parlour with Elmira. She played the piano and they would sing together, Edgar in a fresh young tenor voice, or he would accompany her upon the flute which he played quite well."[15] Allen's only evidence for constructing this musical tryst stems from interviews Royster gave to Edward Valentine in 1875, fifty years later, interviews I've yet to find.[16] We do know, however, that J. Allan, Poe's adopted father, bought at auction in 1812 a flute for twenty-one dollars, which H. Allen suggests is "the same flute upon which Edgar Allan Poe afterwards learned to play in those early, easy days in Richmond which were to permeate his dreams."[17] Poe would have been a toddler at the time.

Along with his flute playing, Poe's singing voice is also romanticized in some critical pieces. Lenhart maintains that "Poe's speaking as well as his singing voice has been frequently praised. It was said that he literally sang his more musical poems,"[18] and similar anecdotes of Poe's speaking and singing voice abound.[19] Other writers claim that Poe's voice was "melodious" even when not singing or reciting one of his pieces. Mary Gove Nichols claims that in speaking, Poe's "voice was melody itself," and Thomas Chivers goes so far as to argue that Poe's "voice was soft, mellow, melodious, and rather more flexible than powerful. It was as musical as Apollo's Lute, and as plaintive in its utterances of his Memnonian Mysteries."[20] Whether the claims are that Poe could sing well, that his voice transformed to the "melodious" when reciting his poetry or that his voice was "musical" when he spoke, writers have perpetuated the image of the musically inclined Poe.

The critical attention to the possibility of Poe's musical abilities does not end with his own singing and alleged flute playing. Lenhart, among others, has also focused on the fact that Poe's young wife Virginia's "fatal illness was ascribed in its day to the rupture of a blood-vessel while she was singing,"[21] a dark romantic image originating with Poe himself. In a letter to George W. Eveleth, Poe laments:

> Six years ago, a wife, whom I loved as no man ever loved before, ruptured a blood-vessel in singing. Her life was despaired of. [. . .] At the end of a year the vessel broke again—[. . .] Again in about a year afterward. Then again—again—again and even once again at varying intervals. [. . .] I became insane, with long intervals of horrible sanity.[22]

Poe's letter describes Virginia's extended decline resulting from a "'death-in-life,' as many people then referred to tuberculosis."[23] Yet, when that anecdote appears in some biographies, the rupture while singing implicitly leads to Virginia's immediate demise. Although it is more accurate to say, as Silverman does, that Virginia "was hemorrhaging from her lungs" over an extended time, critics and biographers prefer to incorporate the detail that she was singing when she "began to bleed from her mouth."[24] Even Silverman begins the paragraph describing Virginia's death with the notion: "The son of a celebrated singer, Poe always encouraged Virginia's own taste for singing,"[25] an idea stemming from Virginia's mother, Maria Clemm, who writes on August 19, 1860, that "Eddie finished Virginia's education himself, and, I assure you, she was highly cultivated. She was an excellent linguist, and a perfect musician."[26] The story, in which Virginia's musicality is defined and influenced by Edgar's, leads to a conflation of Poe's work with the legend of his wife dying in an anti–swan song.

D. H. Lawrence exemplifies the ways in which this anecdote has made its way into some criticism, writing that Poe's "grand attempt and achievement was with his wife; his cousin, a girl with a singing voice. [. . .] It was the intensest nervous vibration of unison, pressed higher and higher in pitch, till the blood-vessels of the girl broke, and the blood began to flow out loose. It was love."[27] In the same piece, Lawrence figures Poe as a "vampire"; Lawrence's defining Virginia as "a girl with a singing voice," in the terms of this aesthetic, links Virginia's blood with her "singing voice," and Poe's pressing her in "nervous vibration" until the "blood-vessels of the girl broke" compounds the images of her singing and his vampirism.[28] Lawrence goes so far as to argue that, to Poe, "the woman, his wife [. . .] was Ligeia,"[29] merging Virginia with one of Poe's characters often associated with music. Lawrence uses the story surrounding Virginia's death to create a mythical connection between Poe and music through the medium of Virginia's own musicality. Ultimately, in spite of the romanticized image of the musical Poe to which some critics subscribe, one cannot prove Poe's extraliterary musicality. The notions that he could sing and play the flute or that he inherited musical talent are based on anecdote, romance, and conjecture.

THE IDEA WITHOUT MUSIC: DECONTEXTUALIZING POE

What we do know about Poe is that he incorporates music in his creative works in a way that develops a story of its own, a story that needs to be uncovered before we can connect Poe's literary music to Poe's historical, literary, or theoretical contexts. It is for this very reason that I decontextualize Poe in this book. Yet, once decontextualized, Poe himself does not leave much at all for anyone to even piece together his understanding of music in an extraliterary space. Studies of Poe and music either begin or end with Poe's own oft-quoted cornerstone definition of music:

> I know that indefinitiveness is an element of the true music—I mean of the true musical expression. Give to it any undue decision—imbue it with any very determinate tone—and you deprive it, at once, of its ethereal, its ideal, its intrinsic and essential character. You dispel its luxury of dream. You dissolve the atmosphere of the mystic upon which it floats. You exhaust it of its breath of fäery. It now becomes a tangible and easy appreciable idea—a thing of the earth, earthy. It has not, indeed, lost its power to please, but all which I consider the distinctiveness of that power. And to the uncultivated talent, or to the unimaginative apprehension, this deprivation of its most delicate grace will be, not unfrequently, a recommendation. A determinateness of expression is sought—and often by composers who should know better—is sought as a beauty rather than rejected as a blemish.[30]

Rather than being indefinite or indefinable, both of which convey a total lack of definition whatsoever, music's "indefinitiveness" connotes a quality of multiple elusive meanings, leading us to believe that we understand these meanings implicitly and can understand them only implicitly, or we destroy its "intrinsic and essential character." Residing at the center of this nondefined definition we are warned not to unpack the mystery of the "true musical expression." We must ask ourselves what that entails and whether Poe believes that such an expression is accomplished only in heard music, music on the page, or whether it is also inherent in poetry (heard or unheard) or prose (heard or unheard).

One looks to Poe's definitions of poetry and prose for an answer, definitions that are nearly indistinguishable by his own theory, and both of which are complicated by his describing them in musical terms. Poe writes, for instance, of Frances Osgood, "her prose is merely poetry in disguise. [. . .] a scrap of verse renders itself manifest; then another and another;—then comes a poem outright, and then another and another and another, with little odd batches of prose in between, until at length the mask is thrown fairly off and far away, and the whole article—sings."[31]

In this quotation alone, not only does Poe conflate the forms of poetry and prose such that they can be found within one another without any of the traditional indicators of form, but he also conflates poetry and song by substituting that the article "sings" for the article becoming poetry. It seems then, that poetry, by Poe's definition, can be take in the same form as prose but with a different, more sacred, subject matter. Because of the subject matter, it inhabits a more lofty order than prose without that subject—but then we are left with the question of what a sacred or lofty subject matter might be. Still, Poe continues to justify this hierarchy:

> A poem, in my opinion, is opposed to a work of science by having, for its immediate object, pleasure, not truth; to romance, by having for its object an indefinite instead of a definite pleasure, being a poem only so far as this object is attained; romance presenting perceptible images with definite, poetry with indefinite sensations, to which end music is an essential, since the comprehension of sweet sound is our most indefinite conception. Music, when combined with a pleasurable idea, is poetry; music without idea is simply music; the idea without music is prose from its very definitiveness.[32]

Setting aside for the moment that, when unraveled, this is merely a stream of indefinite sensations and pleasurable ideas, this appears to reveal a hierarchy that holds poetry above prose. As Thompson explains,

> This particular passage is remarkable for its succinct setting forth of the concerns regarding the nature and function of poetry that will preoccupy Poe to the end of his life [. . .]. Poe's emphasis on music, as the most abstract and mathematical, the least earthbound of the arts, becomes more insistent in later essays. In addition to this abstract indefinitiveness, however, another element, also indefinite, but terrible rather than supernally beautiful, lurks in the background.[33]

The element Thompson describes is the circumscription of the poet's power, and the "paradox of the poet's limitation is also his source of inspiration."[34] In short, this passage gestures toward the importance of music, a possible hierarchy of artistic media, and the struggle of the poet.

Then again, Poe also writes that he has "always regarded the Tale (using this word in its popular acceptation) as affording the best prose opportunity for display of the highest talent. It has peculiar advantages which the novel does not admit. It is, of course, a far finer field than the essay. It even has points of superiority over the poem."[35] While Poe allows the poet access only to the sacred, he writes that a prose work may have "points of superiority over the poem." If indeed these ideas coexist in Poe's mind, there must be something else that defines poetry and prose for Poe beyond that of subject matter.

In fact, as much as Poe obscures his distinction of poetry and prose, he does the same for music and both genres. While many of Poe's descriptions of music could be substituted for that of poetry, Poe does not necessarily preclude tales in his writings on music in literature. He explains that "when music affects us to tears, seemingly causeless, we weep not, as Gravina supposes, from 'excess of pleasure' but through excess of an impatient, petulant sorrow that, as mere mortals, we are as yet in no condition to banquet upon those supernal ecstasies of which the music affords us merely a suggestive and indefinite glimpse."[36] He implies here that music arrives in subject matter and not in form. While music affects the listener in the way that Poe hopes that Ideal Poetry should, by affording the listener or reader a "suggestive and indefinite glimpse" of "supernal ecstasies," the question then becomes how Poe defines music and how he believes it is related to, or used in, poetry and prose. The key for that relationship lies in the effect that both are meant to convey.

As Jerome McGann argues, "Poe's theory is procedural: to know what poetry is you want to observe how it works, and you only achieve that if, like a scientist investigating electricity, you experiment with its actual resources and possibilities."[37] Poe scholars might agree that, no matter their individual determinations of Poe's use of the terms, the way he conceives of poetry, prose, and music remains staunchly difficult to pin down. At least, we may all agree that, according to Poe, *Music, then, is the ideal subject matter of literature embodied*. Music injects an indefinable, yet distinctive feeling of reaching toward God into art. Music, however the artist achieves it, is the primary tool for poetry to attain the same effect. "Determinateness" may be left to the less powerful arts, to unsuccessful poems, to less successful stories, and to essays and criticism altogether, for those do not strive for a spiritual ideal.

The artist is then caught between two worlds. While he may never understand or express fully the supernal beauty of heaven, the full expression of purely worldly things is nothing more than imitation, lacking imagination. And now we are right back where we started. And even with all of his vague definitions of the arts, Poe clearly and separately published his tales from his poems, never conflating the two until his publication of *Eureka—A Prose Poem*, an exception too large to address here. Like *Eureka*, however, the subject matter of this book is often macrocosmic. Incorporating too much of Poe's culture, from the economy of literature, to literature's material history, to cultural and literary historical narratives, would render meaningless any initial foray into Poe's own understanding of music. Because Poe is so obscure when it comes to his use of music, one must untangle his language on its own terms, but he makes even this impossible.

For Poe, the ideal Music our art can never achieve is prelapsarian. We are completely excluded from that past state, so music conveys our dispossession of Eden. Music, in its current and lesser state, represents an attempt to escape from the myths of history and time. Humanity's fall, unheard music, and the escape into timelessness all tie in Poe directly with the idea of absolute music, around which I center my narrative in this book.

"THE RATIONAL AGENT OF ENCHANTMENT ITSELF": ABSOLUTE MUSIC AND THE MUSIC OF THE SPHERES

I primarily use Daniel Chua's language to show the ways Poe conceived of ideal Music. This ideal Music hinges upon concepts of absolute music and the music of the spheres. I chose Chua because here is a strange kinship between his contemporary scholarship and Edgar Allan Poe's creative oeuvre. Daniel Chua's work merges the idea of the music of the spheres with the historical development of the concept of absolute music. He explains the Pythagorean concept of the music of the spheres as follows:

> In Plato's account of creation, music tunes the cosmos according to the Pythagorean ratios of 2:1, 3:2, 4:3 and 9:8, and scales the human soul to the same proportions. This enabled the inaudible sounds of the heavens to vibrate within the earthly soul, and, conversely, for the audible tones of human music to reflect the celestial spheres, so that heaven and earth could be harmonized within the unity of a well-tuned scale. This scale came to be pictured as a monochord that connected the stars to the earth like a long piece of string that vibrated the structure of the universe. Its geometric and astral mathematics represented the binding order of an immutable and crystalline world. So music, as the invisible and inaudible harmony of the spheres, imposed a unity over creation, linking everything along the entire chain of being. [. . .] When music moves, the earth moves with it. Thus music was not simply an object in a magical world, but the *rational agent of enchantment itself.*[38]

Chua's own development of the concept of absolute music takes on a much more mythological and spiritual flavor than other traditional definitions of absolute music. Carl Dahlhaus's working definition of absolute music, for instance, focuses on the development of the nineteenth-century use of the term; absolute music is "independent instrumental music [. . .] consist[ing] of the conviction that instrumental music purely and clearly expresses the true nature of music by its very lack of concept, object, and purpose."[39] Yet Chua adds to this, as seen in the quote above, as he argues that what "the Romantics discovered as absolute music was a mere shadow of what Pythagoras formulated two thousand years earlier, for the absolute music he bequeathed to humanity was not so much a music to be composed as a music that composed the world."[40] In other words, Chua believes that when the German Romantics unveiled their belief in an ideal and pure Music, they were doing so from an actual modern and broken condition, from a postlapsarian standpoint. This holds true for Chua and for Poe, even though the fall of humankind is admittedly difficult for either to pinpoint: "Exactly when the world became modern is difficult to gauge."[41] More than speaking metaphorically, Chua really believes in the metaphysical loss of our ancient Musical ideality—I do not—yet, I think that in many ways, Poe's works themselves (not to be conflated with Poe the individual) deeply parallel Chua's argument.[42]

Rather than the "inaudible sounds" of the heavens that vibrated in the "earthly soul," Poe sees music in its modern condition as vulgarly "heard," "real," and "earthly," and the notion of music as "inaudible" represents a dead connection to the "invisible" and the "otherworldly." As I said, I do not subscribe to Chua's rendering of a musical history that explains a fallen modernity, but it illustrates Poe's expression of a real, audible, or to use Chua's terms, "demythologised music with an empirical rationality," which constantly wars with unreclaimable celestial inaudible music.[43]

This cosmic perspective grants us a nuanced background with which we can look at Poe's works with fresh eyes. For instead of believing that this tuned cosmos still exists, Poe's works reveal a cosmos aligned with Chua's, one that is a shadow, a failure of its former self, reflective of the downfall of humanity. That Pythagorean notion of the "taut string" becomes Poe's "strange sound, as of a harp-string broken."[44] Music of the spheres lowers into a "mere shadow," as Chua posits, of its former self, silent and wholly separated from the fallen modern condition.[45] Poe is no pure Romantic though. More than the Romantics, for whom "the absolute was an 'infinite yearning' for the 'spirit realm,'" Poe recognizes in his yearning the totality of separation between the earth and the ethereal, the present and the mythological past, words and music.[46]

In Poe's cosmic universe, it is easy to see that if there is a point of rupture between the modern world and an ancient Pythagorean universe in which "music tunes the cosmos [. . .] and scales the human soul to the same proportions," the human soul must have ruptured as well.[47] To find the language to describe the soul's break in Poe's work, I turn to Foucault. He famously describes history in terms of "that zero point in the course of madness at which madness is an undifferentiated experience, a not yet divided experience of division itself."[48] Just as Foucault interrogates the modern understanding of insanity as that point "which relegates Reason and Madness to one side or the other [. . .] as things henceforth external, deaf to all exchange, and as though dead to one another," Poe also negotiates a parallel fissure in reason and madness.[49] Because of this fissure, for Poe, Romantic transcendence is impossible.

Indeed, Poe differentiates himself from both Romanticism and that, as Blasing remarks, "which Harold Bloom terms the 'American Sublime,'" or that "integration of the angelic imagination with natural law," such that Poe's work "can only confirm the absolute separation of the eternal and temporal worlds."[50] But, more than this, I find that we may argue far beyond, as Blasing states,

> while the poet can hear the music of the spheres—a harmony that precludes sounds [. . .] —he cannot "name" this "silence" without the means of the music of verse [. . .]. The poet has authority over "the circumscribed Eden" of dreams; the circumscribing or defining words subscribe to another authority and are subject to time and history, thus rendering the dreamed-of paradise unspeakable and unrecoverable. This paradise is both a radiant center before time and a nature before history.[51]

Although I agree that Poe's "poet," or representative voice in his tales and prose fiction, finds his "dreamed-of paradise unspeakable and unrecoverable," that "radiant center before time and history," I argue that he cannot "name" that "harmony that precludes sounds" of the music of the spheres *precisely because he cannot "hear" it.*

NOTES

1. Poe, "Purloined Letter," 993.
2. Poe, "A Decided Loss," 57.
3. See Ingram, "Unpublished Correspondence," 423.
4. Poe, "Von Jung, the Mystific," 294.
5. "Madame Catalani," 344.
6. Quinn, *Edgar Allan Poe*, 65.
7. Merlin and Malibran, *Memoirs and Letters*, 1: lix.
8. "Sontag, Henriette," *Northeastern Dictionary*.
9. Lenhart, *Musical Influence*, 125. Lenhart writes that Poe's grandmother "was one of the most famous vocalists at Covent Garden Theatre Royal" and that his mother, Eliza, was "fine as a vocalist in the light operas of the day." (ibid.) Recently, Kenneth Silverman specified that Eliza Poe was an "admired singer [. . .] [who] became particularly associated with a song entitled 'Nobody Coming to Marry Me.'" See Silverman, *Edgar A. Poe*, 4.
10. Ibid., 9.
11. Lenhart, *Musical Influence*, 126.
12. Ibid., 127.
13. Margaret Hrabe, e-mail message to author, March 13, 2012.
14. See Ackroyd, *Poe*, 23.
15. See Allen, *Israfel*, 119.
16. John Ingram's *Edgar Allan Poe: His Life, Letters and Opinions* contains the published accounts that Allen mentions, but does not contain this piece of information about the flute, implying that Allen takes as his source those of the letters that had never been published when Allen first wrote the biography in 1926. See Ingram, *Edgar Allan Poe*, 118. It is these letters that must contain any evidence that Poe could play the flute. The letters still reside at the University of Virginia in the John Ingram Collection. In my communications with the University of Virginia, I have not been able to locate the specific letter that contains this citation, although that is not definitive proof that it does not exist.
17. See Hervey Allen, *Israfel*, 36.
18. Lenhart, *Musical Influence*, 127.

19. Mary Louise Shew, a friend of Poe, remembers: "Mr. Poe came to town to go to a midnight service with a lady friend and myself. [. . .] [He] sang the psalms with us, and to my astonishment struck up a tenor to our soprano [. . .]. [He] sang the hymn, without looking at the book, in a fine clear tenor." In Ingram, "Unpublished Correspondence," 422.

20. See Nichols, *Reminiscences*, 8; Chivers, *Life of Poe*, 62.
21. Lenhart, *Musical Influence*, 127.
22. Poe, "Letter 259," 639.
23. Silverman, *Edgar A. Poe*, 179.
24. Ibid.
25. Ibid.
26. Maria Clemm to Nelson Poe, 19 August 1860, John Ingram Collection, University of Virginia Library, Charlottesville.
27. Lawrence, "Edgar Allan Poe," 113–14.
28. Ibid., 114.
29. Ibid.
30. Ibid., 1331.
31. Poe, "Literati of New York City," 1197.
32. Poe, "Letter to B—," 11.
33. Thompson, *Circumscribed Eden of Dreams*, 9. Thompson's booklet touches upon many of the themes of this book, from Poe's circularity to his Platonic theories and his relationship to the German Romantics. Readers interested in a focus on the tension between opposing forces outside of music in Poe's works might look here.
34. Ibid., 11.
35. Poe, "Francis L. Hawks," 568.
36. Poe, "Marginalia," 1313.
37. McGann, *The Poet Edgar Allan Poe*, 116. In his book, McGann faces the delicate and demanding task of articulately unpacking Poe's difficult historical and personal relationship with poetry. Any readers interested in following this thread in Poe studies should look to McGann's work. For an example of the kinds of versification studies from which McGann deviates, see Ensley, *Poe's Rhymes*.
38. Chua, *Absolute Music*, 15–16.
39. Dahlhaus, *Idea of Absolute Music*, 7.
40. Chua, *Absolute Music*, 15.
41. Ibid., 9.
42. As much as I discussed, via Chua and others, our modern failed state, I never pinpoint in this book where or how we might have failed according to Poe, as so many of these critics seem not to be able to either.
43. Ibid., 19.
44. Poe, "[Stanzas]," 23.
45. Chua, *Absolute Music*, 15.
46. Ibid., 22.
47. Ibid., 15.
48. Foucault, *Madness and Civilization*, ix.
49. Ibid.
50. Blasing, 23–24.
51. Ibid., 23.

Bibliography

Abel, Darrel. "A Key to the House of Usher." In *Twentieth Century Interpretations of "The Fall of the House of Usher,"* edited by Thomas Woodson, 43–55. Englewood Cliffs: Prentice-Hall, 1969.
Ackroyd, Peter. *Poe: A Life Cut Short*. London: Chatto and Windus, 2008.
Allen, Hervey. *Israfel: The Life and Times of Edgar Allan Poe*. 1926. Reprint, London: Victor Gollancz Ltd., 1935.
Allison, John. "Coleridgean Self-Development: Entrapment and Incest in 'The Fall of the House of Usher.'" *South Central Review* 5, no. 1 (1988): 40–47.
Anderson, Douglas. *Pictures of Ascent in the Fiction of Edgar Allan Poe*. New York: Palgrave Macmillan, 2009.
Anderson, Erland. *Harmonious Madness: A Study of Musical Metaphors in the Poetry of Coleridge, Shelley, and Keats*. Salzburg: U of Salzberg, 1975.
"Auber and His New Opera." *The Evergreen: A Monthly Magazine of New and Popular Tales and Poetry* 1 (1840): 86.
Auerbach, Jonathan. *The Romance of Failure: First-Person Fictions of Poe, Hawthorne, and James*. Oxford: Oxford UP, 1989.
Bailey, J. O. "What Happens in 'The Fall of the House of Usher.'" *American Literature* 35, no. 4 (1964): 445–66.
Baudelaire, Charles. *Baudelaire on Poe: Critical Papers*. Translated and edited by Lois Hyslop and Francis Hyslop. Carrolltown: Bald Eagle P, 1952.
Bell, Robert E. *Women of Classical Mythology: A Biographical Dictionary*. Oxford: Oxford UP, 1993.
Bennett, Maurice J. "'The Madness of Art': Poe's 'Ligeia' as Metafiction." *Poe Studies* 14, no. 1 (1981): 1–6.
Bernhart, Walter. "A Profile in Retrospect: Calvin S. Brown as a Musico-Literary Scholar." In *Musico-poetics in Perspective: Calvin S. Brown in Memoriam*. Edited by Jean-Louis Cupers and Ulrich Weisstein, 115–29. Amsterdam: Rodopi, 2000.
Bieganowski, Ronald. "The Self-Consuming Narrator in Poe's 'Ligeia' and 'Usher.'" In *Critical Insights*. Edited by Steven Frye, 198–211. Pasadena: Salem P.
Blasing, Mutlu Konuk. *American Poetry: The Rhetoric of its Forms*. New Haven: Yale UP, 1987.
Bloom, Harold. Introduction to *Bloom's Classic Critical Views: Edgar Allan Poe*, xii–xiv. New York: Infobase P, 2008.
———, ed. *Edgar Allan Poe*. New York: Chelsea House, 1985.
Bristol, Michael D. "In Search of the Bear: Spatiotemporal Form and the Heterogeneity of Economics in *The Winter's Tale*." *Shakespeare Quarterly* 42, no. 2 (1991): 145–67.
Brown, Calvin S. *Music and Literature: A Companion of the Arts*. Athens: U of Georgia P, 1948.
———. "The Relations between Music and Literature as a Field of Study." *Comparative Literature* 22, no. 2 (1970): 97–107.
Burke, Peter. *Popular Culture in Early Modern Europe*. 1978. Reprint, Farnham: Ashgate P, 2009.
Butler, Shane. *The Matter of the Page: Essays in Search of Ancient and Medieval Authors*. Madison: U of Wisconsin P, 2011.
Campbell, Killis. Introduction to *The Poems of Edgar Allan Poe*, by Edgar Allan Poe. Edited by Killis Campbell. 1917. Reprint, New York: Russell and Russell Inc., 1962.
———. *The Mind of Poe and Other Studies*. Cambridge: Harvard UP, 1933.

Canada, Mark. "Flight into Fancy: Poe's Discovery of the Right Brain." *Southern Literary Journal* 33, no. 2 (2001): 62–79.
Carlson, Eric, ed. *The Recognition of Edgar Allan Poe: Selected Criticism Since 1829*. Ann Arbor: U of Michigan P, 1966.
———. "Symbol and Sense in Poe's 'Ulalume.'" *American Literature* 35, no. 1 (1963): 22–37.
Chivers, Thomas H. *Life of Poe*. Edited by Richard Beale Davis. New York: E. P. Dutton and Co., 1952.
Chua, Daniel. *Absolute Music and the Construction of Meaning*. Cambridge: Cambridge UP, 1999.
Clemm, Maria. Letter to Nelson Poe, 19 August 1860. John Ingram Collection. U of Virginia Library, Charlottesville.
Coulson, Joseph. "Word Music: A Study of American Poetry (Prosody)." PhD diss., State U of New York at Buffalo, 1985.
Dahlhaus, Carl. *The Idea of Absolute Music*. Translated by Roger Lustig. Chicago: U of Chicago P, 1978.
Davidson, Gustav. *A Dictionary of Angels: Including the Fallen Angels*. New York: The Free P, 1967.
Davis, Jack, and June Davis. "Poe's Ethereal Ligeia." *The Bulletin of the Rocky Mountain Language Association* 24, no. 4 (1970): 170–76.
Dayan, Joan. "Poe, Locke and Kant." In *Poe and His Times*. Edited by Benjamin Franklin Fisher, 30–44. Baltimore: The Edgar Allen Poe Society, 1990.
Dayan, Peter. *Art as Music, Music as Poetry, Poetry as Art, From Whistler to Stravinsky and Beyond*. Farnham: Ashgate, 2011.
———. *Music Writing Literature, from Sand via Debussy to Derrida*. Aldershot: Ashgate, 2006.
D'Israeli, Isaac. "Some Ingenious Thoughts." In *Curiosities of Literature*. Vol. 1, 104–108. Boston: Lilly, Wait, Colman, and Holden, 1833.
Dix, Robin C. "The Harps of Memnon and Aeolus: A Study in the Propagation of an Error." *Modern Philology* 85, no. 3 (1988): 288–93.
Du Bois, Arthur E. "The Jazz Bells of Poe." *College English* 2, no. 3 (1940): 230–44.
"Education of the Intellect, the Taste and the Imagination, in English Public Schools." In *The American Eclectic: Selections from the Periodical Literature of All Foreign Countries*. Edited by Absalom Peters and Selah Treat. Vol. 1, 428–46. New York: W. R. Peters, 1841.
Eliot, T. S. "From Poe to Valéry." *The Hudson Review* 2, no. 3 (1949): 327–42.
Ensley, Helen. *Poe's Rhymes*. Baltimore: Edgar Allan Poe Society, 1981.
Evans, May Garrettson. *Music and Edgar Allan Poe: A Bibliographical Study*. 1939. Reprint, New York: Greenwood P, 1968.
Faber, Pamela. "Charles Baudelaire and His Translation of Edgar Allan Poe." *Meta: journal des traducteurs* 34, no. 2 (1989): 253–59.
Fagin, N. Bryllion. *The Histrionic Mr. Poe*. 1949. Reprint, Baltimore: Johns Hopkins P, 1967.
Ferrari, G. R. F., ed. *Plato: The Republic*. Translated by Tom Griffith. Cambridge: Cambridge UP, 2003.
Fisher, Benjamin Franklin, ed. *Poe and His Times*. Baltimore: Edgar Allan Poe Society, 1990.
Fitzlyon, April. *Maria Malibran: Diva of the Romantic Age*. London: Souvenir P, 1987.
Foerster, Norman. "Quantity and Quality in the Aesthetic of Poe." *Studies in Philology* 20, no. 3 (1923): 310–35.
Foucault, Michel. *Madness and Civilization: A History in the Age of Reason*. Translated by Richard Howard. New York: Vintage Books, 1988.
Freedman, William. "Poe's 'Raven': The Word That Is an Answer 'Nevermore.'" *Poe Studies/Dark Romanticism* 29, no. 1 (1996): 23–31.
Frye, Steven, ed. *Critical Insights: The Tales of Edgar Allan Poe*. Pasadena: Salem P, 2010.

Fuller, Sophie, and Nicky Losseff, eds. *The Idea of Music in Victorian Fiction.* Aldershot: Ashgate, 2004.
Gargano, James W. "Poe's 'Ligeia': Dream and Destruction." *College English* 23, no. 5 (1962): 337–42.
Harrison, James A. *The Life of Edgar Allan Poe.* 1902. Reprint, New York: AMS P Inc., 1965.
Heidegger, Martin. *The Event.* Translated by Richard Rojcewicz. Bloomington: Indiana UP, 2012.
Higginson, Thomas Wentworth. "Poe." In *Edgar Allan Poe.* Edited by Harold Bloom, 72–76. New York: Chelsea House Publishers, 2007.
Hirsch, David H. "The Raven and the Nightingale." In *Poe and His Times.* Edited by Benjamin Franklin Fisher, 194–208. Baltimore: The Edgar Allen Poe Society, 1990.
Hoagwood, Terence Allan. *From Song to Print: Romantic Pseudo-Songs.* New York: Palgrave Macmillan, 2010.
Hoffman, Daniel. *Poe Poe Poe Poe Poe Poe Poe.* Baton Rouge: Louisiana State UP, 1972.
Hoffman, Michael J. "The House of Usher and Negative Romanticism." *Studies in Romanticism* 4, no. 3 (1965): 158–68.
Hollander, John. *The Figure of Echo: A Mode of Allusion in Milton and After.* Berkeley: UC Press, 1981.
———. *The Untuning of the Sky.* Princeton: Princeton UP, 1961.
Howey, Ann, and Stephen Raimer. *A Bibliography of Modern Arthuriana (1500-2000).* Cambridge: D. S. Brewer, 2006.
Hrabe, Margaret. "UVa Library re: John Henry Ingram's Poe Collection." E-mail message to the author. March 13, 2012.
Hubbell, Jay. "Poe and the Southern Literary Tradition." *Texas Studies in Literature and Language* 2, no. 2 (1960): 151–71.
Hunter, William, Jr. "Poe's 'The Sleeper' and *Macbeth.*" *American Literature* 20, no. 1 (1948): 55–58.
Huxley, Aldous. "Vulgarity in Literature." Carlson, *Recognition,* 160–67.
Ingram, John. *Edgar Allan Poe: His Life, Letters and Opinions.* 2 vols. 1880. Reprint, Whitefish: Kessinger Publishing, 2007.
———. "Unpublished Correspondence by Edgar Allen Poe." *Appletons' Journal* 4, no. 5 (1878): 421–30.
Jones, Daryl E. "Poe's Siren: Character and Meaning in 'Ligeia.'" *Studies in Short Fiction* 20, no. 1 (1983): 33–37.
Joseph, Gerhard. "Poe and Tennyson." *PMLA* 88, no. 3 (1973): 418–28.
Kent, Charles W. Introduction to *The Poems of Edgar Allan Poe.* Edited by James A. Harrison. 1902. Reprint, New York: AMS P Inc., 1965.
Kramer, Lawrence. "'Longindyingcall': Of Music, Modernity, and the Sirens." In *Music of the Sirens.* Edited by Linda Austern and Inna Naroditskaya, 194–215. Bloomington: Indiana UP, 2006.
———. *Music and Poetry: The Nineteenth Century and After.* Berkeley: U of California P, 1984.
———. "Ocean and Vision: Imaginative Dilemma in Wordsworth, Whitman, and Stevens." *The Journal of English and Germanic Philology* 79, no. 2 (1980): 210–30.
Lavin, Audrey. "A Birder's Re-Reading of Poe's 'Romance.'" *Studies in English* 9, no. 1 (1991): 199–204.
Lawrence, D. H. "Edgar Allan Poe." 1919. In Carlson, Eric, ed. *The Recognition of Edgar Allan Poe: Selected Criticism Since 1829.* Ann Arbor: U of Michigan P, 1966, 110–26.
Lenhart, Charmenz S. *Musical Influence on American Poetry.* Atlanta: U of Georgia P, 1956.
Leppert, Richard. *The Sight of Sound: Music, Representation, and the History of the Body.* Berkeley: U of California P, 1993.
Levine, Stuart, and Susan F. Levine, eds. *The Short Fiction of Edgar Allan Poe: An Annotated Edition.* Chicago: First Illinois, 1990.

Ljungquist, Kent. "'The Coliseum': A Dialogue on Ruins." *Poe Studies* 16, no. 2 (1983): 32–33.

———. "Poe's Nubian Geographer." *American Literature* 48, no. 1 (1976): 73–75.

Lloyd, Rosemary. *Mallarmé: The Poet and His Circle*. Ithaca: Cornell UP, 1999.

Losseff, Nicky. "The Voice, the Breath and the Soul: Song and Poverty in *Thyrza, Mary Barton, Alton Locke* and *A Child of the Jago*." In *Idea of Music in Victorian Fiction*. Edited by Sophie Fuller and Nicky Losseff, 3–26. Aldershot, UK: Ashgate Publishing, 2004.

Lubbers, Klaus. "Poe's 'The Conqueror Worm.'" *American Literature* 39, no. 3 (1967): 375–79.

Mabbott, Thomas Ollive, ed. *Edgar Allan Poe: Complete Poems*. 1969. Reprint, Champaign: U of Illinois P, 2000.

———, ed. *Edgar Allan Poe: Tales & Sketches*. 2 vols. 1969. Reprint, Champaign: U of Illinois P, 2000.

———. "Poe's 'The Sleeper' Again." *American Literature* 21, no. 3 (1949): 339–40.

"Madame Catalani." *Chambers's Edinburgh Journal*. Vol. 11, 342–45. Edinburgh: William and Robert Chambers, 1849.

McGann, Jerome. *The Poet Edgar Allan Poe: Alien Angel*. Cambridge: Harvard UP, 2014.

McLane, Maureen. "Ballads and Bards: British Romantic Orality." *Modern Philology* 98, no. 3 (2001): 423–43.

Merlin, Maria de las Mercedes and Marie Félicité Malibran. *Memoirs and Letters of Madame Malibran*. 2 vols. Philadelphia: Carey and Hart, 1840.

Miller, James. "'Ulalume' Resurrected." *Philological Quarterly* 34 (1955): 197–205.

Minahan, John A. *Word Like a Bell: John Keats, Music and the Romantic Poet*. London: Kent UP, 1992.

Moldenhauer, Joseph J. "Murder as a Fine Art: Basic Connections Between Poe's Aesthetics, Psychology, and Moral Vision." *PMLA* 83, no. 2 (1968): 284–97.

More, Paul Elmer. "A Note on Poe's Method." *Studies in Philology* 20, no. 3 (1923): 302–309.

Newman, Steve. *Ballad Collection, Lyric, and the Canon: The Call of the Popular from the Restoration to the New Criticism*. Philadelphia: U of Pennsylvania P, 2007.

Nichols, Mary Sargeant Gove. *Reminiscences of Edgar Allan Poe*. New York: Union Square Book Shop, 1931.

Nikolopoulou, Kalliopi. *Tragically Speaking: On the Use and Abuse of Theory for Life*. U of Nebraska, 2012.

Omans, Glen A. "Poe and Washington Allston: Visionary Kin." In *Poe and His Times*. Edited by Benjamin Franklin Fisher, 1–29. Baltimore: The Edgar Allen Poe Society, 1990.

Ostrom, John Ward, Burton R. Pollin, and Jeffrey A. Savoye, eds. *The Collected Letters of Edgar Allan Poe*. Third ed. 2 vols. New York: The Gordian Press, 2008.

The Oxford English Dictionary. Second ed. 1989.

"Paean, n." Entry 1. *The Oxford English Dictionary*.

Pahl, Dennis. "Sounding the Sublime: Poe, Burke, and the (Non)Sense of Language." *Poe Studies* 42, no. 1 (2009): 41–60.

Partridge, Richard. "Lute." *The Oxford Companion to Music*. Edited by Alison Latham.

Pearson, Roger. *Mallarmé and Circumstance: The Translation of Silence*. Oxford: Oxford UP, 2004.

Peeples, Scott. *The Afterlife of Edgar Allan Poe*. Rochester: Camden House, 2004.

Peláez, Mónica. "The Sentimental Poe." *Edgar Allan Poe Review* 8, no. 2 (2007): 65–85.

Poe, Edgar Allan. "Al Aaraaf." 1845 [K]. In Mabbott, *Poems*, 99–115.

———. "Annabel Lee—A Ballad." 1850 [K]. In Mabbott, *Poems*, 477–79.

———. "The Assignation." 1850 [F]. In Mabbott, *Tales*, 150–66.

———. "The Bells.—A Song." 1849 [C]. In Mabbott, *Poems*, 434–38.

———. "The Bells." 1849 [G]. In Mabbott, *Poems*, 434–38.

———. "The Black Cat." 1845 [B]. In Mabbott, *Tales*, 849–59.

———. "The Cask of Amontillado." 1850 [B]. In Mabbott, *Tales*, 1256–63.

———. "The Coliseum." 1850 [M]. In Mabbott, *Poems*, 228–29.

———. "The Colloquy of Monos and Una." 1845 [B]. In Mabbott, *Tales*, 608–17.
———. "The Conqueror Worm." 1849 [J]. In Mabbott, *Poems*, 325–26.
———. "The Conversation of Eiros and Charmion." 1845 [D]. In Mabbott, *Tales*, 455–61.
———. "A Decided Loss." 1832 [A]. In Mabbott, *Tales*, 51–61.
———. "A Descent into the Maelström." 1849 [C]. In Mabbott, *Tales*, 577–94.
———. "The Devil in the Belfry." 1850 [F]. In Mabbott, *Tales*, 365–74.
———. "Le Duc de L'Omelette [A]." 1832. In Mabbott, *Tales*, 33–37.
———. "Le Duc de L'Omelette [F]." 1850. In Mabbott, *Tales*, 33–37.
———. "Eldorado." 1850 [B]. In Mabbott, *Poems*, 463.
———. "Eleonora." 1845 [B]. In Mabbott, *Tales*, 638–45.
———. "Eulalie—A Song." 1845 [E]. In Mabbott, *Poems*, 349–50.
———. "The Fall of the House of Usher." 1845 [D]. In Mabbott, *Tales*, 397–417.
———. "Fanny." 1833. In Mabbott, *Poems*, 225–26.
———. "Four Beasts in One; The Homo-Cameleopard." 1850 [E]. In Mabbott, *Tales*, 119–28.
———. "Francis L. Hawks." In Thompson, *Essays and Reviews*, 557–777.
———. "The Haunted Palace." 1850 [R]. In Mabbott, *Poems*, 315–17.
———. "Israfel [A]." 1831. In Mabbott, *Poems*, 173–77.
———. "Israfel [C]." 1841. In Mabbott, *Poems*, 173–77.
———. "Israfel [G]." 1849. In Mabbott, *Poems*, 173–77.
———. "The Lake— To —." 1845 [F]. In Mabbott, *Poems*, 84–86.
———. "Lenore." 1849 [K]. In Mabbott, *Poems*, 336–37.
———. "Letter 12." *before* May 27, 1829. In Ostrom, *Collected Letters*, 26–27.
———. "Letter 52." December 1, 1835. In Ostrom, *Collected Letters*, 113–16.
———. "Letter 112." May 29, 1841. In Ostrom, *Collected Letters*, 272.
———. "Letter 259." January 4, 1848. In Ostrom, *Collected Letteres*, 639–44.
———. "Letter to B—." In Thompson, *Essays and Reviews*, 5–12.
———. "Ligeia." 1848 [F]. In Mabbott, *Tales*, 310–30.
———. "The Literati of New York City." In Thompson, *Essays and Reviews*, 1118–1226.
———. "The Man of the Crowd." 1849 [C]. In Mabbott, *Tales*, 505–18.
———. "Marginalia." 1844–1849. In Thompson, *Essays and Reviews*, 1309–1472.
———. "The Masque of the Red Death." 1850 [C]. In Mabbott, *Tales*, 670–77.
———. "Morella [A]." 1835. In Mabbott, *Tales*, 225–36.
———. "Morella [G]." 1848. In Mabbott, *Tales*, 225–36.
———. "The Murders in the Rue Morgue." 1850 [E]. In Mabbott, *Tales*, 527–68.
———. "A Pæan." 1836 [B]. In Mabbott, *Poems*, 205–207.
———. "The Pit and the Pendulum." 1850 [C]. In Mabbott, *Tales*, 681–97.
———. "The Purloined Letter." 1849 [C]. In Mabbott, *Tales*, 974–93.
———. "The Raven." 1849 [T]. In Mabbott, *Poems*, 364–69.
———. Rev. of *Alciphron, a Poem*, by Thomas Moore. 1840. In Thompson, *Essays and Reviews*, 333–41.
———. Rev. of *The Culprit Fay* and *Alnwick Castle*, by Joseph Drack and Fitz-Greene Halleck. 1836. In Thompson, *Essays and Reviews*, 505–39.
———. Rev. of *Memoirs and Letters of Madame Malibran*, by the Countess de Merlin. In *Burton's Gentleman's Magazine* 6, no. 1 (1840): 248–49.
———. Rev. of *Prose and Verse*, by Thomas Hood. 1845. In Thompson, *Essays and Reviews*, 274–88.
———. "Romance." 1845 [G]. In Mabbott, *Poems*, 128.
———. "Serenade." 1833. In Mabbott, *Poems*, 222–23.
———. "Shadow.—A Parable." 1850 [F]. In Mabbott, *Tales*, 188–91.
———. "Silence—A Fable." 1850 [E]. In Mabbott, *Tales*, 195–99.
———. "The Sleeper." 1849 [J]. In Mabbott, *Poems*, 186–88.
———. "Song." 1845 [F]. In Mabbott, *Poems*, 66.
———. "Sonnet—Silence." 1845 [F]. In Mabbott, *Poems*, 322.
———. "The Spectacles." 1850 [D]. In Mabbott, *Tales*, 886–916.

———. "[Stanzas]." 1827. In Mabbott, *Poems*, 77–78.
———. "The System of Doctor Tarr and Professor Fether." 1850 [C]. In Mabbott, *Tales*, 1002–22.
———. "A Tale of the Ragged Mountains." 1845 [C]. In Mabbott, *Tales*, 939–50.
———. "Tamerlane." 1845 [H]. In Mabbott, *Poems*, 26–61.
———. "To —." 1845 [D]. In Mabbott, *Poems*, 132–33.
———. "To — — —." 1848 [B]. In Mabbott, *Poems*, 406–408.
———. "Ulalume—A Ballad." 1849 [K]. In Mabbott, *Poems*, 415–19.
———. "Von Jung, the Mystific." 1837 [A]. In Mabbott, *Tales*, 292–304.
———. "William Wilson." 1850 [F]. In Mabbott, *Tales*, 426–48.
Pollin, Burton R. *Poe, Creator of Words*. Baltimore: Enoch Pratt Free Library, 1974.
———. "Poe's 'Eldorado' Viewed as a Song of the West." *Prairie Schooner* 46, no. 1 (1973): 228–35.
———. "Poe as a Writer of Songs." *American Renaissance Literary Report* 6, no. 1 (1992): 58–66.
———. "'The Spectacles' of Poe—Sources and Significance." *American Literature* 37, no. 2 (1965): 185–90.
———. "Undine in the Works of Poe." *Studies in Romanticism* 14, no. 1 (1975): 59–74.
Preston, Katherine K. *Opera on the Road: Traveling Opera Troupes in the United States, 1825-60*. Champaign: U of Illinois P, 2001.
Quinn, Arthur Hobson. *Edgar Allan Poe: A Critical Biography*. New York: D. Appleton-Century Company, 1942.
Rayan, Krishna. "Edgar Allan Poe and Suggestiveness." *The British Journal of Aesthetics* 9, no. 1 (1969): 73–79.
Rea, Joy. "Classicism and Romanticism in Poe's 'Ligeia.'" *Ball State U Forum* 8.1 (1967): 25–29.
Relihan, Joel, trans. *The Tale of Cupid and Psyche*. By Apuleius. Indianapolis: Hackett P, 2009.
Riddel, Joseph N. "The 'Crypt' of Edgar Poe." *Boundary 2* 7, no. 3 (1979): 117–44.
Rodriguez, Julian. "Parody and Language in 'The Cask of Amontillado' by E.A. Poe." *Atlantis* 7 (1985): 37–47.
Rollason, Christopher. "Tell-Tale Signs—Edgar Allan Poe and Bob Dylan: Towards a Model of Intertextuality." *Atlantis* 31, no. 2 (2009): 41–56.
Roth, Martin. "Poe's Divine Spondee." *Poe Studies* 12, no. 1 (1979): 14–18.
Scher, Steven Paul. "Notes Toward a Theory of Verbal Music." *Comparative Literature* 22, no. 2 (1970): 147–56.
Scott, Walter. *Minstrelsy of the Scottish Border*. 1802. Reprint, London: Alex Murray and Son, 1869.
———. *Sir Tristrem; A Metrical Romance of The Thirteenth Century*. Edinburgh: Archibald Constable and Co., 1804.
"Serenade, n." Entry 1. *The Oxford English Dictionary*.
Shakespeare, William. *Hamlet*. Edited by George Richard Hibbard. Oxford: Oxford UP, 1987.
———. *The Oxford Shakespeare: Twelfth Night, or What You Will*. Edited by Roger Warren and Stanley Wells. Oxford: Oxford UP, 1994.
Shirt, David J. *The Old French Tristan Poems*. London: Grant & Cutler, 1980.
Silverman, Kenneth. *Edgar A. Poe: A Biography: Mournful and Never-Ending Remembrance*. New York: Harper Perennial, 1991.
"Sontag, Henriette." *The Northeastern Dictionary of Women's Biography*. London: Macmillan, 1998.
Stedman, Edmund C., and George E. Woodberry, eds. *The Poems of Edgar Allan Poe*. 1895. Reprint, New York: Charles Scribner's Sons, 1914.
Stovall, Floyd. "An Interpretation of Poe's 'Al Aaraaf.'" *Studies in English* 9 (1929): 106–33.
———. "Poe's Debt to Coleridge." *Studies in English* 10 (1930): 70–127.
———. "The Women of Poe's Poems and Tales." *Studies in English* 5 (1925): 197–209.

Sullivan, Jack. "New Worlds of Terror: The Legacy of Poe." In *New World Symphonies*, 61–94. New Haven: Yale UP, 1999.
Sweet, Charles A. "Retapping Poe's 'Cask of Amontillado.'" *Poe Studies* 8, no. 1 (1975): 10–12.
Thibault, Jean-François. "Debussy's Unfinished American Opera: *La chute de la maison Usher*." In *Opera and the Golden West: The Past, Present, and Future of Opera in the U.S.A.* Edited by John L. DiGaetani and Josef P. Sirefman, 198–206. London: Associated UP, 1994.
Thompson, Gary Richard. *Circumscribed Eden of Dreams: Dreamvision and Nightmare in Poe's Early Poetry*. Baltimore: Edgar Allan Poe Society, 1984.
———, ed. *Poe: Essays and Reviews*. New York: Library of America, 1984.
Vines, Lois Davis, ed. "Stéphane Mallarmé and Paul Valéry." *Poe Abroad: Influence, Reputation, Affinities*, 171–76. Iowa City: U of Iowa P, 1999.
Whalen, Terence. *Edgar Allan Poe and the Masses: The Political Economy of Literature in Antebellum America*. Princeton: Princeton UP, 1999.
Whitt, Celia. "Poe and the Mysteries of Udolpho." *Studies in English* 17, no. 1 (1937): 124–31.
Wilbur, Richard. "The House of Poe." 1959. In In Carolson, Eric, ed. *The Recognition of Edgar Allan Poe: Selected Criticism Since 1829*. Ann Arbor: U of Michigan P, 1966, 255–77.
———. "The Poe Mystery Case." Rev. of *The Recognition of Edgar Allan Poe: A Collection of Critical Essays*, ed. Eric W. Carlson, and *Poe: A Collection of Critical Essays*, ed. Robert Regan. *New York Review of Books* July 13, 1967: N. pag.
Williams, Michael. *A World of Words: Language and Displacement in the Fiction of Edgar Allan Poe*. Durham: Duke UP, 1988.
Williams, Paul O. "A Reading of Poe's 'The Bells.'" *Poe Newsletter* 1, no. 2 (1968): 24–25.

Index

Abel, Darrel, 41–42, 45
"Al Aaraaf," 55, 86–93
Allen, Hervey, 132
Allison, John, 23
Anderson, Douglas, 44, 107, 120
Anderson, Erland, 63
angels, 23–24, 40, 53, 56, 68, 76, 79, 81, 89, 93–98, 105, 117, 121–122, 127
animality, 12–14, 15, 125
"Annabel Lee — A Ballad," 27, 38–40, 52, 56
Apuleius, 34, 36, 37, 66
articulation, 17, 45, 50–51, 66, 96, 122, 127. *See also* materiality, utterance
"The Assignation," 25
audibility, ix, x–xi, xii, 1, 2, 3, 5, 7, 21, 24, 25, 44, 50, 53, 55, 57, 58, 64, 65, 66, 69, 70, 72, 74, 76, 80, 81, 84, 84–85, 85–86, 88, 90, 90–91, 91, 92, 93, 94, 95, 98–99, 105, 107, 116, 117, 118, 125–126, 127, 134, 137, 138. *See also* silence, unheard
Auerbach, Jonathan, 50, 54

Bailey, J. O., 24, 42
ballad, 23, 25–31, 34, 37, 38, 40, 43, 45, 49, 58, 63, 67, 82, 104, 115. *See also* Song
Barthes, Roland, 75–76, 127, 128
Baudelaire, Charles, 127
"The Bells," 62, 63, 64, 73, 96, 112–119
bells (disambig.), 16, 42, 45, 64, 73, 108–111, 113, 127
Bennett Maurice, 54, 86
birds, 67–76, 103
"The Black Cat," 49–50, 107, 114
Blasing, Mutlu Konuk, x, xi–xii, 74, 138–139
Bloom, Harold, 125, 138

breath (disambig.), 33, 34, 41, 50, 51, 53, 57, 66, 72, 76, 86, 87, 89, 91, 93, 108, 120, 121, 122, 127, 134. *See also* soul, spirit
Bristol, Michael, 29
Burke, Peter, 108

cacophony, 11, 13. *See also* discord
Carlson, Eric, 32, 34–35
"The Cask of Amontillado," 108–111, 119
Chivers, Thomas, 132
choir, 81, 94, 95. *See also* hymn, song
Chua, Daniel, x–xi, 27, 28, 41, 66, 84, 127, 137, 138
Clemm, Maria, 133
"The Coliseum," 42–43, 93
"The Colloquy of Monos and Una," 81–82, 111
"The Conqueror Worm," 25, 121–122
"The Conversation of Eiros and Charmion," 107

Dahlhaus, Carl, 137
Damnation, 16, 23, 49, 50, 119. *See also* Fall, Postlapsarian, Underworld
Dayan, Joan, 55, 56
Dayan, Peter, x, 75–76, 80, 84–85, 92, 97, 98, 108, 127, 128
"A Decided Loss," 131
demon, 24, 37–38, 40, 42, 45, 50, 51, 56–57, 58, 68, 76, 106, 114, 127, 128
"A Descent into the Maelström," 49–50
"The Devil in the Belfry," 15
discord, 10, 11, 12–17, 29, 42, 44, 44–45, 58, 64, 114, 125. *See also* cacophony
divinity, 9–10, 34, 42, 50, 53, 54, 69, 76, 86, 87, 90, 90–91, 93, 97, 99, 121, 125, 126–127. *See also* ideality
Dix, Robin, 43

dreams, xii, 22, 24, 25, 32, 33, 39, 40, 52, 55, 56, 58, 61, 65, 65–66, 67, 68, 70, 73, 76, 77, 90, 97, 105, 106, 111, 119, 120–121, 125, 127–128, 132, 134, 139. *See also* liminality

echo, xi–xii, 42, 43, 43–44, 45, 56, 58, 63, 68, 76, 88, 98–99, 105, 106, 106–108, 119, 120, 120–121
"Eldorado," 67, 103–104, 104–105
"Eleonora," 52–53, 88
ethereality (disambig.), 33, 34–35, 36, 41, 53, 68, 73, 74, 76, 79, 84, 88, 99, 120, 134, 138. *See also* ideality, liminality, otherworldly
"Eulalie—A Song," 62, 63, 125

Faber, Pamela, 61
Fagin, N. Bryllion, 105
failure (disambig.), ix, xi–xii, xii, 10, 25, 36, 37, 43, 56, 58, 67, 76, 79, 82, 84, 86, 88, 90, 91, 95, 99, 122, 127–128, 138. *See also* Damnation, Fall, Postlapsarian, Underworld
Fairy, 32, 35, 37, 87, 91, 99, 131
Fall (disambig.), xi, 36, 37, 70, 84, 87, 89, 91, 93, 99, 118, 125, 127, 137, 138. *See also* Damnation, failure, Postlapsarian, Underworld
"The Fall of the House of Usher," ix, 9, 19–27, 32, 35, 36, 39, 40–42, 44–45, 50, 50–51, 56, 72, 107–108, 127
"Fanny," 68–72, 75, 85, 116
flute, 63, 132, 133
Fool, 21, 22, 109
Foucault, Michel, x–xi, 12, 13, 15, 22–23, 25, 39, 109–110
"Four Beasts in One; The Homo-Cameleopard," 13–15, 25, 125
Freedman, William, 74
Frye, Steven, 95, 96

ghosts, 75, 85, 92, 98–99, 117. *See also* revenants
guitar, 23–24, 25–26, 27, 41

harp, 21, 23, 25, 26–27, 29, 41, 43, 53, 64–65, 66, 72, 84, 93–94, 95, 96, 97, 103, 138

"The Haunted Palace," 25–26, 40, 40–45, 93, 105
Heidegger, Martin, 33
Hirsch, David, 74–75
Hoagwood, Terence, 27–28, 29, 31, 35
Hoffman, Daniel, x, 30–31, 38–39, 70, 71, 87, 91–92, 93–94
Hoffman, Michael, 26
Hollander, John, x, 43, 64–65, 68, 72, 81, 82, 106, 117
howl, 12, 16, 49, 49–50
Hunter, William, 86
Huxley, Aldous, 61
hymn, x, 14–15, 25, 79, 91, 91–92, 95, 107, 118. *See also* choir, song

ideality (disambig.), ix, x, xi, 20, 25, 27, 28, 30, 33, 34, 36, 37, 38, 40, 41–42, 43–44, 45, 54, 56, 58, 65, 67, 71, 73, 74, 76–77, 80, 83, 86, 87, 88, 90, 91, 95, 96, 96–97, 98, 118, 119, 120, 121, 122, 134, 136–137
indefinite (disambig.), 17, 32–35, 36, 41, 50, 53, 70, 73, 75, 76, 89, 90, 108, 113, 121, 125–126, 127, 129, 134, 135, 136
informing voice, 50–51, 53. *See also* articulation, voice
"Israfel," 23, 93–97, 97, 97–98

Jones, Daryl, 55
Joseph, Gerhard, 19, 44

knowledge of music (Poe's), 2–3, 6
Kramer, Lawrence, x, 8, 50, 55–56, 69, 71, 75, 94, 103

"The Lake—To—," 92–93
Lalande, Henriette, 3, 6–7
Lavin, Audrey, 71
Lawrence, D. H., 51, 133
"Le Duc de L'Omelette," 16
Lenhart, Charmenz, 6, 132, 133
Leppert, Richard, 1–2, 112, 125–126
Ligeia (disambig.), 10, 20, 25, 51, 53, 53–58, 66, 89, 90, 90–91, 91, 133. *See also* sirens
liminality (disambig.), 22–23, 25, 32, 35, 37, 38, 39, 40, 42, 45, 53, 56, 58, 67, 71, 76–77, 85, 98, 99, 103, 104, 106,

111, 115, 117, 120, 125, 126
Ljungquist, Kent, 42
Losseff, Nicky, 65–66, 93
low voice (disambig.), 6, 7–8, 8, 10, 12, 51–52, 53, 54, 57, 65, 70, 107, 110, 111
lute, 23, 41, 42, 43, 44, 45, 64–65, 66, 72, 77, 93, 94, 94–96, 132
lyre, 23, 41, 43, 64–65, 66, 70, 71, 72, 77, 93, 94, 94–95, 96, 98, 98–99, 106

Mabbott, Thomas, 6, 12, 13, 23, 31, 34, 40, 43, 67, 82, 86, 92, 97
madness (disambig.), x–xi, 9, 9–10, 10–14, 15, 15–17, 21–23, 24, 25, 27, 32, 37, 38, 39, 40–41, 42, 44, 45, 49, 51, 52, 56, 58, 76, 85, 88, 97, 106, 108, 109, 110–111, 125, 126, 138. *See also* unreason
Malibran, Maria, 1, 2–10, 13, 83, 126, 131
"The Man of the Crowd," 29
"The Masque of the Red Death," 119–122
materiality (disambig.), ix, 5, 6, 7, 9, 11, 13, 15, 15–17, 29, 49, 51, 52–53, 54–55, 57, 73, 74, 81, 85, 87, 89, 90, 105, 114, 117, 119, 128, 136. *See also* articulation, utterance
McGann, Jerome, 103, 136
McLane, Maureen, 30
melody, 16, 43, 44, 45, 49, 53, 54–55, 57, 67, 72, 88, 89, 90, 91, 92, 93, 95, 96, 98, 111, 112, 113, 132
Merlin, Maria, 3
Miller, James, 32, 35
Minahan, John, 118–119
"Morella," 25, 57–58
mortality (disambig.), 10, 40, 44, 51, 54–55, 74, 75, 81, 86, 87, 88, 89, 95, 96, 98, 109, 127, 136
Mousike, 81–82. *See also* true musical expression
"The Murders in the Rue Morgue," 54
murmur, 51–52, 53–54, 56, 57–58, 76, 88, 90, 92, 93, 95–96, 97, 99, 107, 108
music of the spheres, xi, xii, 68, 81–86, 91, 94, 96, 113, 122, 127, 129, 137–139
musical notation, 1–2, 5–6, 7–9, 11, 12, 14, 16, 24, 25, 112, 125

naming (disambig.), xii, 4, 6, 7, 9, 10, 20–22, 25, 31, 37, 39, 51, 53, 55, 57, 58, 63, 68, 68–69, 69, 73, 75–76, 95, 97–98, 104, 106, 108, 116, 127, 128, 139
Newman, Steve, 30
Nichols, Mary, 132
Nikolopoulou, Kalliopi, 33
notes (musical), ix, xi–xii, 6, 7–8, 8–9, 12, 17, 26, 43, 73, 96, 98–99, 107, 111, 112, 113, 117, 117–118, 118, 119, 119–120, 127, 131

Omans, Glen, 96–97
Orpheus, xi–xii, 25, 64–65, 75–76, 98, 108, 127, 128
otherworldly, ix, x, xi, xii, 25, 34, 38, 40, 53, 56–57, 58, 67, 71, 73, 74, 77, 85, 86, 87, 88, 91, 92, 93, 96, 99, 104, 107, 111, 113, 115, 120, 127, 128–129, 138. *See also* ethereality, ideality, liminality

"A Paean," 62, 115, 115–117
Pelaez, Monica, 98
"The Pit and the Pendulum," 112
Poeisis, 33
Pollin, Burton, 6, 28, 62–63, 94, 99, 104–105, 126
Postlapsarian, x, 138. *See also* Damnation, failure, Fall, Underworld
power of words, 61, 96–99
Psyche, 34, 35–38, 39, 66, 93
"The Purloined Letter," 131

Quinn, Arthur, 40

"The Raven," 51, 61, 68, 71, 73–76, 89, 105, 115
Rea, Joy, 54
real-world music, ix, xii, 1–2, 2, 3, 5, 9, 10, 11, 12–13, 15, 16, 24, 25, 27, 28, 29, 30, 31, 35, 41, 49, 54, 56, 58, 63–64, 65, 66, 68, 69, 74, 76, 80, 81, 85, 91, 95, 104, 105, 107, 112–113, 113, 114, 115, 117, 125–126, 127, 131
revenants, 75, 76, 108. *See also* ghosts
Riddel, Joseph, x, 61

Rollason, Christopher, 25
"Romance," 70–72
Romanticism, ix–x, 8, 26, 27, 28, 30, 35, 41, 53, 63, 66, 69, 74, 75, 84, 93–94, 95, 103, 127, 133, 137, 138
Roth, Martin, x, 118

Scott, Walter, 20–21, 23, 25, 26, 27, 29, 30
"Serenade," 62, 64–65
shadows (disambig.), 57, 70, 73, 84, 103, 104, 104–105, 106, 106–107, 107–108, 109, 110, 114, 119, 127, 128, 128–129, 137, 138
"Shadow.—A Parable," 105–108, 109, 119
Shirt, David, 20
shriek, 11, 49–50, 51–52, 52–54, 56, 58, 66, 76, 114
sigh, 36, 51–52, 53–54, 127, 131. *See also* breath
silence, xi, xii, 13, 20, 22–23, 33, 42, 43, 49, 50, 55, 57, 64, 64–65, 69, 71, 72, 75, 80, 81, 84–85, 85–86, 88, 89, 90, 90–91, 91, 91–92, 93, 94, 95, 96, 99, 104, 106, 111, 114, 120, 126, 127, 128, 138, 139. *See also* audibility, unheard
"Silence—A Fable," 49
Silverman, Kenneth, 133
song (disambig.), ix, x, xi, 1, 3, 4–5, 7, 7–8, 8–10, 12, 13, 14, 15, 25, 26–27, 27–28, 29–30, 30–31, 31, 42, 44, 54, 54–56, 58, 62–64, 66–67, 67, 68, 68–70, 70–71, 71, 72–73, 73, 74–75, 75, 76–77, 81, 84, 89, 91, 91–92, 93, 94, 94–97, 97, 98, 98–99, 103, 104, 105, 106–108, 111, 115, 116, 117, 119, 125–126, 127, 131, 132–133, 134–135. *See also* ballad, choir
sirens, 54–56, 81. *See also* Ligeia (disambig.)
"The Sleeper," 85–86, 116
solemnity, 10, 25, 51, 68, 68–69, 69, 85, 104, 109, 111, 112, 114, 115, 116
"Sonnet—Silence," 104, 105
soul, x–xi, 7–8, 12, 35, 37, 38, 40, 49, 51, 57, 57–58, 65, 65–66, 69, 72, 76–77, 79, 81–84, 89, 93, 95, 95–96, 97, 98, 99, 104, 108, 110, 117, 118, 120, 122, 125, 126, 129, 137, 138. *See also* breath, spirit
"The Spectacles," ix, 1, 2, 3–9, 10, 14, 16, 34, 63, 66, 125
spirit, ix, x, 13, 15, 19–20, 24, 33, 37, 40, 41, 45, 51, 52–53, 58, 66, 67, 70, 72, 77, 79, 81, 84, 85, 87, 88, 89, 90, 91, 93, 98, 99, 103, 105, 107, 117, 121, 128, 129, 131, 136, 137, 138. *See also* breath, soul
"[Stanzas]," 72, 96
Stedman, Edmund, and George Woodberry, 67–68
Stovall, Floyd, 87, 90–91
strings, 23–24, 42, 43, 64, 70, 72–73, 81, 84, 91, 93, 94, 95, 96, 99, 127, 137, 138. *See also* guitar, harp, lute, lyre
Sullivan, Jack, 19
swan song, 68, 69, 70, 72, 76, 77, 133
"The System of Doctor Tarr and Professor Fether," ix, 1, 2, 4, 6, 8–13, 14, 16, 24, 125

"A Tale of the Ragged Mountains," 107
"Tamerlane," 79–80, 85, 85–86, 105, 127
Thompson, George, 135
transcendence, ix–x, 36, 40, 74, 86, 95–96, 117, 138
"true musical expression," 32–38, 41, 75, 129, 134. *See also* indefinite, Mousike

"Ulalume," 27, 30–32, 34, 37–38, 38, 39, 40, 41, 42, 61, 85, 115
underworld, 36, 37, 75. *See also* damnation, failure, fall, postlapsarian
unheard, ix, xii, 43, 54, 69, 71, 72, 74, 76, 76–77, 88, 91, 116, 134, 137. *See also* audibility, silence
unreason, 12, 13. *See also* madness
utterance, 6, 7–8, 45, 51–52, 54, 57, 58, 65, 66, 69, 70, 71, 73, 74, 85, 88, 97, 107, 117, 120, 125, 127, 132. *See also* articulation, materiality

Veil of the Soul / Ventum Textilum, 33–34, 36, 38, 40, 41, 65–66, 76, 93, 99, 122, 128

voice (disambig.), 3, 5, 6, 7, 8, 9, 10, 11, 12, 31, 38, 42, 43–44, 45, 49, 49–51, 53–58, 65, 65–66, 68, 69, 70, 72–73, 74, 76, 79, 88, 89, 90–91, 93, 95, 95–96, 96, 97, 98, 103, 106, 107–108, 109–110, 114, 116, 117, 120, 120–121, 122, 125, 126–127, 128, 132, 133, 139
Von Weber, 25
"Von Jung, the Mystific," 131

water (disambig.), 19–20, 21–23, 25, 30, 31, 31–32, 35, 36, 37, 38, 39–40, 44, 49, 50–51, 52–53, 56–57, 57–58, 68, 70, 88, 89, 92, 99, 104, 108, 117
whisper, 57–58, 89, 93, 119
Wilbur, Richard, 42, 45, 56, 67, 68, 70
"William Wilson," 19, 45
Williams, Michael, 106, 108
Williams, Paul, 113, 115

About the Author

Charity McAdams grew up in a small town nestled in the shadow of the Superstition Mountains and first became interested in nineteenth-century art and literature during her undergraduate studies at Arizona State university. She went on to earn her PhD in English Literature at the University of Edinburgh, and she has taught in Scotland as a Postdoctoral Teaching Fellow and in Arizona as a professor at Arizona State University's honors college. She has since returned to her mountain roots, now residing in the Cascades, and continues to write and teach as a professor in Washington state.

In her spare time, Charity enjoys attempting the *New York Time s* crossword puzzle and taking too many pictures of her miniature labradoodle, Graeme. Every year she trains unsuccessfully for a half-marathon. This is her first book.

www.ingramcontent.com/pod-product-compliance
Lightning Source LLC
Chambersburg PA
CBHW022014300426
44117CB00005B/192